40.—

19 JAN 2012

THE NEW SHELLEY

Series Standing Order

If you would like to receive future titles in this series as they
are published, you can make use of our standing order
facility. To place a standing order please contact your
bookseller or, in case of difficulty, write to us at the address
below with your name and address and the name of the
series. Please state with which title you wish to begin your
standing order. (If you live outside the UK we may not have
the rights for your area, in which case we will forward your
order to the publisher concerned.)

Standing Order Service, Macmillan Distribution Ltd,
Houndmills, Basingstoke, Hampshire, RG21 2XS, England.

The New Shelley

Later Twentieth-Century Views

Edited by

G. Kim Blank

Associate Professor of English
University of Victoria, British Columbia

MACMILLAN

© Macmillan Academic and Professional Ltd 1991

First published 1991

Published by
MACMILLAN ACADEMIC AND PROFESSIONAL LTD
Houndmills, Basingstoke, Hampshire RG21 2XS
and London
Companies and representatives
throughout the world

Typeset by Footnote Graphics, Warminster, Wiltshire

Printed in Hong Kong

British Library Cataloguing in Publication Data
The New Shelley: later twentieth-century views.
1. Poetry in English. Shelley, Percy Bysshe, 1792–1822
I. Blank, G. Kim 1952–
821.7
ISBN 0–333–44331–4

For Jenner and Acia

I stand, as it were, upon a precipice, which I have ascended with great, and cannot descend without greater, peril, and I am content if the heaven above me is calm for the passing moment.

Shelley, to John Gisborne, 18 June 1822

Contents

Contents

Notes on the Contributors

P. M. S. Dawson is the author of *The Unacknowledged Legislator: Shelley and Politics* (1980) and articles on Shelley and other Romantic poets. He is presently a Lecturer at the University of Manchester.

Barbara Charlesworth Gelpi, author of *Dark Passages: The Decadent Consciousness in Victorian Literature*, teaches English at Stanford University. She has published essays on Victorian literature and feminist theory and was editor of *Signs: Journal of Women in Culture and Society*. She is presently completing a book entitled *Shelley's Goddess: Language, Subjectivity and Incest in the Writings of Percy Bysshe Shelley*.

Jean Hall is Professor of English at California State University, Fullerton, and the author of *The Transforming Image: A Study of Shelley's Major Poetry* (1980) and *A Mind that Feeds Upon Infinity: The Deep Self in Romantic Poetry* (forthcoming).

William Hildebrand is Professor of English at Kent State University. The author of two monographs and numerous articles on Shelley, he has also written on Fitzgerald and Melville. He presently is at work on a book-length study of Shelley and the problematic of consciousness.

Jerrold E. Hogle is Professor of English at the University of Arizona. Recently the recipient of a Guggenheim Fellowship and a Mellon Foundation Fellowship to the Huntington Library, he is the author of *Shelley's Process: Radical Transference and the Development of his Major Works* (1988), as well as essays on Romantic poetry, literary theory, Shakespeare, and Gothic fiction.

Angela Leighton is Lecturer in English at the University of Hull. She is author of *Shelley and the Sublime* (1984) and *Elizabeth Barrett Browning* (1986), and has published articles on Shelley, Jane Austen, Elizabeth Barrett Browning, Christina Rossetti, nineteenth-century women poets and contemporary feminist theory. She is currently writing a book to be called *Victorian Women Poets*.

Stuart Peterfreund teaches at Northeastern University, where he also edits *Nineteenth-Century Contexts* (formerly *Romanticism Past and Present*). He is also the editor of *Literature and Science: Theory and Practice* (1989), and is in the process of completing *Shelley: The Idea of Language*, a study about the relationship of language to the social construction of order.

Tilottama Rajan is Professor in the Department of English and the Centre for the Study of Criticism and Theory at the University of Western Ontario. She is the author of *Dark Interpreter: The Discourse of Romanticism* (1980) and *The Supplement of Reading: Figures of Understanding in Romantic Literature and Theory*, as well as articles in the areas of Romanticism and literary theory. She is currently working on a book on Romantic narrative.

Charles J. Rzepka is an Associate Professor of English at Boston University. In addition to *The Self as Mind: Vision and Identity in Wordsworth, Coleridge, and Keats* (1986), he has written articles on Wordsworth, Coleridge, Keats, Shelley and De Quincey. He is writing a book on the socio-economic contexts of the Sublime in the work of Wordsworth and De Quincey.

Lisa M. Steinman teaches English and humanities at Reed College. Her most recent books are *Made in America: Science, Technology, and American Modernist Poets* (1987) and *All That Comes to Light* (1989). She has recently spent a year as a Rockefeller Scholar, working on a book primarily about English Romantic poetry.

Ronald Tetreault teaches Romantic literature and critical theory at Dalhousie University. He is the author of *The Poetry of Life: Shelley and Literary Form* (1987) and a number of articles on Shelley.

Ross G. Woodman is Professor Emeritus of English at the University of Western Ontario. He is the author of *The Apocalyptic Vision in the Poetry of Shelley* (1964) and numerous articles on the English Romantics.

Introduction

G. Kim Blank

The New Shelley represents a collection of pictures of Percy Bysshe Shelley taken in the late 1980s by a number of photographers, each bringing different attitudes and approaches to the subject. These photographers have focused on different features from different angles: some went for close-ups, others for broader perspectives; some took profiles, others full-frontal views; some wanted to capture the visionary gaze, while others wanted to expose the virtuoso intellect. But perhaps this volume should not be considered an exhibition of single works by single hands, but as a photo-montage, a re-picturing without a final or clear image of Shelley. Shelley himself would certainly have liked the idea of undecidability and refiguration. And since Shelley was keen to point out that figurative language allows meaning to be approximated via unapprehended relations, he might also have approved of the extended metaphor used to describe a volume that witnesses his presence in a poetic scene just short of his two-hundredth birthday.

This volume is assembled on the basis that in the last two decades or so the business of researching and writing about Shelley has changed in positive and significant ways. There are a number of reasons for these changes, many of which have to do with creating a field of scholarly credibility and critical acceptance around Shelley. But three forces, if you will, are most obviously at work here. First, there is the multi-volume project initiated out of the considerable holdings of the Carl H. Pforzheimer Library in New York, and entitled *Shelley and His Circle, 1773–1822*. Kenneth Neill Cameron published the first two volumes in 1961, but with volumes 3–4 published in 1970, volumes 5–6 in 1973 (and now under the general editorship of Donald H. Reiman), and 7–8 in 1986, the whole enterprise, with its superb facsimiles, manuscript transcriptions, and excellent commentary, has served not only to bring respectability to Shelley studies, but also, by example, to the business of literary scholarship in general. *Shelley and His Circle,*

1

1773–1822, has not just compiled and supplied background research material, some standard texts, and critical insight, but,
perhaps more importantly, it has also connected Shelley to the
context of his own time and contemporaries. The gathering of such
information naturally enhances the material understanding of
Shelley for our own time; that is, it connects us with Shelley's
connections in a new way.

A second impetus behind a new picturing of Shelley can be
attributed to the 'sceptical idealism' now perceived to be prevalent
in Shelley's thought. C. E. Pulos's *The Deep Truth: A Study of
Shelley's Scepticism* (1954) is particularly important here, but Earl R.
Wasserman's *Shelley: A Critical Reading* (1971) has for later
twentieth-century readers rendered Shelley's complexity in a complex way, and this complexity is largely the result of examining
that sceptical strain.[1] Despite Wasserman's forcing of the 'One
Mind' theory on Shelley's thought and poetry, no 'one' Shelley
emerges out of Wasserman's book; rather it is a Shelley who in his
poetry moves between hope and fear, optimism and doubt, faith
and uncertainty, permanence and mutability, feeling and reason,
mind and world, causation and origin, transience and constancy,
utopianism and immortality, atheism and perfectibility. These
dialectical constructs inform a great deal of our modern readings
and understanding of Shelley; that is, his work is no longer
considered to be the result of having, as T. S. Eliot held, a confused
mind (Eliot, 1933, p. 81), but rather of attempting poetically and
intellectually to negotiate such conflicting and contrary pulls.

As a result, particular Shelleyan characteristics which were once
deemed negative are now re-viewed as critically engaging qualities.
Shelley, of course, hasn't changed; but in the last two decades critical
methods and interpretative values have. Just over twenty years ago
one of my editor-predecessors, R. B. Woodings, wrote in *Shelley:
Modern Judgements* about the kinds of issues raised by Shelley's work:

> For his poetry draws attention to certain constant problems in
> literary theory. Shelley's own theorising, and the nature of his
> poetic practice, brought him up against the apparent critical
> trespasses that he was committing: the yoking together of
> didacticism and aestheticism; the reliance on the precise,
> detailed word beside the emotive, general one; the unity of the
> personal and the mythic, self-communion and public expression.
> (Woodings, 1968, p. 12)

At this present moment, theory is at least as prolific as it is problematical, and today theory goes beyond being merely an issue of style or personal disposition. It puts under question the very notions of literature and criticism, goodness and badness, marginality and canonicity, signification and textuality. That is, theory is no longer a subordinate or derivative aspect of literary studies. And theory is the third and final impetus behind the formulation of a new Shelley.

Theory today as *critical* theory is its own business and genre, and does not succumb to rationalizations of being just another tool of literary investigation. Such displacement within the discipline manifests itself in a number of different reconsiderations in examining the text, the tradition, the author: today the primary text no longer stands in a superior or differentiated position relevant to its interpretations; the reader's response sometimes subjugates not only the author's experience but also the text being read; the problems of language and signification have supplanted the finality of meaning as the premise for critical study; bourgeois history is unwritten by Marxist analysis; phallocentric discourse has been appropriately defiled by feminist readings; and literary criticism (and more generally hermeneutics) has become the ground over which struggling ideologies display themselves and then struggle for privileged positions. The end result of all this, which has in one way or another been referred to as the crisis in English studies, is that the late 1980s have been characterized by a plethora of conferences and colloquia on canonisation, at which the canon itself has often come under fire.

Shelley figures in this history in that F. R. Leavis, the century's most influential canoniser, was particularly tough on Shelley (see especially Leavis, 1936, pp. 203–32). Leavis, in his desire to name for us the great literature, the first-rate writers, and the true tradition, claims that:

> it is impossible to go on reading him [Shelley] at any length with pleasure; the elusive imagery, the high-pitched emotions, the tone and movement, the ardours, ecstasies, and despairs, are too much the same all through. The effect is of vanity and emptiness (Arnold was right) as well as monotony.
>
> (Leavis, 1936, p. 211)

Here and elsewhere Leavis dismisses Shelley for two general

reasons. First, and following from Matthew Arnold's readily quotable portrayal of Shelley as an 'ineffectual angel' (Arnold, 1905, pp. 203–4), Leavis does not approve of Shelley because he considers him weak, self-regarding without possessing self-knowledge, ephemeral, and over-emotional. These charges are obviously more dispositional than professional;[2] moreover, they are very much open to debate. Second, and more important, Leavis objects to Shelley's particular style: the 'elusive imagery' where there is a 'general tendency of the images to forget the status of the metaphor or simile that introduced them and to assume an autonomy and a right to propagate' (1936, p. 206). Leavis is right, except in the forgetting business; Shelley doesn't lose sight; he simply changes or refocuses it. Shelley's figurative language does 'propagate'; it does, so to speak, take on and create a life of its own, and not necessarily in its own image. But Shelley was always very purposeful in the style and form of his poetry and in the selection of his words and images, as William Keach has shown so carefully in *Shelley's Style* (1984). What Leavis objects to is that in Shelley's poetry language calls out to (or falls upon) other language; it is often reflexive, and Leavis wants poetry firmly to grasp the actual, to signify, to refer and not defer.

Leavis is particularly uneasy with the suggested relationship between thought, language and metaphor that Shelley's poetry promotes. His idea of poetry simply cannot take into account Shelley's theory and practice of poetry, where language is, in Shelley's words, 'vitally metaphorical' and 'has relation to thoughts alone' (Shelley, 1977, p. 482–3). For Shelley, one of the reasons the world of objects is impossible to know is because we have to name these objects, and in naming them the names call out to other names which have significance (or signing power) different from themselves. Meaning in this process is thus always already deferred: Shelley writes that 'almost all familiar objects are signs, standing not for themselves but for others, in their capacity of suggesting one thought, which shall lead to a train of thoughts: – Our whole life is thus an education of error' (Shelley, 1977, p. 477). This 'standing not for themselves' and leading 'to a train of thought' is not unlike Jacques Derrida's notion of *differance* (Derrida, 1973, pp. 129–60), given that for Shelley meaning and language, and especially poetry as written language, stand some distance apart. In Shelley's negative epistemology there is a loss and substantial difference between conception and expression. Thus poetry, being in Shelley's view the highest point of the latter, can be nothing more than a 'feeble shadow' of the former (Shelley, 1977, p. 504). Moreover, for Shelley, language holds no *logos*. There is no centre at which a name can be found. In post-structuralist terms, there is no transcendental signified; in Shelley's terms, 'the deep truth is imageless' (*Prometheus Unbound*, II.iv. 116);[3] it cannot be pictured, being (like Demogorgon) powerful, shapeless and ultimately unknowable.

Shelley is aware that language in its drive for meaning works as a kind of surplus, and his style of poetry often uses this surplus. His poetry is just as likely to follow the logic of sound and figurative language as the logic of idea. When Shelley's poetry follows both, which happens in his best work, the result is some of the most remarkable poetry in the language. In a negative light, Shelley's poetry can be described as both excessive and dense; put more objectively, this is a poetry of radical self-consciousness and reflexivity. Leavis and the New Critics were not ready for a poetry where the play of language is at least as esteemed as the work of signification. Roland Barthes and post-structuralist critics were ready for such texts – texts, that is, that point to their own textuality; and Barthes, with a bias towards works that are pluralistic and indeterminate, and where meaning is suspended, would certainly have approved of Shelley's poetry as '*writerly*' as opposed to '*readerly*' or '*classic*' (Barthes, 1974, pp. 4–11).

Shelley's ideas seem, then, to take up the most important issue of post-structuralist theory – the confrontation of language and meaning. As he puts it in one of his fragmentary essays,

> The words *I*, and *you* and *they* are grammatical devices invented simply for arrangement and totally devoid of the intense and exclusive sense usually attached to them. It is difficult to find terms adequately to express so subtle a conception as that to which the intellectual philosophy has conducted us. We are on that verge where words abandon us, and what wonder if we grow dizzy to look down the dark abyss of – how little we know.   (Shelley, 1977, p. 478)

There is, for Leavis, altogether too much gasping in Shelley's poetry and not nearly enough grasping. Leavis, armed with unqualified calls for poetry to be specific and concrete, would, of course, never consent to a poetics or poetry underwritten by and executed with such uncertainty and vertiginous abandonment.

Post-structuralism, however, would consent to such a poetry and poetics, and Shelley's poetry can be seen to challenge the problematics of meaning and language; indeed, this challenge constitutes the actual content of the poems themselves. It may be somewhat presumptuous to call Shelley a 'proto-deconstructionist' or 'pre-post-structuralist', but Pulos and Wasserman have in a way 'prepared' Shelley for critical theory by having firmly placed him in the tradition of radical scepticism, and as a poet this scepticism is very forcefully and perhaps uniquely manifest in both his themes and use of language. As Tilottama Rajan notes in a more general context, 'romantic literature marks the dawning of an age of linguistic anxiety' (Rajan, 1984, p. 317); and as Stephen Heath notes, 'Romanticism ... is the *essence* of literature, the force of a will to unity that knows in its figures, the tropes of its expression, all of the impossibility of the wholeness it intends' (Heath, 1989, p. 40). No poet of the period displays quite as much 'anxiety' as Shelley about the 'impossibility' of the relationship between the world and the word.

Many of Shelley's major poems can thus be read as allegories of the confrontation between knowing and articulation. In *Alastor* the young hero, the Poet, finds that external knowledge is inadequate and that internal knowledge or self-knowledge is both seductively deceptive and ultimately unattainable. The Poet's quest, which is framed by and then interwoven with imagery of darkness and secrecy (that is, of the unknowable), can only end in death and silence, suggesting the failure of the Poet, and of poetry itself as a representation of or means of discovering knowledge and truth. Yet the narrator of *Alastor*, himself going to some lengths to invoke favorable expression (1–49), while admitting at the end of the poem that 'Art and eloquence/ ... are frail and vain' (710–11), paradoxically manages to articulate loss and failure within a discourse of success and gain – the poem itself; a poem that, moreover, claims in its Preface to possess instructional qualities. What the Poet cannot know or say within his own story, the narrator attempts to know and say outside of the story yet still within the confines of the poem. Both figures are poets, but *Alastor* raises the issue of what poets and poetry can do, or at least what certain kinds of poets and poetry can do. What we have even so early in Shelley's career is a clear recognition of the limits of language, knowledge and poetry, yet a development of strategies – stylistic, rhetorical, narratological, intellectual – that confront and challenge those limits. In more conventional terms, this confrontation is one of the important sources of tension and irony in Shelley's poetry.

Mont Blanc works through the problematic distinction between mind and world, the problem of knowing the world and the source of its power. Although the poem begins by suggesting that the mind is overwhelmed by powerful, external and transcendent influences, as *Mont Blanc* comes to a close it appears that the capital-M Mountain, the symbol for those influences, is itself contingent upon the mind's own power to create the Mountain as such a symbol of mystery and power. In an uncanny way the Mountain and the mind trade places: with its power of image-making, with its imagination, the mind has made the Mountain's 'voice' (80) indistinguishable from its own sounds – that is, thought and speech. *Mont Blanc*'s organising tropes are appropriately sound/articulation and darkness/mystery. The poem enacts Shelley's desire to know and speak of the world as the knowable Other, but since the Other is seemingly interchangeable with the mind, the mind itself and its products of thought and speech become figures of inaccessibility and mystery. Power is *there* in the mountain; the mountain and the mind create and image each other; Power is *there* in the mind. The mind cannot know itself, yet *Mont Blanc* is about searching for a voice that articulates such negative confirmation and an image that represents such power.

Julian and Maddalo also clearly allegorises the confrontation between knowing and articulation. The two characters purposefully set out to test their respective views (free will vs. determinism, idealism vs. nihilism, hope vs. despondency) by the example and interpretation of the Maniac's 'talk' (200). But his impressive 'speech' (290), a speech not unlike a written text (286), overwhelms the issue altogether, and the poem's agenda becomes hidden or forgotten in the unwritten history of the Maniac. That is, in the same way and by the same logic through which the Maniac, who exclaims 'How vain/Are words!' (472–3), can 'hide/Under ... [his own] words' (503–4), the poem ends by withholding knowledge. *Julian and Maddalo* is thus about the resistance of completion – completion, that is, in the sense of complete meaning and knowledge; in narratological terms there is, as so often in Shelley's poetry, closure without disclosure.

As in *Alastor*, *Mont Blanc* and *Julian and Maddalo*, closure without disclosure and knowledge without knowing also stand as the

problematic centre of much of Shelley's other major poetry. The
Ode to the West Wind constitutes Shelley's painful search for
powerful and pervasive eloquence using a trope he can identify
with and, indeed, become: 'Be thou, Spirit fierce,/My spirit! Be
thou me. . .!' (61–2). Yet having rhetorically effected the transference, the poem closes by opening a question about the very
possibility of finding its own voice in prophecy. *To a Sky-lark* is also
a plea for a voice, the difference being that now the subject of
transference is an unseen bird rather than an invisible wind. The
poem is premised on the acquisition of two items of knowledge:
first, the speaker wants to know what the bird says; second, he
wants to know how to say what the bird says. One unsettling
translation of this is: the speaker is willing to say something he
cannot understand. At the centre of the poem there is a series of
metaphoric approximations in an attempt to know what the
Sky-lark is 'like' (36–60), all of these being the result of the
statement 'What thou art we know not' (31). Metaphor thus
presents the only possibility of knowledge. But again, since we
have a poem that closes with expectation rather than knowledge,
we have a text that desires a transcendent voice it cannot assume
owing to its clearly formulated limitations:

>   Teach me half the gladness
>   That thy brain must know,
>   Such harmonious madness
>   From my lips would flow
>   The world should listen then – as I am listening now.
>   (101–5)

We are listening to a text listening to a voice it is promoting as
unknowable. These two poems have an eternal 'then' stifled by a
momentary 'now'. So like many of Shelley's other poems, these
express an awareness of their own possible failure.

   One of the reasons Shelley might have been able to achieve so
much in *Prometheus Unbound* is that he found a figure and story
through which he could, on a grand, mythopoeic scale, allegorise
the power and problems of language and knowledge. Prometheus
is, after all, portrayed as the giver of knowledge (I. 542) who, by
being a little too loose with his words, loses the power of the word.
Put rather more respectfully, in the Prometheus myth Shelley had
a narrative structure where words could be misused, lost, and then

restored to a performative status. *Prometheus Unbound* resonates with voices, echoes, sounds and choruses, and if the poem suffers from anything, even in terms of its main characters, it is logorrhoea, various speech defects, and more generally problems with language: Jupiter is deluded by his grandiloquence; Prometheus, who was once magniloquent, has for a few thousand years been afflicted with aphoria; and Demogorgon, who is at the centre of *Prometheus Unbound*, is the 'voice unspoken' (I.i.191) who admits that words can never approximate truth. In this work language is shown to be at once impenetrable, restrictive, redemptive and liberating. Shelley's calling his work 'A Lyrical Drama' now makes more sense: it is a dramatisation of words, a drama of words about words; the words are the players; the players are words. In this reading the title now appears to have a useful and deliberate punning: the 'unbound' Prometheus represents the freeing of words and pages from the limits of closure, or at least it opens up the possibility of an appropriate re-ordering, of creating a new order. As in the final section of the *Ode to the West Wind*, Shelley is working towards an image of spreading words (scattering leaves) to the world.

Teresa 'Emilia' Viviani and John Keats, the ostensible subjects of *Epipsychidion* and *Adonais* respectively, were real people, but both poems go out of or away from these real subjects towards idealised representations of these figures. The poems seem to perform such movements in very different ways, *Epipsychidion* being more impassioned and *Adonais* more controlled; but both of these figures serve a similar function: they allow for Shelley's displacement of that idealised figure for his own rhetorical desires, desires that are in fact held back by the language of desire. (In Shelley's poetry 'love' for an Other often collapses under the pressure of narcissism.) In *Epipsychidion* Shelley once more rehearses the quest for the idealised Other, for becoming one with that Other, for indeed becoming that One. This is the same strategy of displacement that we see in the *Ode to the West Wind*, where the plea to the Wind as Other finally becomes 'Be thou me, impetuous one!' (62). Likewise in *Epipsychidion*, the hope is not to be subject *to* the idealised Other, but subject *with* that Other: 'Ah me! I am not thine: I am a part of *thee!*' (51–2). The poem emotionally dizzies itself (both the poem's 'Muse' and speaker being 'moth-like', 53, 220–1) in attempting to express the history of this desire, until at last it reaches the point of actually writing itself:

> The winged words on which my soul would pierce
> Into the height of love's rare Universe,
> Are chains of lead around its flight of fire. –
> I pant, I sink, I tremble, I expire!
>
>   (588–91)

The failure here, the heavy, agonising restraint, are the 'words'. They simply cannot break through. The last line here is not, as some of Shelley's earlier detractors have maintained, a display of some kind of pathological weakness on Shelley's part; it is Shelley coming up against the limits of language.

The formal demands of pastoral elegy prevent *Adonais* from overtly displacing its idealised subject, but the poem nonetheless manages to put the 'one frail Form' (271) at the centre of the poem, and the metaphorical attempts to come to *terms* with Death greatly outnumber the specific praises of Adonais, a.k.a. John Keats. Shelley did not know Keats all that well anyway; but then again, Shelley always preferred dead poets over living ones. *Adonais*, as an expression of rhetorical agnosticism, remains a poem about a poet-subject (Keats) and poet-speaker (Shelley) being misunderstood. Moreover, *Adonais* is premised on the view that the subject of the poem was killed by words, yet the poem is an act of grammatological resurrection.

The Triumph of Life retreats into itself, going deeper and deeper as a vision within a vision within a vision, as if in the hope that somehow this pattern of narrative collapse might, after falling through each successive level, at last land upon some kind of final image or conclusion where Truth is unveiled and pictured (in words) before us. But at each level in the poem knowledge is withheld and the ultimate question is left unanswered. The only possible centre of the poem (that is, in the poem as we have it) appears to be the 'shape all light' (352), but this is a figure representing the erasure of thought. Yet *The Triumph of Life* goes beyond acting out a conflation of levels of consciousness and knowledge; it actually negates them. Closer to its narrative line a pessimistic view of life, aspirations and knowledge is paraded before us, with all of the deluded participants amounting to naught – Life as an endless and confused procession; History as going nowhere; Knowledge as impossible. This is where *The Triumph of Life* leads us and what it beckons us to ask: How do we get to Truth and Meaning in poetry? How do we break down the boundary between knowing and articulation?

These are the kinds of questions Shelley's poetry poses. This may present for us a somewhat dismal vision, but it does not mean that Shelley's poetry, even with its negative epistemology, is without hope. It only suggests that for Shelley answers only lead to other questions; that victory is necessarily temporary; that faith is contingent upon fear; that inspiration is fleeting; that thought needs to confront language; that understanding is an arbitrary construct; and that, in spite of all, one must go on, pushing further, looking for answers, hoping for victory, holding faith, seeking inspiration, expressing the inexpressible, and attempting to understand. If Shelley's poetry can be accused of anything, it is its simultaneous pushiness and fragility: its soaring and crashing, aspiring and expiring, salvation and damnation, ecstasy and agony. And here the content of Shelley's poetry is often reflected in its form: both themes and style tend to operate in excess.

Of course, the kinds of readings above limit the extraordinary range of Shelley's interests. The dimensions of Shelley's political, historical, personal and literary concerns go *beyond* his sceptical disposition as it influences his stand on language and knowledge, but more often than not those concerns are negotiated *through* that sceptical disposition. In other words, it cannot be said that Shelley dismisses language as a tool of social change or method of historical reflection or means of emotional expression; nor can we say that Shelley's work is without dogmatic or (despite what he says in the Preface to *Prometheus Unbound*) didactic aims. Indeed, Shelley felt that poetry had the potential to teach real lessons, describe real moments, and inspire real action. It simply remains that Shelley was at the same time hyper-aware that all of man's constructions, including language, have fallibility built within them. Like the traveller from the antique land in *Ozymandias*, Shelley looks upon the work of man, man's fractured inscription in the cold face of history, and despairs. Yet Shelley's desire for language to recover and make manifest the original power of conception shows at once his hope that the word can shape and shake the world, and his fear that the world cannot hear his words – it can only listen for the voice and wait for Spring.

The New Shelley offers some essays that contextualise Shelley in our own scene of critical practice, and others that place him in his own scene of poetic production. In his own scene the 'new' Shelley of this volume thus marks a return to or more closely approximates the original Shelley. Here we see the formation of Shelley's attitudes towards motherhood and the maternal deity, his consciousness of class, his life experiences and aesthetic consciousness conflicting with each other, and his identification with and deconstruction of contemporary poets. This last item marks the bridge to seeing Shelley in our own scene of critical practice: how his use of language and sceptical bent connect him with the deconstructive turn, how his use of language moves between a belief in a transcendental signified and a nihilistic materialism, and how in his poetry language, love and power seductively negotiate each other. Language indeed is the make-or-break issue with Shelley. We can choose to ignore or embrace his personality and politics, but we will always be left with his words. Shelley once wrote: 'I have found my language misunderstood like one in a distant and savage land' (Shelley, 1977, p. 473). In our own 'distant' land at the end of the twentieth century we can not know whether we finally understand Shelley or not. But, at least for the moment of this volume, the land is not so savage. It welcomes him.

Part I
Issues

1

Shelley: Style and Substance

Ronald Tetreault

In this day of political handlers and image consultants, it has become fashionable to say that we value style at the expense of substance. The pervasiveness of electronic media constantly reminds us that we live in a world of appearances, a *tele*-world far off from a reality we can no longer conceive of as immediate. Instead, the 'reality' in which we function is one of mediation, a realm of images and signs that come to have a substance of their own. The voice on the phone, the picture on the screen, the words on the page all mimic presence, deceiving us into thinking that they are the 'thing itself'; but this essence always seems to escape, if only by the time it takes to blink an eye or draw a breath, our desire to pin it down.[1] Nevertheless, that desire persists and urges us to the pursuit of the sense beyond sound, of the content beyond form, of the substance beyond style that we call reading. What we are coming to appreciate, though, are the ways in which style can arouse that desire and in the process complicate the possibilities of substance.

Where to locate substance is very much a problem raised by deconstruction. As a method alive above all to the rhetorical strategies operating in texts, it gives precedence to the signifier over the signified. Resistant to all claims to truth and totalisation, deconstruction denies that language is transparent and concentrates on the material conditions of language as sound or as a series of black marks on a page. This opacity of language makes its customary referential function unclear or indeterminate, and forces the reader's attention back on the substantiality of words themselves. The ordering of words we call style is thus placed in the foreground, while their meaning is deferred.

This problematisation of substance has had an impact on all literary culture, but it affects Shelley studies in particular because

15

his work has always been subject to the charge that it is all style and no substance. Wordsworth's judgement that 'Shelley is one of the best *artists* of us all: I mean in workmanship of style', seems just a bit grudging (Wordsworth, 1876, III, p. 463); he seems to have admired Shelley's artistic power, but is notably reticent about his ideas. Matthew Arnold implied that Shelley was all sound and no sense when he stated in a footnote to his essay on Maurice de Guerin (1863) his belief that 'the right sphere for Shelley's genius was the sphere of music' (Arnold, 1962, p. 34). Leavis echoes this attitude when he objects to the poet's ' "quivering intensity", offered in itself apart from any substance' (Leavis, 1936, p. 211). Such responses undeniably acknowledge the richness and force of Shelley's language, though Leavis is less perceptive than his nineteenth-century forebears about the order and organisation that underlie Shelley's verbal intensity. But what these readers do by strictly distinguishing between form and content in Shelley is damn him with faint praise. A good writer with bad ideas, he can be accorded a place in the literary pantheon while his content is evaded.

For some nineteenth-century readers, after all, Shelley did have a definite content. In the generation after his death, his poetry was esteemed almost exclusively by radicals who saw him as primarily a political poet. Friedrich Engels recorded his understanding of Shelley's significance in 1845:

> The most important modern works in philosophy, poetry and politics are in practice read only by the proletariat ... It is the workers who are most familiar with the poetry of Shelley and Byron. Shelley's prophetic genius has caught their imagination.
> (Engels, 1958, pp. 272–3)

Valued as a poet of the people, Shelley was hailed as an advocate of liberty and a champion of the oppressed. But he was not, like Byron, regarded simply as a voice of protest; above all, his poetry was prized because it could envision forms of social organisation towards which readers were invited to strive. His style stirred the masses to action, and his substance was the picture of the world remade according to a political ideal.

Those modern readers who have been generally sympathetic to Shelley's progressive ideology also identified idealism as his subject, but have preferred to view it as of the more abstract and metaphysical variety. Writers from Carl Grabo (1936) through James A. Notopoulos (1949) to Earl R. Wasserman (1971) have traced Shelley's debt to the tradition of Western philosophical inquiry. Even here, though, there is considerable dispute over what species of idealism Shelley's poetry is to be aligned with. Shelley's Platonism has been put aside by the very influential study of Shelley's allegiance to scepticism undertaken by C. E. Pulos (1954), and continued by Wasserman, who reads Shelley's poetry as the embodiment of 'metaphysical speculations' that 'recapitulate the course of eighteenth-century empiricism and result in a special brand of idealism rooted in a persistent epistemological skepticism' (Wasserman, 1971, p. 136).

One result of the modern reading of Shelley's poetry as being preoccupied with an apprehension of the ideal has been to narrow the comprehensive social vision of the text, perceived by readers like Engels, down to the pursuit of an individual spiritual quest through the exploration of personal consciousness. Harold Bloom's (1970) study of the internalisation of quest romance, indebted to M. H. Abrams's thesis that the Romantics turned inward as their disappointment with the course of the French Revolution grew, is adumbrated in *Shelley's Mythmaking*, where he argues that Shelley's project is the establishment of an I-Thou relationship with the natural world (Bloom, 1959). This transcendence of the dichotomy between subject and object became the very essence of Romanticism for Abrams, who reads Shelley for moments of visionary apocalypse, instances of revelation in which 'man's imaginative vision, suddenly liberated, penetrates to the inner forms, both of man and his world, which had been there all the time, beneath the veil' (Abrams, 1971, p. 344). A promise is held out here of the recovery of truth in the fullness of its presence beyond time, a wish very much at odds with Shelley's scepticism. Any attempt to penetrate 'beneath the veil' of temporal phenomena was very much distrusted by Shelley, who warns in a memorable sonnet:

> Lift not the painted veil which those who live
> Call Life; though unreal shapes be pictured there
> And it but mimic all we would believe
> With colours idly spread, – behind, lurk Fear

> And Hope, twin Destinies, who ever weave
> Their shadows o'er the chasm, sightless and drear.
>   (Shelley, 1977, p. 312)

The melancholy fate of 'one who had lifted it', not any specific historical personage but a generic quester who 'strove for truth' but 'found it not', is recounted in the remaining lines. This poem depicts 'Life' as a realm of appearances, the transcendence of which is shadowed by anxiety and desire. Supposed moments of bardic insight admit, as Bloom himself says, 'the precariousness of mythmaking', and are thus qualified by a 'prophetic irony' (Bloom, 1959, pp. 94–5), phrases that herald with marvellous self-awareness the deconstructive turn in the reading of Shelley.

The affinity between deconstruction and scepticism may be what makes Shelley such an apt subject for this type of reading. The extent to which deconstruction is identical with scepticism and no more, however, is also tested in the reading of Shelley. Just as Shelley's creative achievement cannot be understood (much less appreciated) on the basis of his sceptical tendency alone, so deconstruction would be a barren discipline indeed if all it did was to point out the delusions under which authors and readers alike labour. In pointing out the sources of error in reading, deconstruction does not thereby render without value the texts it reads so much as draw attention to the rhetorical techniques by which the text's values are created and conveyed. In resisting belief, deconstruction may help us to understand how a text can generate conviction by explaining not what the text 'means' but how it functions.

The difficulty with deconstruction as a critical method arises when we ask just who best represents its potentialities. To read *The Triumph of Life* with Paul de Man is to encounter the most extreme version of Shelley's sceptical moment. De Man begins by drawing attention to the unanswered questions about origins and ultimate ends that punctuate the poem: ' "And what is this?/Whose shape is that within the car? & why?" ', ' "Whence camest thou? and whither goest thou?/How did thy course begin," I said, "and why?" ', ' "Shew whence I came, and where I am, and why" ', to which we might add the question with which the poem all but breaks off, ' "Then what is Life?" I said' (de Man, 1979b, p. 39). The resistance of these questions to any satisfactory answer is implicated by de Man in the inadequacy of language to experience, for at the centre of his analysis is the deceptive 'Shape all light', which he argues is 'the model of figuration in general' and 'the figure for the figurality of all signification' (de Man, 1979b, pp. 61, 62). Resistant (unlike Rousseau) to the Shape's power, he concludes that *'The Triumph of Life* warns us that nothing, whether deed, word, thought or text, ever happens in relation, positive or negative, to anything that precedes, follows or exists elsewhere' (de Man, 1979b, p. 69). The way the poem poses questions that can only raise further questions 'arrests the process of understanding' (de Man, 1979b, p. 44) and frustrates any desire for meaning. Yet that desire is surprisingly resilient in Shelley, for it attaches itself to the things that were most problematic for him – language, life, and love. Arising out of the life-force of eros, Shelleyan desire is an impulse towards relation with the other that can be achieved in language only by a process of figural substitution, a process that establishes the relation of words to things and self to other selves by means of metaphor.

That Shelley hungered for such relationship is evident in his poems no less than in the essay *On Love*, where understanding is both comprehension and sympathy:

> If we reason, we would be understood; if we imagine, we would that the airy children of our brain were born anew within another's; if we feel, we would that another's nerves should vibrate to our own . . .   (Shelley, 1977, p. 473)

Shelley's lament in this same piece over 'language misunderstood', however, betrays a doubt whether such relation, either in love or in life, can ever be perfected. His despairing note, 'These words are inefficient and metaphorical – Most words so – No help –' (Shelley, 1977, p. 474), questions whether metaphor can establish any connections that are real rather than illusory. Life seems ineluctably clouded by deception and error.

That metaphor depends on illusion comes as no climactic and crushing revelation at the end of Shelley's career. The inadequacy of language is a recurring theme in Shelley, and the questions Rousseau and the speaker raise in *The Triumph of Life* are nothing new. The limits of verbal cognition are explored in the essay *On Life*, where similar questions lead to 'that verge where words abandon us, and . . . we grow dizzy to look down the dark abyss of – how little we know' (Shelley, 1977, p. 478). As early as *Alastor*,

Shelley's visionary quester raised questions of origins and ends for which he could find no answer:

> 'O stream!
> Whose source is inaccessibly profound,
> Whither do thy mysterious waters tend?
> Thou imagest my life. . .'
>
> (502–5)

A similar moment of bafflement before the mystery of life occurs in *Adonais* when the speaker tries to comprehend the permanence of loss amid the passing of time:

> Woe is me!
> Whence are we, and why are we? of what scene
> The actors or spectators? Great and mean
> Meet massed in death, who lends what life must borrow.
> As long as skies are blue, and fields are green,
> Evening must usher night, night urge the morrow,
> Month follow month with woe, and year wake year to sorrow.
>
> (183–9)

In *Adonais*, life desperately tries to 'borrow' meaning from death: 'No more let Life divide what Death can join together' (477), but can do so only at the cost of one's will to live 'when hope has kindled hope, and lured thee to the brink' (423). This failure to achieve unity with an object of desire occurs again at the end of *Epipsychidion*, another poem in which Shelley pushes language up against its limits:

> One hope within two wills, one will beneath
> Two overshadowing minds, one life, one death,
> One Heaven, one Hell, one immortality,
> And one annihilation. Woe is me!
> The winged words on which my soul would pierce
> Into the height of Love's rare Universe,
> Are chains of lead around its flight of fire.
>
> (584–90)

The desire to find a means to 'pierce/Into the height of Love's rare Universe' arises from a need to find a vantage point outside of language, but that need is checked by a reliance on metaphor to make the leap beyond life.

Throughout his career Shelley is aware that he can only play by the rules of the game of figuration, beyond which is a vast undifferentiated void of the unknowable. Over and against this is the phenomenal world of differences, troped at the climax of *Adonais* by images of light and the rainbow that will reappear in *The Triumph of Life*:

> The One remains, the many change and pass;
> Heaven's light forever shines, Earth's shadows fly;
> Life, like a dome of many-coloured glass,
> Stains the white radiance of Eternity,
> Until Death tramples it to fragments.
>
> (460–4)

If life deceives, it seems to invite a violence that 'tramples it to fragments'; one can only ask at the end of the poem whether error may, after all, be preferable to destruction.

What is remarkable about all these poems is the way in which what de Man calls 'the radical blockage that befalls' *The Triumph of Life* (de Man, 1979b, p. 68) has been encountered before and survived. Shelley's scepticism is a constant in his verse, but it has not previously led to nihilism. To claim, as de Man does, that '*The Triumph of Life* can be said to reduce all of Shelley's previous work to nought' (de Man, 1979b, p. 66) is to over-reach a poem that itself resists completion. The distinction drawn by Balachandra Rajan between a fragment and that which is incomplete is useful here, for the incomplete may still be finished in a variety of ways while the fragment as a reminder of something that was once complete indicates a necessary conclusion. Reading in a somewhat less apocalyptic mood than de Man, Rajan finds the questioning mode of *The Triumph of Life* 'creatively uncertain':

> Placed between surrender and negation, its enterprise (which must in its nature be unfinished) is to find a third way which partakes of neither. (B. Rajan, 1985, pp. 187–8)

The difference between scepticism and nihilism is precisely this openness to possibilities. Perhaps there are possibilities in the poem that de Man's rhetoric closes off but which Shelley's allows us to explore.

To be true to deconstruction, we should be prepared to read even de Man's text with an eye to its covert rhetorical strategies. Perhaps inevitably, critical reading must rely on synecdoche and therefore can never be exhaustive. To the extent that de Man makes *The Triumph of Life* stand for Shelley's creative achievement, and especially when he claims cancellation of the latter by the former, he takes a partial view. *The Triumph of Life* is another instance of the periodic resurfacing of a sceptical tendency in Shelley's work; that it comes at the 'end' of his career is owing merely to the accident of his death and not to any arc of creative necessity. Apart from the urge to impose a neat narrative closure on Shelley's career, there is no reason to believe that he could not have recovered from this glimpse into 'the abyss of how little we know' as he had from all the others, especially if the poem is as radically open-ended as Rajan thinks.

Synecdoche is evident again in de Man's selection for interpretive purposes of certain images in the poem and not others. For example, de Man concentrates on images of light, emphasising their elusive quality:

> Light covers light, trance covers slumber and creates conditions of optical confusion that resemble nothing so much as the experience of trying to read *The Triumph of Life*, as its meaning glimmers, hovers and wavers, but refuses to yield the clarity it keeps announcing.   (de Man, 1979b, pp. 52–3)

Light had been used in a similar way in *Alastor*, where the Visionary pursues his dream-maiden 'Obedient to the light/That shone within his soul' (492–3), much as Rousseau in *The Triumph* is taken in by the female 'shape all light' (352). As little as the Visionary does Rousseau realise that his female guide may be no more than the narcissistic projection of his own desire. Yet in commenting on *Alastor*, Shelley had found a degree of error to be essential to the maintenance of imaginative vitality:

> They who, deluded by no generous error, instigated by no sacred thirst of doubtful knowledge, duped by no illustrious superstition, loving nothing on this earth, and cherishing no hopes beyond ... have their apportioned curse. They languish, because none feel with them their common nature. They are morally dead.   (Shelley, 1977, p. 69)

This repression of love and hope is a tragic consequence of a preference for 'clarity' over the wavering light of 'doubtful knowledge'.

De Man does of course stress instances of evanescence in *The Triumph of Life*, though he tends to view them negatively. He attends to water as a sign for instability in the poem, but he concentrates almost exclusively on the passage in which the sea's waves wash away all trace of presence on the shore, in a figure for erasure that de Man calls 'disfiguration' (de Man, 1979b, pp. 45–6). This is surely a matter of partial emphasis again, for water is prominent in other ways among the many image patterns in *The Triumph of Life*. Once again, the poem reaches back to *Alastor* in using the 'stream' metaphor to image Life. In fact, the first turn of phrase used to express the speaker's attempt to comprehend Life's processes depends upon this very figure:

> As in that trance of wondrous thought I lay,
>   This was the tenour of my waking dream
> Methought I sate beside a public way
>
>   Thick strewn with summer dust, and a great stream
> Of people there was hurrying to and fro...
>
> (41–5)

The unthinking onrush of Life's captives is figured by more actively moving water shortly thereafter:

>   Old age and youth, manhood and infancy,
>   Mixed in one mighty torrent did appear...
>
> (52–3)

These lines are reminiscent of the passage beginning 'Great and mean/Meet massed in death' in *Adonais* (185–6), except that now temporal succession is conveyed by the moving water imagery of the stream of life. This river is figurally transformed to ocean as the procession wears on:

>   Imperial Rome poured forth her living sea
>   From senate-house and prison...
>
> (113–14)

One does not have to reach very far to see the similarity that enables the substitution of the way rivers run into the sea for the way life leads to death. In a related manner, the poem's lament for temporal loss and destruction invokes the dissipation of a wave's kinetic energy upon the shore:

> . . . the chariot hath
> Past over them; nor other trace I find
> But as of foam after the Ocean's wrath
>
> Is spent upon the desert shore.
>   (161–4)

This image of bubbling foam is equivocal, however, for though it is the sign of an absence it is still the bearer of a 'trace' of a previous presence. That it can hint at future presences too is evident in Rousseau's description of how he himself is 'borne onward' by the stream of life:

> But all like bubbles on an eddying flood
> Fell into the same track at last and were
>
> Borne onward. – I among the multitude
> Was swept. . .
>   (458–61)

Being 'swept' along by life does not, of course, imply recovery of what has been previously lost, but neither does it exclude encounters with new experiences in the succession of temporality. The visual representation of bubbles vanishing and reforming in the ebb and flow of time carries a value that the aural impression of bubbles popping does not. De Man says that 'the property of the river that the poem singles out is its sound' (de Man, 1979b, p. 53), but there are manifestly other possibilities cast up by the poem's water imagery.

De Man makes an important contribution when he says that *The Triumph of Life* turns upon a 'structure of "forgetting"' (de Man 1979b, p. 50), though negation is not the final stage in a poem that so resists closure. Disfiguration is succeeded by constant refiguration in the poem, just as the water's turbulence replaces vanished bubbles with new ones. The way the Shape replies to the plea for

absolute knowledge suggests the way in which cognition is mimed
by the successions of figural substitution in Shelley's poetry:

> 'Shew whence I came, and where I am, and why –
> Pass not away upon the passing stream.'

> 'Arise and quench thy thirst,' was her reply.
> And as a shut lily, stricken by the wand
> Of dewy morning's vital alchemy,

> I rose; and, bending at her sweet command,
>   Touched with faint lips the cup she raised,
> And suddenly my brain became as sand

>   Where the first wave had more than half erased
> The track of deer on desert Labrador . . .

(398–407)

It is true that the waves erase Rousseau's memory of something he
has lost, but it is *also* true that in their temporal succession they
replace his loss with something fresh:

> Whilst the fierce wolf from which they fled amazed

> Leaves his stamp visibly upon the shore
>   Until the second bursts – so on my sight
> Burst a new Vision never seen before.

(408–11)

The incessant successive replacement of deer's track by wolf's
stamp by some new trace after the next wave images the play of
substitution that characterises what William Keach calls the 'most
productive poetic impulse' of Shelley's style.[2] There is no nostalgia
for a lost origin nor any impulse to a revelatory ending in this play,
for it accepts a succession of appearances within time. The vigour
of Shelley's figurative play takes its impetus from such a world of
shifting phenomena where, as Derrida says, 'Nothing . . . is
anywhere ever simply present or absent. There are only, everywhere, differences, and traces of traces' (Derrida, 1981, p. 26).[3]

In his reading of *The Triumph of Life*, de Man is chary of play. He
seems less alive than other deconstructionists to what J. Hillis

Miller praises as 'the equivocal richness' that arises from 'the fact
that there is no conceptual expression without figure' (Miller, 1979,
p. 223). My experience of reading Shelley (not to mention other
texts) is that his work is replete with 'equivocal richness', and this
is no less true of *The Triumph of Life* than it is of his other poems.
The play on water as a signifier in the poem is a case in point. The
significance of water imagery in the poem cannot be confined to
erasure, as de Man claims. In its many transformations in the
poem, water is linked to light imagery by the visual potential of
bubbles to reflect an image. At one point the speaker, whose
growing frustration with a world of appearances associates him
with the elegiac mood of the speaker of *Adonais*, threatens to reject
life; Rousseau's reply, however, hints at the wonder still to be
found even in the foam that time casts upon the shores of this
world:

> > > > > 'Let them pass' –
> I cried – 'the world and its mysterious doom
>
> > Is not so much more glorious than it was
> > That I desire to worship those who drew
> New figures on its false and fragile glass
>
> > As the old faded.' – 'Figures ever new
> Rise on the bubble, paint them how you may;
> > We have but thrown, as those before us threw,
>
> > Our shadows on it as it past away.'
> > > > > > > (243–51)

It is difficult to decide in this poem whether to regard Rousseau's
attitude to figuration as one of hope or fear, a wish for the future,
or anxiety over its uncertainty. But that Shelley can project an
alternative to despair from the same imagery is evident in the
second chorus of *Hellas*. There, a group of captive women welcomes the flux of temporal appearance for the new possibilities it
can offer:

> > > Worlds on worlds are rolling ever
> > > > From creation to decay,
> > > Like the bubbles on a river

> Sparkling, bursting, borne away.
> But *they* are still immortal
> Who through Birth's orient portal
> And Death's dark chasm hurrying to and fro,
> Clothe their unceasing flight
> In the brief dust and light
> Gathered around their chariots as they go;
> New shapes they still may weave,
> New Gods, new Laws receive,
> Bright or dim are they as the robes they last
> On Death's bare ribs had cast.
>
> (197–210)

These accept the stream of life with lyric joy, and seek to shape meanings within it, even though these meanings may be no more lasting or substantial than 'bubbles on a river'. These meanings depend on glimpsing in 'the brief dust and light' of appearances thrown up by the relentless progress of the chariot of life constantly shifting figurations that help us to resist death by veiling it in 'robes' of language. Whether Rousseau or the speaker in *The Triumph of Life* can summon the mental agility to play the game of life is, as has been said, debatable, but that such a willingness to play exists elsewhere in Shelley's text is not.

The temptation that would make one particular poem stand for the whole of Shelley's 'text', or one set of images, read a particular way, stand for his 'meaning', is what makes synecdoche, as de Man himself admits, 'the most seductive of metaphors' (de Man, 1979a, p. 11). My reading as much as his gives in to it, for I can make no claim to have grasped the totality of Shelley's text, though I feel justified in pointing out other parts of it that can bring his reading into question. Still, since all critical reading relies on synecdoche, it seems unduly harsh to single out de Man for blame, until of course it is appreciated just how much his insistence on critical rigour distrusts all figuration. 'Figuration', he writes in his essay on *The Triumph of Life*, 'is the element in language that allows for the reiteration of meaning by substitution . . . But the particular seduction of the figure is not necessarily that it creates an illusion of sensory pleasure, but that it creates an illusion of meaning' (de Man, 1979b, p. 61).

De Man sternly resists the play of substitution in literature in the interest of something beyond the pleasure principle, and openly warns against the ways 'literature seduces us with the freedom of its figural combinations' (de Man, 1979a, p. 115). Evidence that there can be no conceptual thinking without the use of figures of speech, however, is found in his own text. The danger of being taken in by 'an illusion of meaning' generated by figurative language he habitually expresses in terms of a sublimated sexual metaphor – it is a 'seduction', an exercise of subtle powers designed to deceive, not through masculine force but through feminine beguilement. Christopher Norris notes that de Man associates the rhetoric of falsity with a 'will to resist these distinctly *female* blandishments' of language found in male philosophers and critics (Norris, 1988, p. 66). Indeed, de Man's identification of the plainly female 'shape all light' as 'the figure for the figuration of all signification' (de Man, 1979b, p. 62) makes her into a temptress in the context of his reading of *The Triumph of Life*, and attributes Cleopatra-like powers of bewitchment to language. De Man therefore does not deny the power of words, but it is a power his metaphor of seductive deceit identifies with a power of women to make the false seem true.

The Nietzschean trope that identifies truth as a dissimulative woman is a common theme in deconstruction, though Derrida takes a much more positive view of it than de Man. In a meditation on Nietzsche that responds less to the gloom than to the playful side of the philosopher, Derrida equates woman's artifice with the 'artist's philosophy' and insists that 'hers is an affirmative power' (Derrida, 1979, p. 67). Women's power is a favourite theme in Shelley, and though he is aware of its dark side, as the case of Beatrice Cenci shows, he more commonly celebrates its beneficial effects. One has only to think of characters like Cythna and Asia to be reminded of how Shelley portrays woman's subtlety as an indispensable supplement to masculine will. Though it can deceive, woman's power is more often a sustaining force in Shelley's poetry, a force akin to the power of language in its affirmative rather than analytical mode. Indeed, woman figures poetry in Shelley, from 'the still cave of the witch poesy' in *Mont Blanc* to the title character in *The Witch of Atlas*, who allegorises the 'subtler language' that Cythna wove in *The Revolt of Islam*.

It is perhaps not coincidental, then, that in *The Witch of Atlas* Shelley's 'lady-witch' is described as 'A lovely lady garmented in light' (81), an image that should call into question the unmixed malevolence of the female 'shape all light' in *The Triumph of Life*, thus allowing her a degree of ambiguity. As her purer ancestor, Shelley's witch is a holy innocent, and her behaviour is characterised by playfulness rather than seduction.[4] Throughout the poem she is associated with beauty, poetry and play, until in the end she is bidden farewell with the promise of future encounters in mind:

> These were the pranks she played among the cities
> Of mortal men, and what she did to sprites
> And gods, entangling them in her sweet ditties
> To do her will, and show their subtle slights,
> I will declare another time. . .
>
> (665–9)

She returns to her heterocosm, fixed at the poem's opening as somewhere prior to 'Error and Truth' (49–51), which is the dwelling place of metaphor. There she weaves out of natural beauties and the heart's desire 'a subtle veil' that clothes 'the chasm of death' but does not close it, for it supplements life without replacing it.

Even while he questions it, Derrida understands this desire for connections that metaphor fulfils amid the disconnectedness of the temporal world, where it is all too easy to conclude that 'nothing ... ever happens in relation ... to anything that precedes' (de Man, 1979b, p. 69). Such nihilism is not Shelley's, for though he cannot penetrate the veil of life, he finds compensation for cognitive lack in poetry's veil of figures. Poetry, he writes,

> defeats the curse which binds us to be subjected to the accident of surrounding impressions. And whether it spreads its own figured curtain or withdraws life's dark veil from before the scene of things, it equally creates for us a being within our being.   (Shelley, 1977, p. 505)

Shelley always lets us know that his illusions are made, that the fictive activity of the imagination works through metaphor to make connections that would not otherwise exist. Language, which is 'arbitrarily produced by the Imagination', is 'vitally metaphorical', writes Shelley in the *Defence of Poetry* (Shelley, 1977, pp. 482–3); 'it marks the before unapprehended relations of things', and whether those relations are true or false seems to matter less than the pathos they leave behind in the reader.

Derrida is far from being hostile to the figured curtain of poetry. He understands that 'the poet ... is the man of metaphor':

> While the philosopher is interested only in the truth of meaning, beyond even signs and names; and the sophist manipulates empty signs ... the poet plays on the multiplicity of signifieds.
>
> (Derrida, 1982, p. 248n)

Like Shelley, he allows poetry a place between truth and falsehood where our desires can have free play. While de Man cultivates an ascetic self-denial that amounts almost to an abnegation of the desire to read, Derrida is much more alive to the force of desire in our response to literary language, and so is more willing to enter into the game of the poet.[5] By highlighting the element of play in language, Derrida helps us to understand both how and why Shelley tried to mediate the conflict between the impetus of love and the restraints of life through figurative language.

Late in *The Triumph of Life*, Dante is praised for telling 'the wondrous story/How all things are transfigured, except Love' (475–6). De Man neglects the positive attraction of love for Shelley, for he can see it only as an occasion for seduction. Though he knows it can be a trap, love is not exclusively deceit in Shelley, for he can figure it as a harmonising agent, as he does in the dance in the fourth act of *Prometheus Unbound*. Shelley also figures life as a dance in *The Triumph of Life*, though one less attractive: 'If thou canst forbear/To join the dance, which I had well forborne' (188–9), cautions Rousseau. But the alternative to the dance of life is death, as the waning lines of the poem make clear:

> And some grew weary of the ghastly dance
>
> And fell, as I have fallen by the way side,
>   Those soonest from whose forms most shadows past,
>   And least of strength and beauty did abide.
>
> (540–3)

Those who deprive themselves of the 'shadows' of 'strength and beauty' fall into an even lower form of existence than that depicted in the dance of life. Avoidance of this apathy is also what motivates

Nietzsche to continue living, even though only in a world of mere appearance:

> I suddenly woke up in the midst of this dream, but only to the consciousness that I am dreaming and that I must go on dreaming lest I perish – as a somnambulist must go on dreaming lest he fall. What is 'appearance' for me now? . . . Appearance is for me that which lives and is effective and goes so far in its self-mockery that it makes me feel that this is appearance and will-o'-the-wisp and a dance of spirits and nothing more – that among all these dreamers, I, too, who 'know', am dancing my dance; that the knower is a means for prolonging the earthly dance and thus belongs to the masters of ceremony of existence.   (Nietzsche, 1974, p. 116)

For all his sceptical doubts, Shelley is in love with life and with the possibilities that it offers. Its very impermanence is to him a recommendation, not just because it contrasts with the permanence of death, but for the potential for change it can offer. And this is how we may answer de Man's challenge to dispose of Shelley's body (de Man, 1979b, p. 67): let us inscribe it within the structure of forgetting that is the text of his poetry and not seek outside the text for extra-linguistic factors that call into question values that can only be generated by verbal play within language itself.

Like Nietzsche, Shelley is dancing as hard as he can. He cannot evade death, nor even postpone it, but he can keep the thought of it at bay while he seeks ways to live. The role of the imagination is crucial here, for it projects the possibilities of living, and in so doing stimulates our desire to realise them. This is why Shelley thought the imagination indispensable to moral (and political) life:

> The great instrument of moral good is the imagination; and poetry administers to the effect by acting upon the cause. Poetry enlarges the circumference of the imagination by replenishing it with thoughts of ever new delight . . . Poetry strengthens that faculty which is the organ of the moral nature of man, in the same manner as exercise strengthens a limb.
>   (Shelley, 1977, p. 488)

Without the ability to 'imagine intensely and comprehensively', human beings cannot improve their conditions, and without the imaginative sympathy to 'put himself in the place of another and of many others' no one would bother to desire improvement. Love sustains language and language sustains life (which in its turn makes love and language possible): this imaginative economy is not an evasion of death so much as an interpretation of existence, a moral choice made authentic by Shelley's glimpse 'down the dark abyss of how little we know'. Even if it is true that life is killing him, his preference for the evil he knows makes him rather bear the ills he has than fly to others that he knows not of.

That the maintenance of existence depends on the play of illusion seems not to worry Shelley, or at least not to incapacitate him. It is a condition of the 'poetic faith' he inherits from Coleridge that he accept the inadequacy of language to ultimate truth, affirm life through the play of imaginative fictions, and count on his readers' desire for meaning to cope with the free-play of signs. To prevent illusion from growing into delusion, Coleridge knew that such 'willing suspension of disbelief' could only be a *'negative* faith which simply permits the images presented to work by their own force, without either denial or affirmation of their real existence by the judgement', which is to admit language's power 'for the moment' but not its reference to lasting and 'absolute truth' (Coleridge, 1956, pp. 169, 256). Derrida writes that there can be two attitudes to this loss of the transcendental signified:

> Turned towards the lost or impossible presence of the absent origin, this structuralist thematic of broken immediacy is there- fore the saddened, negative, nostalgic, guilty, Rousseauistic side of the thinking of play whose other side would be the Nietz- schean affirmation, that is the joyous affirmation of a world of signs without fault, without truth, and without origin which is offered to active interpretation.   (Derrida, 1978, p. 292)

Shelley's poetry is on balance just such an affirmation of a world of signs, a sceptical affirmation of a life without truth but with many possibilities for meaning. The attitude to life expressed by the guilty and nostalgic Rousseau of *The Triumph of Life* is not exhaus- tive of those possibilities, and his torpor is not Shelley's. The exuberance of Shelley's play affirms signs as it affirms life, and is the source of his power as an artist.

To say that in Shelley the play of signifiers generates a multiplicity of signifieds is to re-inscribe the way style modifies substance in

Shelley. It is not that Shelley's style exists 'apart from substance', as Leavis would have it. Instead, Shelley's 'artistic power', so much praised by Wordsworth, derives from the extravagance of his play with language.[6] This play, far from effacing meaning, generates potentials for meaning that can be produced in different ways by different readers. In helping us understand how his text 'is offered to active interpretation', deconstruction points to the variety of ways in which his text can be experienced and verifies its richness. The figural productivity of Shelley's text means that, far from having no substance at all, Shelley has a surfeit of it, for the reader who responds to the power of his language and the play of his style.

2
Shelley and Class
P. M. S. Dawson

There are three main problems in locating and explicating Shelley's political identity. First, there is the extent to which the expression of his views was influenced by tactical considerations which entailed some compromising of his real opinions. Second, there is the question of how far elements of his background and upbringing continued to coexist uneasily with his consciously worked-out political philosophy. Third, there is the equivocal political situation of the intellectual, a problematic issue for literary scholars as much as for their subject of study.

The first question is the least problematic. The techniques of scholarship, properly applied, are generally adequate to ascertain when and to what degree Shelley was accommodating his views to his audience. His apparent endorsement of 'the Laws of your own land ... The old laws of England' in *The Masque of Anarchy* (327, 331), a poem intended for publication, is a tactical appeal to a political tradition which Shelley himself, as a consistent opponent of custom and prejudice, would on other occasions be the first to treat sceptically. Shelley himself was fully conscious of the problem, and tried to think it through in some of his writings. The work known as the *Essay on Christianity* is able to present Christ with considerable sympathy, because Shelley sees him as facing his own dilemma as a reformer. Christ was able to influence his hearers because he 'accommodated his doctrines to the prepossessions of those whom he addressed'. Generalising from Christ's situation in order to include his own, Shelley concluded that 'All reformers have been compelled to practice this misrepresentation of their own true feelings and opinions' (Shelley, 1926–30, VI, p. 243). This discussion should be kept in mind by all Shelley scholars when trying to extricate his 'true feelings and opinions' from the evidence of his statements on various occasions and for various purposes.

Fortunately the time has long since passed when Shelley's

political views were judged either irrelevant to his poetry (as for his Victorian admirers) or unworthy of serious consideration (as for T. S. Eliot and F. R. Leavis). Enthusiasm has its own dangers, and readers of Paul Foot's *Red Shelley* (Foot, 1980) will sometimes suspect an attempt to convert Shelley retrospectively to Foot's own socialist views. In fact Foot is aware of the tension in Shelley's views between radicalism and moderation – he simply insists on finding the 'true' Shelley in the former. This attitude may sometimes lead him to cut knots rather than disentangle them, but it probably does Shelley more real service than a pretence at a more dispassionate consideration. As an activist, Foot sees political issues as finally resolvable only by taking sides, and he reminds us that this was also part of Shelley's situation. It remains true that we will only partially understand Shelley's political decisions if we are unaware of the concerns that underlie them. But scholarship is on the whole good at reconstructing such intellectual schemes, and the 'philosophical anarchism' that Shelley shared with Godwin has been persuasively elucidated by Michael Scrivener (1982). This philosophy provided Shelley with a systematic foundation for the liberal positions inherited from his Whig background, while its strenuous gestures towards philosophical rigour allowed him to avoid the bad faith with which those ideals were more preached than practised by his family and its political patrons. Philosophical anarchism is the intellectual's political philosophy, stressing Independence and Opinion in a way that privileges the supposed autonomy and influence of the thinker and man of letters. Its progenitor, Godwin, took as his models thinkers like Montesquieu and Helvetius rather than an activist like Paine, and he indeed belongs along with Bentham and the Mills to the select group of British *philosophes* in the tradition of the continental Enlightenment. As Carl Woodring (1970) has astutely pointed out, such an enlightened or utilitarian radicalism exists in tension with other Romantic values.

The other questions, involving as they do the issue of class position, are more resistant to treatment at the level of conscious awareness. There is enough evidence to establish that Shelley was unusually sensitive to questions of what we would now call class. This is illustrated by an anecdote recorded in 1811 which he himself called 'striking':

My window is over the kitchen; in the morning I threw it up, & had nearly finished dressing when 'for Charitys dear sake' met my ear, these words were pronounced with such sweetness that on turning round I was surprised to find them uttered by an old beggar, to whom in a moment the servant brought some meat. I ran down and gave him something: – he appeared extremely grateful. I tried to enter into conversation with him – in vain. I followed him a mile asking a thousand questions; at length I quitted him finding by this remarkable observation that perseverance was useless. 'I see by your dress that you are a rich man – they have injured me & mine a million times. You appear to be well intentioned but I have no security of it while you live in such a house as that, or wear such clothes as those. It wd. be charity to quit me.'

(Shelley, 1964, I, p. 120)

The beggar's rejection of Shelley's advances is based on a clear if rudimentary class consciousness – there can be no real community between 'they' and 'me & mine'. In Shelley the encounter evidently helped to spark off – or allowed him to record – the consciousness of class that fuels his reformist passion. Such incidents were to lead him to the conclusion that, as he wrote to Hunt in 1820, 'The system of society as it exists at present must be overthrown from the foundations with all its superstructure of maxims & of forms before we shall find anything but dissapointment in our intercourse with any but a few select spirits' (Shelley, 1964, II, p. 191). It is significant that Shelley rarely uses the poor and oppressed as figures in his poetry, except in the most clearly propagandistic way. He was not able, as Wordsworth was, to appropriate such figures for the purposes of self-dramatisation, however strong his feelings of alienation and isolation.

Shelley's consciousness of class was inevitably a guilty one; it identified him as one of the privileged, an 'oppressor' who benefited from an unjust system. 'I am one of these aristocrats', he confessed in 1811 (to a social inferior). 'In me . . . the same machinery of oppression is preparing, in order that I also in my turn may become an oppressor' (Merle, 1841, p. 706). He did all that he could to escape from his class and the position that his birth into it had prepared for him. His spectacular acts of youthful rebellion – defending atheism, a misalliance, fomenting revolution among the Irish – served to burn his social bridges. But it is questionable whether the entanglements of class affiliation can be escaped so easily. As his friends pointed out, he always kept the manners of the born gentleman (Hogg, in Wolfe, 1933, I, p. 133; II, p. 108; Medwin, 1913, p. 343; Hunt, 1828, p. 49). More significantly, it could be argued that he also preserved many of the social and political instincts of the born aristocrat. He was not unaware of the danger, and recognised that the opinions even of the dissident, 'which he often hopes he has dispassionately secured from all contagion of prejudice and vulgarity, would be found, on examination, to be the inevitable excrescence of the very usages from which he vehemently dissents' (Shelley, 1926–30, VII, p. 83).

Donald Reiman has argued persuasively that 'Shelley – benevolent and generous though he was and possessing a highly sensitive social conscience though he did – was not himself exempt from being unconsciously swayed in his social, economic, and political theories by inbred class prejudices' (Reiman, 1979, p. 11). His attitude to the bourgeoisie is a telling example of this. While opposed on principle to all 'aristocracies', he was particularly opposed to the new financial aristocracy of the middle class, and freely confessed that his 'republicanism' 'would bear with an aristocracy of chivalry, & refinement, before an aristocracy of commerce and vulgarity' (Shelley, 1964, I, p. 352; see Reiman, 1979, pp. 9–10).

If Shelley's background set him against the bourgeoisie, it also complicated his stance towards the working class. Despite his sympathy for the exploited, he harboured considerable fears about the results of their taking a hand in redressing the wrongs done to them. While allowing for popular resistance as a last resort, he preferred a reform guided by the enlightened and influential – a position hard to distinguish from the paternalism of the Whig aristocracy: 'the change should commence among the higher orders', he assured Peacock in 1819, 'or anarchy will only be the last flash before despotism' (Shelley, 1964, II, p. 115). No doubt he would have sympathised with the comment of his family's political patron, the Duke of Norfolk, on the French Revolution that 'when the people reformed for themselves, they reformed miserably' (see Dawson, 1980, p. 21). When in 1819 Shelley addressed himself to 'the people' in *A Philosophical View of Reform* and a number of poems, most notably *The Masque of Anarchy*, one can sense a considerable nervousness about the possible effects of his intervention. *The Masque of Anarchy* shifts from visionary inspiration very reminiscent of Blake, to advice as to how the reform campaign should be managed which the reformers could only have found condescending. Significantly, Shelley made little attempt to circumvent the caution of his friends in England, and these works remained unpublished in his lifetime.

If Shelley never divested himself of his aristocratic instincts, neither did he acquire a working-class consciousness. More to the point, he did not recognise any need to do so. His consciousness of class is not to be identified with class consciousness. His response to the existence of divisions in society was not an acceptance of the inescapability of class consciousness, but a recourse to an Enlightenment universalism that promised to abolish such divisions. Shelley's allegiance, as he saw it, was not to the interests of his own class, or of any class, but to certain potent abstractions – Justice, Equality, Benevolence, Reason. It could be argued – and it was argued by Marx – that these were merely the cloak assumed by the class interests of the revolutionary bourgeoisie – a cloak that could also be assumed by other classes willing to ally with it. This analysis is a necessary one, but it should not be allowed to obscure the possibility that individuals pursuing these ideals in ignorance of their class determination may find themselves committed to acting against their own class interests – and the more so when the ideals themselves prescribe a sacrifice of personal interest to the general good. One can imagine the frustration of Shelley's family, faced with his determination to shape his conduct by those Whig liberal values which they knew (but could hardly say) were intended for public consumption only. Timothy Shelley professed to be an atheist, but of course he attended the established worship; his Whig commitment to religious liberty did not prevent him from consistently voting against Catholic Emancipation. We can also appreciate Shelley's impatience with such institutionalised hypocrisy.

The equivocal class situation of the intellectual stems from the fact that the very logic of the intellectual project will lead him (or her) to prefer the ideals of his class to its practice, but will then leave him to pursue these ideals in a social vacuum. He will articulate them in their most extreme and logically consistent form, as Shelley rejected Whig liberalism and even Paineite republicanism in favour of Godwin's philosophical anarchism, however careful he was to recognise that theoretical rigour must not preclude flexibility in practice. What the intellectual cannot control is the reception of his work, which will be determined by considerations of class interest. His own class will recuperate his work in so far as it pays lip service to its professed values, while detaching it from any relevance to practice. Shelley could be an angel for respectable readers of the nineteenth century on the condition of being ineffectual. His commitment to revolution was received as the protest of a fine spirit against the restrictions of mortal existence, rather than accepted as a valid demand for political change. When a writer's devotion to universal values leads him to plead the cause of another class, that class will appropriate his writings, but in a necessarily limited and tactical way. The working-class movement of the nineteenth century valued the political support of Shelley and Byron precisely because they were aristocrats.

The intellectual, having severed the organic links with his own class while forming only precarious alliances outside it, is in danger of running into damaging delusions concerning political change and his own place within it. Those universalist values which serve to express material interests are taken to be the causes rather than the consequences of political change, and those who articulate them are tempted to arrogate to themselves a correspondingly privileged position, as 'the unacknowledged legislators of the world'. The phrase is, of course, Shelley's conclusion to *A Defence of Poetry*, where he bestows on poets alone the honorific title that in *A Philosophical View of Reform* he had accorded to poets and philosophers (Shelley, 1926–30, VII, p. 20). The same optimism concerning the potential role of the intelligentsia is present in Coleridge, who actually proposed to institutionalise it in the form of a 'clerisy' (Coleridge, 1976). Coleridge deplored the class divisions within his society, and his remedy was the 'estate' of the clerisy, which would have no interest of its own apart from the national interest. Though Coleridge would not be happy to recognise the fact, it could be argued that his 'clerisy' does exist in the form of teaching, media and publicity professions. The ability to reshape society that Coleridge dreamt of for such an intellectual class has in practice been severely compromised by the class backgrounds of the individuals who staff it and the class pressures across society which constitute the environment within which it must work. Shelley recognised that there is a crucial ambiguity as to whether intellectual formulations are the causes or consequences of significant political changes. He notes that 'an energetic development' of English literature 'has ever followed or preceded a great and free development of the national will', and claims that poetry is 'the most unfailing herald, or companion, or follower, of a universal employment of the sentiments of a nation to the production of beneficial change' (Shelley, 1926–30, VII, p. 19). It is possible that Shelley's anarchist beliefs would have prevented him from putting his trust in an intellectual class which would do the nation's thinking for it. But in order to retain his faith in the positive and beneficial role of writers and intellectuals, he is obliged to leave obscure the actual relations between intellectual formulation and social change.

The ultimate source of this vagueness is the fallacy which Marx and Engels found and denounced in their Young Hegelian opponents:

> Since the Young Hegelians consider conceptions, thoughts, ideas, in fact all the products of consciousness, to which they attribute an independent existence, as the real chains of men (just as the Old Hegelians declare them the true bonds of human society), it is evident that the Young Hegelians have to fight only against these illusions of consciousness. Since, according to their fantasy, the relations of men, all their doings, their fetters, and their limitations are products of their consciousness, the Young Hegelians logically put to men the moral postulate of exchanging their present consciousness for human, critical or egoistic consciousness, and thus of removing their limitations.
>
> (Marx and Engels, 1976, pp. 35–6)

As Jerome McGann has argued, there is a 'Romantic ideology' which is, in its fundamental idealism, identical with the 'German ideology' so trenchantly criticised by Marx and Engels: 'This idea that poetry, or even consciousness, can set one free of the ruins of history and culture is the grand illusion of every Romantic poet' (McGann, 1983, p. 137). Both the enslavement and the liberation of Shelley's Prometheus are presented as mental acts: Prometheus will be free once he has come to recognise that it is his own limited perceptions that enslave him. But this is neither an answer to the problem nor an adequate explanation of it. Prometheus' self-enslavement remains inexplicable in the absence of the recognition that mental slavery is an expression of a condition of historical oppression. To be sure, the chains will not be broken until their existence is recognised, but this recognition does not in itself undo the condition of oppression. ' "Liberation" ', as Marx and Engels remark, 'is a historical and not a mental act' (Marx and Engels, 1976, p. 44).

The point is not to denounce Shelley for intellectual errors that are the understandable result of his own historical condition. To have recognised the real conditions of liberation would only have faced him with his own impotence and prevented him from making what contribution he could. It is more to the point to note that, as McGann argues, 'Today the scholarship and interpretations of Romantic works is dominated by an uncritical absorption in Romanticism's own self-representations' (McGann, 1983, p. 137) – though to call this merely 'uncritical' might imply more ideological innocence than is actually involved. Shelley scholarship faithfully repeats his delusion without his excuse. The reduction of human unfreedom to Blakean 'mind-forg'd manacles' is a kind of political wisdom that continues to appeal to professional intellectuals, less because they see in this insight the key to human liberation in general than because it allows them to believe in mental liberation as available to the intellectual himself, however stubbornly the world at large refuses to transform itself in accordance with his insights. This soured elitism has rather less to recommend it than the more optimistic idealism of the Romantics, and the latter should not be used to underpin the former.

3

The Nursery Cave: Shelley and the Maternal

Barbara Charlesworth Gelpi

The months of 1792 during which Elizabeth Pilfold Shelley was pregnant with her first child were a time when her condition was so enviable that fashion dictated 'the sixth-month pad' as an undergarment for all women, regardless of age or marital status (Werkmeister, 1967, pp. 328–30). The outcry against padding – voiced primarily by men – soon assigned pads to oblivion, but in its brief appearance this humble piece of clothing served as a visible sign of a domestic ideology that was firmly in place at the time of Percy Bysshe Shelley's birth.

Historians differ over the time at which this particular ideology of family relationships first appeared, the class in which it originated, the social forces that gave rise to it, and its effects; but the material facts, however differently interpreted, remain constant. The palpable evidence of conduct manuals, medical advice books, magazine articles, paintings, imaginative literature, children's stories, and hymns gives the certainty that by the middle of the eighteenth century upper- and middle-class women were barraged with instructions to remain in the sphere of the home in intimate and constant contact with their infants and young children: breast-feeding them, supervising and participating in their play, guiding them into the spoken and written use of language, socialising, amusing, cleansing, and instructing them. Grudgingly it was allowed that the mother's tasks might to some extent be supervisory in that she could delegate some of them to servants part of the time – but never to the point where a servant's relationship to the child would have anything of the immediacy, importance or power of her own.[1]

This amassed evidence cannot, of course, serve as an historical record of women's actual ideas or actions. In a certain way, it serves as negative evidence. If women were in fact conforming with these social norms, what need would there be to continue spending time, money and human energy urging them so to conform? At the same time, this powerful ideology makes a real impingement upon consciousness and so has real effects. No matter how particular mothers around Shelley (including his own) were behaving, he was necessarily influenced by the ideology of motherhood in place while he grew up.

The ideology restricted women to a separate, domestic sphere, but obviously if women are, without overt coercion, to step mildly into their sphere and remain there, its restrictions should ideally be experienced as liberatory, even flattering, proof of female control. Yet the power thereby ascribed to women could be made to appear so great that it threatened the masculine dominance it was designed to maintain. The line the argument must take, then, becomes a tight-rope across what Leonore Davidoff and Catherine Hall describe as 'the contradictions between the claims for women's superiority and their social subordination' (Davidoff and Hall, 1987, p. 149).

The contradiction manifests itself in the very word 'sphere'. When used to define, indeed restrict, women's social position, 'sphere' has the sixth meaning assigned it in the *New English Dictionary* (*NED*): 'A province or domain in which one's activities or faculties find scope or exercise, or in which they are naturally confined; range or compass of action or study'. The words 'domain' and 'scope' suggest full control, while 'confined' and 'compass' carry seemingly opposed notions of restriction. Behind this contradiction lies the ancient 'signified' of this signifier, in the *NED*'s second definition of 'sphere': 'one of the concentric, transparent, hollow globes imagined by the earlier astronomers as revolving around the earth and respectively carrying with them the several heavenly bodies' (*NED*, 1919, IX, pt. 1, pp. 584–5). *These* separate spheres are those Ptolemaic globes that rise concentrically above the Earth – the Moon, Mercury, Venus, Sun, Mars, Jupiter, Saturn – each of which serves as both domain of and containment for its guiding Intelligence, the source of its 'influence'.

Thomas Gisborne consciously uses the word with the restrictive signification contained in the *NED*'s sixth definition when warning young women against excessive ambition. There are, he laments, female malcontents who 'are occasionally heard to declare their opinion, that the sphere in which women are destined to move is so humble and so limited as neither to require nor to reward assiduity' (Gisborne, 1799, p. 11). However, even in his sentence the resonant juxtaposition of 'sphere' with 'destined to move' calls up the possibility that the sphere to which a woman is 'limited' is also the one in and from which she acts as a tutelary deity. For along with its ancient astronomy, the signifier 'sphere' trails the ancient belief in those divinities named as the ruler of each. The planets, as C. S. Lewis points out, 'had, after all, been the hardiest of all the Pagan gods'. He adds:

> Modern readers sometimes discuss whether, when Jupiter or Venus is mentioned by a mediaeval poet, he means the planet or the deity. It is doubtful whether the question usually admits of an answer. Certainly we must never assume without special evidence that such personages are in Gower or Chaucer the merely mythological figures they are in Shelley or Keats. They are planets as well as gods. Not that the Christian poet believed in the god because he believed in the planet; but all three things – the visible planet in the sky, the source of the influence, and the god – generally acted as a unity upon his mind.
>
> (Lewis, 1964, pp. 104–5)

Lewis's use of the reductive phrase 'merely mythological' assumes that Shelley and Keats cannot participate in medieval Christianity's complex appropriation of pagan worship. I question that assumption and hold rather, with Donald Reiman, that 'there is still room for further exploration of the relationship of Shelley's mythmaking to the tradition of allegorising ancient religions and mythologies' (Reiman, 1988, p. 392). Specifically, I hold that the language used during Shelley's formative years to describe the maternal function and influence, including the concepts implied by the term 'sphere', fosters his imaginative participation in a mythology centred upon a maternal deity: Aphrodite, to give her only one of her many names.

When examining the literature produced by the same maternal ideology in eighteenth- and early nineteenth-century Germany, Marilyn Massey makes the point that the feminine 'soul' constructed to fill society's purpose 'began to refer to a female God. At that point, belief in the feminine soul ceased to serve as an ideological force to shape women for their place in the social order and flickered with the promise of subverting and transforming that order' (Massey, 1985, p. 43). My own analysis of the ideology's potential for subversion is not as positive as Massey's. I would, for instance, argue against the claim that it made Shelley a 'proto-feminist', but I do hold that the texts produced by a first child, a son, reared as Shelley was within a strong ideology of mother-hood, should be read with that ideology in mind. Such a reading has both psychological and political dimensions; it illuminates Shelley's conflicting thoughts about the nature of subjectivity, and it helps in understanding the strategy and imagery involved in his struggle to subvert the political, religious and social institutions of his time. To phrase my thesis in other terms, I wish to argue that Shelley was (in an admittedly complicated way) a worshipper in the ancient cult of the Great Mother and to suggest what that allegiance meant.

Such phrasing makes my thinking vulnerable to an acceptance of the very reified, external absolutes that, as Jerrold Hogle argues, Shelley deplores and resists (Hogle, 1988, p. 54). For Shelley, true human creativity flows from the understanding that life involves a constant transaction or sharing, a 'transference', in Hogle's term, which he defines as 'any "bearing across" between places, moments, thoughts, words, or persons' (Hogle, 1988, p. 15). Despite the Freudian associations of the term 'transference', this dialogic concept of subjectivity is Bakhtinian rather than Freudian, as Hogle himself suggests when he notes that Shelley 'prefigures Bakhtinian concepts of "heteroglossia" and the process of self-composition' (Hogle, 1989, p. 346).

A gloss, therefore, on the term 'transference' is Bakhtin's state-ment that 'consciousness is essentially multiple . . . The very being of man (both external and internal) is the *deepest communion. To be* means *to communicate* . . . To be means to be for another, and through the other, for oneself' (quoted in Emerson, 1986, p. 33; Bakhtin's emphasis). Bakhtin himself uses the maternal relation to the inter-uterine infant, but only as an *analogue* for this communion: 'Just as the body is initially formed in the womb of the mother (in her body), so human consciousness awakens surrounded by the consciousness of others' (quoted in Todorov, 1984, p. 96). In fact, the mother/infant relationship after parturition can serve not just as an analogue but as the primary *example* of consciousness awakening through interaction with other(s). In Shelley's poetry the mother goddess functions as mythic representation of that inner psychological process and not as a reified external deity.

Nonetheless, Shelley cannot truly be considered a protofeminist because the dialogic process described above can only serve as stable grounding for the subject when women, including – indeed, particularly – mothering women, are granted full subjectivity. Shelley reflects the attitudes of his society in that he cannot bring himself to do so. Evidence of this failure, even with the biographical record to one side, is his objection to the possibility of women's suffrage.[2]

As the ruling intelligences of their assigned sphere, mothers in the late eighteenth century were goddesses, while out of that sphere they had no status. Neither case allowed them to function as full human subjects. In such a situation, given the transferential nature of subjectivity and the formative role of the mother in its creation, *all* subjectivity, masculine and feminine, becomes problematic, even delusory. Shelley recognises but never answers this Lacanian problem; he could not do so, indeed, so long as he sought the answer in the locus of the problem, i.e. in 'woman's' Otherness. But if in this way he was the creation of his age – to paraphrase his own words in the Preface to *Prometheus Unbound* (Shelley, 1977, p. 134) – he was also a creator in recognising the liminal or border nature of subjectivity, and in seeing that quality as itself only a microcosm of the shifts, exchanges, interpenetrations and cross-fertilisations characterising all life.

Shelley's most succinct statement of that insight comes in his meditation on the nature of pronouns in *On Life:*

> [T]he existence of distinct individual minds similar to that which is employed in now questioning its own nature, is . . . a delusion. The words, *I, you, they,* are not signs of any actual difference subsisting between the assemblage of thoughts thus indicated, but are merely marks employed to denote the different modifications of the one mind . . . We are on that verge where words abandon us, and what wonder if we grow dizzy to look down the dark abyss of – how little we know.
> (Shelley, 1977, pp. 477–8)

That dizziness could at different moments be for Shelley either terrifyingly nihilistic or sublimely visionary. And in either form the *entirety* of the experience – the revelation, the attendant feelings, and the language expressing both – was best evoked for him by the figure of the goddess who traditionally has been the sign of life's mysterious interconnectedness.

Sometimes she is the overt subject of a poem, as in *Adonais* or as the figure of Asia in *Prometheus Unbound*. Cythna is avatar of the 'foam born' in *Laon and Cythna*; in the *Ode to Liberty* the goddess is 'written' iconographically over the prayer that Liberty may lead forth Wisdom 'as the morning-star/Beckons the Sun from the Eoan wave' (XVIII, 257–8). Indeed, though the word may be inelegant, one can only say that she is scrawled iconographically across all of Shelley's work. Multiplied examples can only give a notion of her pervasiveness, and it would be impossible to draw up an exhaustive list. Also, though her signs are everywhere, they have different, at times contradictory, at times multivalent, meanings; each demands its own reading. In *To a Skylark* her unseen or scarcely seen planet in the daylight sky seems to signify a beneficent, inspirational presence resembling the 'Power' of *The Hymn to Intellectual Beauty* that 'Floats though unseen among us' (2), while in *The Triumph of Life* a series of juxtaposed images carries the suggestion that the guidance seemingly preferred by the goddess's 'star' is in fact delusory (412–31). The goddess's moon-boat carries Asia back to Prometheus (II.v.156–7), but the horned moon also impassively watches the expiration of the Poet in *Alastor* (645–7).[3]

Intellectually, Shelley could find precedent for 'seeing' Aphrodite as such a power in any number of sources, with Lucretius as the most salient. Experientially, his fascination with this goddess is rooted in his culture's understanding of the maternal. As shown by his comments in both *On Love* and *On Life*, the bond between mother and infant was an exemplary one for Shelley and a demonstration of the way in which the weaving, interweaving and unweaving of life's filaments is at work in the world. He left no detailed account of what he thought the nature of that infant experience to be. We can, however, learn much about his assumptions through analysing the way in which the relationship between mothers and their children was being constructed during Shelley's infancy, childhood and youth.

In middle- and upper-class nurseries of the period, children were receiving the same ideology as their mothers and from similar sources. While the omnivorous breadth of Shelley's reading, including his absorption in 'Gothics' and other novels directed towards a female readership, has long been taken for granted, scholarly attention tends to shift quickly to Shelley's precocious philosophical, scientific and 'high' literary interests and away from the comparatively ephemeral works of popular culture. Yet such productions, at any period in history, have if anything more influence upon the consciousness through introjection and identification than do the consciously studied works of high culture; they serve as our imagination's fare at a more highly impressionable period of life. And later, our relatively unconscious absorption of these materials gives them unnoticed strength.

The ideology of motherhood 'in the air' would have reached Shelley from any number of sources: the primers in which he was taught to read, the story books read to him, the attitudes of his caretakers as they were shaped by advice books, the popular literature – stories, novels and poems – that he soon could read for himself. I turn now to look at a cross-section of these different ideological media in order to catch certain quintessential characteristics of the idealised feminine, the ensphered goddess or goddess-like figure who offers an alternative to the violence and injustice of the Jupiterean, patriarchal sphere.

One of the striking characteristics about the many stories in women's magazines on the theme of the mother-educator is the dichotomy set up between a blameless wife and mother and a scapegrace and even vicious husband. After a time, she abandons the attempt to turn him from his dissolute ways and devotes her total, loving attention to the education of her child, usually a daughter. The husband, moved by her example, eventually returns to a domestic routine ordered under her direction.[4]

This scenario carries the clear message that women *must* undertake full responsibility for child-care, not because men have shrugged off boring tasks, but because men are incapable of the selfless sense of duty demanded. So, paradoxically, the more bullying, rapacious, irresponsible and ungrateful men are represented to be, the stronger the argument for women's dedicated, self-abnegating service. While ideologically canny – as one can tell from its long life right up to the present moment – this strategy has a telling circular effect upon the 'family romance' already created by strengthening the bond between mother and infant. It sets up a rivalry between child and father in which they compete for her sexual notice and her maternal nurturance. Such fantasies also lessen the likelihood that fathers will serve as models for moral action, since they make mothers the primary reservoir of moral power.

What was the mother's powerful ordering of life supposed to involve? What was this paragon doing when, in domestic retirement, she devoted herself to the 'education' of her infants and children? First of all, she was to have them constantly under her eye. But simply observing the children to keep them from physical harm – as well as from moral, particularly sexual, wrong, *bien entendu* – is only part, perhaps even the lesser part, of the task. The mother is to involve herself in the children's activities, both passively as a model for behaviour, and actively as one who uses the countless incidents of the day to inculcate intellectual curiosity and moral awareness. 'Mrs. Lovechild' (Lady Eleanor Fenn) introduces her *Rational Sports*, a compendium of dialogues based on such imagined incidents, by saying, 'It is the province of the mother to tincture the mind' (Fenn, n.d., p. xiii).

Books like *Rational Sports* poured from the presses in multiple editions as reading, spelling and grammar texts. Typically such books, written and illustrated to appeal to very young readers, include a preface directed specifically to mothers, encouraging them in their task as educators, and suggesting specific uses for the little text. Such a preface to Fenn's *The Infant's Friend* presupposes an interaction between mother and child in which every physical movement of the mother's lips, teeth, tongue and throat serves as the child's visible model and oral guide:

> There is seldom sufficient attention paid to a very obvious method of leading on the Learner; namely that of giving him the vowel or diphthong of that particular word ... Suppose him to be at a loss for the sound of *cheat*; only ask him *e,a,t*; then *h,e,a,t*; then *c,h,e,a,t*.   (Fenn, 1797, pp. x–xi)

It is impossible to follow the suggested exercise without the mother's and the child's mouths mirroring one another in the way I have described. Fenn's very presentation makes it obvious that she conceives of the learning process as achieved through a constant dialogue between mother and child. Thus, in *The Infant's Friend* her exposition on the teaching of syllables is constructed as an imaginary conversation initiated by the mother: '– Well! now you think you know every letter, meet with it where you may: – I have a mind to try you: – Shew me *m* – Very well! – Now shew me *a*; – *m* and *a* spell *ma* ... I believe I may indulge you with a lesson of syllables' (Fenn, 1797, p. 6).

Again, the child's sounds, produced through the manipulation of tongue, teeth and lips, are both instituted and echoed by the mother's voice. Also, the crossover from verbal to written signs is made with the mother's voice as bridge, while at the same time her voice creates an affective content that is constantly relational; the child's pride in achievement and so pleasure in receiving the mother's notice gets recognition and response in the opening statement, though accompanied by a new challenge and a demand for further effort. The reward – 'I believe I may indulge you with a lesson of syllables' – is the mother's further interest and attention along with the chance for future praise.[5]

In another manual, *Parsing Lessons for Young Children*, Fenn makes the customary point that women alone are capable of fulfilling the demands of child-care and, as was again a virtual cliché, creates an associational link between Providential and maternal concern: 'Certainly Providence has designed our early youth should be under the guidance of Females; they must supply milk; they must support the tottering steps of infancy in a figurative as well as a literal sense' (Fenn, 1798, p. vi). In this instance the mother functions as Providential agent, with no metaphorical link between the two guardianships. Often, however, the connection becomes one in which the mother's selfless and constant attention to the child's needs acts as a 'figure' or 'sign' of God's beneficent watchfulness. At the point of explicit or implied comparison – mother/God – the unstated difference always present in metaphor can easily lose its impact before the resonance created between the two terms. A contradictory factor operates as well: in a religious tradition which conceives God as a triply reinforced masculine Person, the element of difference is so strong in a mother/God comparison that the trope functions more effectively in conveying an idea about mothers than it does in describing the nature of God. If religious faith weakens, the God-term of the trope fades, while the mother-term transforms into the reified divine. Furthermore, in the general dismissal of men as possible caretakers, the Providential mother shares power with no masculine consort.

To approach the point from a slightly different direction, this literature calls up 'the fantasy of the perfect mother' (Chodorow and Contratto, 1982, p. 54), both as a way of inspiring religious devotion to God and as a further inscription upon women's subjectivities about their 'nature' as mothers. But for the reasons discussed above, the image can have more effect on the way mothers perceive themselves and are perceived by others than on people's experience of the Divine.

An edifying passage from Samuel Richardson, anthologised both in Mary Wollstonecraft's *The Female Reader* and in Anna Letitia Barbauld's *The Female Speaker*, uses an extended simile to describe Providence as a fond mother, but the affect lavished on motherhood is so strong that the comparison stands on its head, and we 'see' the mother as Providential:

See the fond mother encircled by her children; with pious tenderness she looks around, and her soul even melts with maternal love ... to these she dispenses a look, and a word to those; and whether she grants or refuses, whether she smiles or frowns, it is all in tender love. Such to us, though infinitely high and awful, is Providence.
(Wollstonecraft, 1789, p. 369; Barbauld, 1811, pp. 14–15)

Among any number of other possible examples, the most forthright appears in William Nesbit's 1809 edition of a household staple, William Buchan's *Domestic Medicine*, which also contained the revered doctor's *Advice to Mothers*. In his introduction to the *Advice*, Nesbit includes this quotation from Buchan about the mother's social significance:

The more I reflect ... on the situation of the mother, the more I am struck with the extent of her powers, and the inestimable value of her services. In the language of love, women are called angels; but this is a weak and silly compliment; they approach nearer to our ideas of the Deity: they not only create, but sustain their creation and hold its future destiny in their hands.
(Buchan, 1809, p. xiii).

The phrasing of such a passage offers yet more evidence, if any were needed, of an earnest Christianity already at work in Regency England to create the mores that we call 'Victorian'. However, the clothing imagined upon these Providential mothers would not at this point have been the many-layered costume of the 'passionless' Victorian angel, but rather the fluttering draperies modelled upon those worn by the nymphs and goddesses decorating the classical 'antiquities' that were pouring into England, particularly from Italy.

Relevant also is an eroticisation of the maternal body and a maternalising of the erotic effected by the extensive literature on breast-feeding. Texts such as James Nelson's *An Essay on the Government of Children* (1756), Sarah Brown's *Letter to a Lady on the Best Means of Obtaining the Milk* (1777), and William Moss's *Essay on the Management, Nursing, and Diseases of Children* (1794) convey a good deal more than medical information as they dwell on the size, shape, fullness and health of the breasts and nipples needed for optimal breast-feeding. Erasmus Darwin makes their implied eroticism explicit in the aesthetic theory outlined in *Zoonomia*, a book that we know was familiar to Shelley (Shelley, 1964, I, p. 342). Darwin writes, 'The characteristic of beauty ... is that it is the object of love', and goes on to argue that *the* object to which all others arousing the experience of beauty are merely analogous is the maternal breast, which the infant 'embraces with its hands, presses with its lips, and watches with its eyes' (Darwin, 1803, p. 109).

A somewhat tangential but extremely important point related to the culture's emphasis on breast-feeding lies in the conviction that just as the discourse of the mother-educator 'tinctures' the mind of the child, so the mother's milk infuses the infant with her personality traits. The author of *The Nurse's Guide* writes that, 'at the same time that she [the mother] gives him her Milk to suck, she makes him suck in the Principles of Virtue' (Anon., 1729). We know that this conviction of liminality in the mother/infant relationship had an impact upon Shelley because when Harriet refused to breast-fed Ianthe and insisted on hiring a wet-nurse, Shelley's horror, allegedly so strong that he attempted to suckle the child himself, stemmed from the fact that 'The nurse's soul would enter the child' (White, 1940, I p. 326).

Thus in the ideology and attendant discourse of motherhood permeating the upper and middle classes during Shelley's formative years, one finds the possibility of a fusion of Christian Providential imagery with the classical evocations of the mother goddess under her many different names and forms of worship. My discussion of the specifically Christian side of the two traditions, is not meant to suggest that Shelley's fascination with the goddess myths shows 'displaced' Christian feeling. What interests me rather is the way in which a conflation of motherhood and divinity present in the culture gives imaginative élan to a concept of divine motherhood 'imported' from both the geographical and the historical distance of the ancient Mediterranean world.

This eclectic cultural importation had as its material base the 'Oriental' as well as Greek and Roman artifacts arriving in crates at the doors of the British Museum. Besides its classical acquisitions, the rapidly expanding Museum was described in an early *Synopsis* of its contents as the depository for 'trophies of our Egyptian expedition' (Anon., 1814, p. xxiii) – and there were many other similar spoils. English scholars and explorers, along with English soldiers and merchants, were taking possession of Middle Eastern and Far Eastern territories politically and economically but also textually – both through the texts they collected at sites and by the transformation of sites into texts (Said, 1979, p. 94). Shelley's interest in these sources is well-known; not so explicitly recognised is the fact that this knowledge was so widespread as to be 'middle brow' and a general cultural phenomenon.

Women's magazines, for instance, carried reviews and digests of 'Oriental' materials as a matter of course, and the tone of the reviewers suggests that they know themselves to be addressing a well-educated readership. The reviewer in *The Lady's Monthly Museum* of Fra Paolino Da San Bartolomeo's *A Voyage to the East Indies*, for instance, takes it for granted that the readers are aware of the scholarship compiled in *Asiatic Researches* and not only know Sir William Jones's *Works* but will agree that they have been imperfectly edited (Anon., 1799a, p. 477). The October 1808 issue of another women's magazine, *La Belle Assemblée*, contains a discussion of Zoroastrianism (1808d, pp. 203–10) and an 'Account of the City of Palmyra. Collected from Various Authors' (Anon., 1808c, pp. 154–9). The principal authors used are Constantin Volney, Robert Wood and James Bruce; again, the readers' acquaintance with their works is assumed.

The gender politics so noticeable in the hortatory stories of the women's magazines surfaces also in one of these authors' works about another ancient site: Wood's *The Ruins of Balbec*. There Wood is at some pains to contrast the fearful obeisance to a tyrannical and destructive male god with loving trust in deities associated with the feminine, with the night sky and the stars – a re-enactment on a grandly cosmic scale of the domestic split between a demanding and self-centred father and a beneficent mother. The sun-god Baal, whose name means 'Lord' and 'Master', lays waste to the earth, but the night sky gives confidence in the existence of a recuperative advocate blessing human concerns:

> No where could we discover in the face of the heavens more beauties, nor on earth fewer, than in our night-travels through

the deserts of Arabia; where it is impossible not to be struck with this contrast: a boundless, dreary waste, without tree or water, mountain or valley, or the least variety of colours, offers a tedious sameness to the wearied traveller; who is agreeably relieved by looking up to that cheerful moving picture, which measures his time, directs his course, and lights up his way.   (Wood, 1757, p. 15)

The general cultural fascination with the remains of ancient civilisations which made Volney's *Ruins* one of Shelley's 'Sacred Books', juxtaposed with a cultural inclination towards beneficent female deities, informs the modifications Shelley made in Volney's plot-line in the writing of *Queen Mab*. When Queen Mab carries the spirit of the sleeping Ianthe to a celestial palace, the first thing she points out on the tiny, circling orb of Earth is 'Palmyra's ruined palaces' (II, 110). Shelley thereby acknowledges his debt to Volney, since the 'scaffolding' in the *Ruins* for an overview of world history is a dialogue which begins in Palmyra. The male narrator, who has come there to brood over why *'empires rise and fall'* and to discover *'on what principles ... the peace of society and the happiness of man [can] be established'* (Volney, 1890, p. 13; author's emphasis) is visited by a male Phantom who carries him to a similarly celestial perch for a vision of universal history and a prophecy of its future course.

Shelley alters Volney's male-oriented scenario by putting two feminine presences into colloquy over the evils of past history, the lamentable state of the world at present, and the hope for a better future. The verse paragraphs in which he imagines a renewed world also offer a very different solution from Volney's remodelled patriarchy, described as a 'community of citizens who, united by fraternal sentiments ... make of their respective strength one common force, the reaction of which on each of them assumes the noble and beneficent character of paternity' (Volney, 1890, p. 209). Shelley gives Time, 'the conqueror', a masculine gender and makes him the patriarchal destroyer of destructive patriarchal rule. When 'the morn of love' gradually dawns, Time flees; in the renovated human life that ensues, the mythic representation of the power(s) serving as ground of the psyche's being has Godwinian nomenclature, feminine gender, and iconographic links to the mother goddess:

Reason was free; and wild though passion went
Through tangled glens and wood-embosomed meads,
Gathering a garland of the strangest flowers,
Yet like the bee returning to her queen,
She bound the sweetest on her sister's brow,
Who meek and sober kissed the sportive child,
No longer trembling at the broken rod.

(IX, 50–6)

The language describing passion's movements 'through tangled glens and wood-embosomed meads', calls up associations with the maenads, frenzied votaries of Dionysus, but more particularly – since passion is represented as female with allegiance to another female – with the sexual licence ritually demanded in women's celebration of the goddess whom Herodotus calls 'Aphrodite' when describing these rituals (Herodotus, 1987, p. 124 [1.199]). Shelley's bee simile creates a further link between 'Reason' and Aphrodite. Herodotus notes without explanation that 'Mylitta' is 'the Assyrian name for Aphrodite', but Jacob Bryant's *New System*, a work almost certainly familiar to Shelley, gives an extended discussion of the word's significance. Bryant's notation grows out of his *idée fixe* on the unity of the Biblical and the Greek philosophical traditions. In this instance he associates Noah's Ark with 'Seira, or *the hive of Venus* alluded to by Natalis Comes: *Let us celebrate the hive of Venus, who rose from the sea: that hive of many names: the mighty fountain, from whence all kings are descended: from whence all the winged and immortal loves were again produced'* (Bryant, 1775, II, 371–2; author's emphasis). Bryant comments further: 'We may perceive that Seira was no other than Damater, the supposed mother of mankind; who was also styled Melitta, and Melissa [Melitta, *a bee*]; and was looked upon as the Venus of the east . . . The priests of the Seira were called Melittae and Melissae from this Deity whom they worshiped' (II, 373; sic).

With the bee-line as my clue, I shall look in the remainder of this chapter at three significant appearances of bee imagery in *Prometheus Unbound* that demonstrate how cultural presumptions about maternal power, the maternal relation to language, and the maternal 'tincturing' of an infant's subjectivity weave themselves into Shelley's text for a renovated human life.

The first of these passages is the song with which the Fourth

Spirit solaces Prometheus after the Furies have tormented him. Their ultimate temptation to despair lies in the suggestion that the violent injustices of history have irreparably warped the human species; the Spirit avers, on the contrary, that the poetic capacity to imagine transfigured human beings gives earnest of their future existence. So goes the paraphrase, but in the song itself the poetic imagination contemplates bees:

> On a Poet's lips I slept
> Dreaming like a love-adept
> In the sound his breathing kept;
> Nor seeks nor finds he mortal blisses
> But feeds on the aerial kisses
> Of shapes that haunt thought's wildernesses.
> He will watch from dawn to gloom
> The lake-reflected sun illume
> The yellow bees i' the ivy-bloom
> Nor heed nor see, what things they be;
> But from these create he can
> Forms more real than living man,
> Nurslings of immortality! –
> One of these awakened me
> And I sped to succour thee.
>
> (I.i.737–51)

The striking word 'love-adept' makes eroticism an important component of the Spirit's solace. An ambiguity in the meaning of the word 'like – 'in the same way as' or 'along with' – offers the possibility, confirmed in the poem's fourth line, that both the spirit and the poet on whose lips he sleeps are love-adepts. Hildebrand notes in his fine essay on these songs that 'The lips are the organ of love and of the Word. They are peculiarly the poet's organ, and for Shelley they are "the seat of the imagination"' (Hildebrand, 1971, p. 95). Connection is the great work of the imagination, and the lips function, after the umbilical cord is severed, as the very first organ of connection, literally the point of contact between the infant and the source of its life. The specific mention of lips, of feeding, and of the rhythmic sound of common breathing in the first three lines, create an effect of montage: our focus on the poet's lips where the spirit lies sleeping, while (as we shall hear shortly) the poet contemplates a natural scene, becomes overlaid with images of a suckling infant as well as of a skilful lover.

Having aroused these possibilities, the spirit straightaway (lines 740–2) denies – and reinforces – their relevance in language that links physical pleasures (gustatory/visual/sexual) to the play of the imagination (hide-and-seek, tag) with its received impressions. Never unmindful of the fact that to the conscious subject all experience is mediated by consciousness and so is symbolic, Shelley suggests here that the love-adept poet can nonetheless through the imagination make a connection of some kind, an aerial kiss, with lived experience. 'But feeds on the aerial kisses/Of shapes' also implies that the poet is feeding on the sight of shapes kissing one another. This ambiguity prepares for the lyric's three central lines (743–5) where we learn what the poet as participant/ voyeur is feeding on: 'yellow bees i' the ivy bloom' illumined by a 'lake-reflected sun'.

The latter phrase exemplifies one of those many self-reflexive images in Shelley's work which, it is generally agreed, show his fascination with narcissism, although opinions differ widely on the moral significance of that interest. It is also typically Shelleyan in its Platonism, though it revises Plato in an important way. Shelley's poet becomes associated, through the image of the 'lake-reflected sun', with that Platonic enlightened leader in *The Republic* who, climbing painfully out of the cave of common opinion and into the light outside, is able to look upon the sun 'and not mere reflections . . . in the water' (*Republic*, 516b). In Shelley's poem, however, the poet appears not to strive for some final, sun-identified transcendence of the human mind's limitations. Instead he rests, lake-identified, at Plato's second-to-last stage, with reflected sun his source of illumination. Metaphorically, the poet's situation predicates subjectivity as created by a positive form of narcissism or mirroring which cancels the division between subject and object. Such cancelling does not involve appropriation of all the 'not me' into one sun-identified subjectivity. It results rather from a dual, lake-identified recognition: first, each subjectivity is formed through introjection of the 'not me', but second, each subjectivity is also an object to other subjects.[6]

After this epistemological prelude, there follows the metonymic heart of the rune: 'yellow bees i' the ivy bloom'. Again there is a mirroring: each bee is a little yellow sun reflection. These are also Platonic bees; in a passage from the *Ion* among the portions of that work which Shelley later translated, Socrates compares the souls of poets to bees 'wandering over the gardens and meadows of the honey-flowing fountains of the Muses' and returning 'laden with the sweetness of melody; and arrayed as it were in the plumes of imagination' (Shelley, 1926–30, VII, p. 238).

As the bees feed, their furry bodies transfer pollen from the male stamens of the flower to the female pistil, a process that Erasmus Darwin in *The Botanic Garden* anthropomorphises constantly into a variety of erotic positions and modes of intercourse matching those known to the most learned and supple of love-adepts (Darwin, 1794, II, *passim*). Ironically, the bees, while such important participants in this erotic activity, are neuter females, as Shelley knew (*Queen Mab*, LXVIII, 5). At the same time, the fertile – and sexual – queen-bee historically has dual sexuality. The ancients, as James Frazer notes in *The Golden Bough*, 'mistook the Queen bee for a male, and hence spoke of King bees' (Frazer, 1911, II, p. 136); Shelley would have seen such an allusion to king-bees in Virgil's *Georgics*, which he had been reading shortly before he began writing *Prometheus Unbound* (Shelley, M., 1987, I, p. 223).

This ancient misattribution of bees' sexuality gets mention in Frazer's work because bees, 'King Bees', are associated with the worship of the many-breasted Diana of Ephesus, a mother-goddess whose heredity lies with 'Asiatic goddesses of love and fertility' (Frazer, 1911, I, p. 37). In *Description of Greece*, a work familiar to Shelley (Shelley, 1964, I, p. 549), Pausanias writes that the goddess was worshipped at Ephesus by a cortege of male priests called Essenes or King Bees who during their year's term of office had to observe strict chastity (Frazer, 1911, II, p. 133). Erotic but, during the period of their priesthood, non-genital, they are represented as bees on the statues of Diana of Ephesus. In his Roman sight-seeing Shelley would have come upon such representations of the goddess in several museums: the Vatican, the Lateran, and the Palazzi dei Conservatori on the Capitol (Frazer, 1911, I, p. 38). Also, female priestesses of Artemis, as Frazer notes, 'were undoubtedly called Bees, and it seems not improbable that ... they represented the goddess in her character of bee' (Frazer, 1911, II, p. 136). The poet, then, has as one part of his day-long meditation the divine mother, metonymically represented by the bee and mirrored by bee-servitors of both sexes. She is asexual, dually sexed; self-fertilizing; and source of all creative energy and production, including the honey of verse.

Equally labyrinthine in its significance is the ivy-bloom, Shelley's particular choice for the bees' forage. Like the bees, the plant merges and unifies dual sexual characteristics, since it is bisexual. That is not unusual in plants, but the ivy's duality-in-unity is particularly striking. As Shelley knew, ivy is sacred to Dionysus; Walter Otto describes its growth cycle as 'suggesting the two fold nature of Dionysus': 'First it puts out the so-called shade-seeking shoots, the scondet tendrils with the well-known lobed leaves. Later, however, a second kind of shoot appears which grows upright and turns toward the light. The leaves are formed completely differently, and now the plant produces flowers and berries' (Otto, 1965, p. 154). This doubleness mirrors not only Dionysus' being the 'twice-born', as Otto suggests, but also the god's dual sexual nature. A phallic deity, Dionysus is also female-identified: women are his principal followers, and he bears such epithets as 'Gynnis (the womanish), Arsenothetys (the man-womanly), Dyalos (the hybrid), Pseudanor (the man without true virility)' (Hillman, 1972, p. 259).

So, like the bees, the ivy is a highly charged erotic symbol but also an ambiguous, bisexual one. The juxtaposition of these images also creates an associative transfer between ideas of renewed humanity and mingled allusions to Aphrodite and Dionysus that we saw earlier in the passage from *Queen Mab*. In the final lines of the Fourth Spirit's song, the poet, brooding over these mystic 'signatures', comes to a vision of life not as it is but as it might be. His answer involves mirrored bisexualities, an erotic, fruitful, and creative – but non-genital – merging of bee and bloom. Functioning both as metaphor for an unnamed process and as metonymic displacement of that unspoken because unspeakable interaction, it is a fantasy of incest, of a conscious subjectivity's return to the narcissistic yet intrasubjective stage in the construction of subjectivity. Because conscious, it is not regressive but creates the possibility of mother-centred subjectivities communicating through mother-given language.[7]

For further understanding of what that language is and how it functions, we turn to another bee song, the Echoes' directions to Asia for her journey to the Cave of Demogorgon:

> As the song floats, thou pursue
> Where the wild bee never flew,
> Through the noontide darkness deep,

By the odour breathing sleep
Of faint night flowers, and the waves
At the fountain-lighted caves,
While our music, wild and sweet,
Mocks thy gently-falling feet
Child of Ocean!

(II.i.179–87)

Shelley substituted 'wild bee' for what in the draft version was 'night bird' (Shelley, 1968, p. 118). Changed thus, the line alludes explicitly in both language and metre to Ariel's 'Where the bee sucks, there suck I' (*Tempest*, V.i.88), but suggests farther and more daring flights. This very simple example of intertextuality bears upon Shelley's sense of his purpose and method in writing *Prometheus Unbound*. He wants, through the construction of what is, admittedly, an 'insubstantial pageant', to lay bare the evils of society and to offer the vision of a better one. But while Ariel, as Prospero's agent, uses his sleights to lead characters into self-betrayal of their mendacity or brutality, his magic does not explore those hidden areas of the psyche from which the motivations for such acts arise. So *this* Ariel song will take up where the other left off.

If, as Asia is shortly to say, 'Speech created thought' (II.iv.71), then the exploration of human subjectivity in *Prometheus Unbound* can also be considered an enquiry into language. Lines 181–4 of the Echoes' song forward that purpose, though they do so by offering an exemplification rather than an analysis of the way language works. In paraphrase the lines say: 'Follow [the sound of our voices] past night-blooming flowers, difficult to see because of this deep shade and because they are now closed up, it being noon. You can, though, smell the perfume they give off. You will also pass the fountain sources of streams which, reflecting the little light there is, cast prismatic shimmerings upon the cavern walls overarching your way.' However, the grammatical syntax of these phrases gives the informational aspect of their function a place secondary to their auditory effect. Syntactical boundaries blur as different parts of speech shift into one another. For instance, every significant word, including 'faint', in the phrases governed by the prepositions 'by' and 'of', is a possible noun, although some take on an adjectival function in context – once we know the context. So, as we set out, spatially oriented through the presence of 'by', we first meet 'odour', then 'breathing', then 'sleep'. Each elicits a response from different senses: olfactory (and the closely related gustatory), auditory, and proprioceptive. And while linear, grammatical logic gives 'odour breathing' the function of a participial phrase modifying 'sleep', a nominativeness in each word disorients that logic, while the words' juxtaposition gives them a triply synesthetic physicality.

These lines have an effect much like that created by the 'literal language', in Margaret Homans's phrase, used by Mrs Ramsay in *To the Lighthouse* to lull her daughter Cam to sleep. Cam is told that she 'must shut her eyes and go to sleep and dream of mountains and valleys and stars falling and parrots and antelopes and gardens, and everything lovely' (Woolf, 1927, p. 115). Explaining her term 'literal language', Homans writes: 'The words matter as sounds, monotonous and rhythmic, issuing from and returning to the body . . . a language of presence in which the presence or absence of referents in the ordinary sense is quite unimportant' (Homans, 1986, p. 16).[8]

Anne Fernald makes a distinction between arbitrary and non-arbitrary aspects of language that gives additional concreteness to Homans's definition of 'literal language' and to Julia Kristeva's related concept of 'the semiotic'. Without disputing Saussure's dictum on the arbitrary nature of language, Fernald argues as well that

the infant's early experience of language builds upon relationships between sound and meaning that are not arbitrary . . . Just as the child learns 'how to mean' by expressing intentions through intonation and gesture, the infant learns how to perceive meaning by responding to the mother's intentions and affective states, also expressed through intonation and gesture . . . (Fernald, 1984, p. 25)

Like Woolf in the passage cited by Homans, Shelley in the Echoes' song takes linguistic liberties with language in order to manifest this still operative paralinguistic signification. Woolf's strategy is to use essentially visual images in juxtapositions that, though grammatical, have no internal logic – 'stars falling and parrots and antelopes' – creating a slight rational disorientation in order to highlight the non-arbitrary, affective, kinesthetic and presence-laden attributes to language. Shelley creates a similar effect through the synesthetic disorientation produced through the grammatical ambiguities of his verse sentence. In Shelley's lines no mother figure appears as she does in Woolf's passage, but by association such non-referential yet affective language, experienced first and most vividly in the communications between mother and infant, necessarily invokes the maternal.

My point is not that Shelley is writing a treatise on infant behaviour or that he had visionary insight into recent linguistic research in developmental psychology. Rather it is that, both in the connections made among speech, song and rhythmic movement and in the disorientation of strict linear meaning in order to capture the affective power of language, the Echoes' song exemplifies the 'true' language that Shelley hopes will vanquish the false Jupiterean language repudiated by Prometheus in Act I. This redemptive language reflects the kind of communication existing between child and mother-educator.

The implied correspondences among language, music and rhythmic movement made in the song just discussed become explicit in the Echoes' pun at the end of the next stanza: 'In a world unknown/Sleeps a voice unspoken;/By thy step alone/Can its rest be broken,/Child of Ocean!' (II.ii.190–4). The Echoes encourage Asia to follow because her presence alone has the power to release a potential energy dormant so far and hidden from others' knowledge. Their words also associate that untapped potential with language now holding a 'rest' – as interval of silence – albeit a very long interval. Her 'step' becomes the conductor's baton that prompts its renewed sound. By following the Echoes, Asia is told, she will open up a form of language now lost and so create a new humanity living in a new world.

The first speech of the unbound Prometheus describing the Cave in which he and the tri-partite mother goddess will pass the future uses a bee simile more complex and allusive than the one employed in *Queen Mab* to depict the interaction between 'Reason' and 'passion', but with a similar contextual effect:

> And hither come, sped on the charmed winds
> Which meet from all the points of Heaven, as bees
> From every flower aerial Enna feeds
> At their known island-homes in Himera,
> The echoes of the human world, which tell
> Of the low voice of love, almost unheard,

And dove-eyed pity's murmured pain and music,
Itself the echo of the heart, and all
That tempers or improves man's life, now free.

                                          (III.iii.40–8)

The simile transforms the Cave into Bryant's 'hive of Venus', the
home, resource, and care of a human race who all might now be
'called Melittae' (Bryant, 1775, p. 373) in that all manifest the spirit
of the beneficent mother goddess. The allusion to the soil of 'aerial
Enna', torn up by Pluto's chariot when he rose up from under it to
ravish Kore, but now whole and flower-strewn once more, underscores a contrast underlying all of *Prometheus Unbound* between the
spirit of the mother goddess and one of rapacious, tyrannical
paternal power.

The tenor of those 'echoes of the human world', these murmur-
ings of love and pity, moved a Victorian critic to grumble that
Prometheus 'cares no more for man, but all his thoughts are bent
on the enjoyment of the most effeminate sort of domestic bliss'
(Shelley, 1959, p. 329). While eschewing the judgemental, I would
agree: this Cave of Prometheus is at once a shrine to the mother
goddess and a well-managed English nursery, circa 1800. The lines
even provide us with a scenario for the kind of activity occurring in
this nursery. Made up, as Olwen Campbell noted, of 'changes
wrung upon aspirated and unaspirated vowel sounds' (Campbell,
1959, p. 246), Shelley's words themselves demonstrate the play
whereby the mother's throat and mouth and tongue imprint
themselves upon the child's language.

4

'These Common Woes':
Shelley and Wordsworth

Lisa M. Steinman

We know that Shelley was exposed to Wordsworth's poetry by 1811, during his stay in the Lake District (Blank, 1988, p. 26). On 2 January 1812, Shelley wrote out from memory Wordsworth's poem, *A Poet's Epitaph*, to send to Elizabeth Hitchener, explaining that he found the first stanzas 'expressively keen', and describing his hope that the poem would give 'some idea of the Man' (Shelley, 1964, I, p. 218). Yet within the week, Shelley wrote again to Elizabeth Hitchener. A 7 January letter suggests that Shelley already suspected that Wordsworth would fail to fill the exemplary role in which the earlier letter tried to cast him. This second letter is most explicit about Shelley's disappointment with another member of the Wordsworth circle, Southey, whom he characterises as a kindly man, but without 'the great character which once I linked him to ... *Once* he *was* this character, everything you can conceive of practised virtue ... Wordsworth & Coleridge I have yet to see' (Shelley, 1964, I, p. 223). The conclusion at very least sounds a challenge to the two poets whom Shelley was never, as it turned out, to meet in person, but in whom he maintained a life-long interest.

It is difficult to deny that Shelley's letters reveal some anxiety about the influence of these older poets (see Blank, 1988, *passim*). At the same time, like Godwin to whom Shelley compared him (Shelley, 1954, p. 309), Wordsworth and more generally the group of poets with whom Wordsworth was associated seem to have held out for Shelley the possibility of an ideal community of poets and men. As Shelley says later in a somewhat different context, 'one is always in love with something or other; the error, and I confess it is not easy for spirits cased in flesh and blood to avoid it, consists in seeking in a mortal image the likeness of what is perhaps eternal' (Shelley, 1964, II, p. 434). I will argue that Shelley, at least during one important period of his life, tried to see in Wordsworth such a mortal likeness, and that the lesson voiced in the letter just quoted was one Shelley learned, in part, from his dialogue with the Lake Poets, who presented images against which Shelley tested himself, seeing the older poets not always as rivals, but often as figures in whom he found his own impulses and beliefs embodied. My endeavour is to examine some of the tensions between man and poet, poet and activist, self and community that Shelley explores through his responses to Wordsworth.

I wish to focus on three moments in Shelley's life. The first of these moments occurs in 1812 just following Shelley's visit to Southey. Immediately following his words of disappointment about Southey in his letter of 7 January to Elizabeth Hitchener, Shelley copies out a poem of his own, which he describes as follows: 'the subject is not fictitious; it is the overflowings of the mind this morning'; he adds that it is to be thought of 'as a picture of [his] feelings not a specimen of [his] art' (Shelley, 1964, I, pp. 223, 226).

Shelley's appeal to truth, that is to the reality of his narrative, combined with his appeal to his own intellectual and emotional processes, are worth considering in some detail. First, his description of poetry as revealing the mind sounds a note repeated again in slightly different form later the same month in a letter to Godwin: 'If any man would determine sincerely and cautiously at *every* period of his life to publish books which should contain the real state of his feelings and opinions, I am willing to suppose that this portraiture of his mind would be worth many metaphysical disquisitions' (Shelley, 1964, I, p. 242). This same language is used in Shelley's descriptions of the poems from the *Esdaile Notebook*, many of which – as the editor of that notebook argues – he had hoped to publish in an 1813 volume of poems just because the work gave a portrait of his mind and despite his knowledge that the work was uneven (Cameron, 1964, p. 4). In all of these cases Shelley's point seems to be that poetry does give some idea of the man and, implicitly, that the self to which poetry thus testifies will appear different at different times of life. Presumably it is this view of the self in flux, too, that dictates Shelley's emphasis in his description of his early poem: it is the overflowings of the mind of a particular morning. Indeed, a closer look at Shelley's criticism of Southey reveals a similar emphasis. Southey's former character, Shelley writes, included 'practised virtue' – that is, virtue put into practice, or in motion. What corrupted him, as Shelley explains it, was 'the world, [he was] contaminated by Custom', which I take to mean at least in part that, for Shelley, Southey's fall from grace was occasioned by the repetition that characterises the habitual or customary (Shelley, 1964, I, p. 223).

The mind's freedom from custom would come to be one of Shelley's persistent themes, a theme presumably fed and complicated by the metaphysical disquisitions that Shelley ordered from his bookseller by December 1812 (Shelley, 1964, I, p. 342). In Hume, for example, he would have found the idea that the self is not one entity, but 'a bundle or collection of different perceptions, which succeed each other with an inconceivable rapidity, and are in a perpetual flux and movement' (Hume, 1964, p. 534). Shelley's own writings on epistemology and identity from the period between 1812 and 1815 draw heavily on Hume, as is indicated in his note that 'beyond the limits of perception and thought nothing can exist' (Shelley, 1954, p. 183). I shall have more to say on Shelley's developing views about personal and poetic identity; here my main point is that Shelley's remarks on Southey as well as on his own poetic efforts in 1812 reveal already, on the one hand, a metaphysical understanding of the poetic self as Humean, figured only as a series of perceptions, and, on the other hand, a desire to link his poetry to the real or historical world.

Indeed, when Shelley writes that the world has corrupted Southey, he presumably has in mind most immediately the pressures of the external world that blasted Southey's (and his generation's) hopes for radical reform. The diagnosis is not completely unfair. In 1812, Shelley entered the political arena in Ireland, Wales and England, and wrote with admiration to the author of *Political Justice*. In contrast, Southey and Wordsworth, although they too had earlier admired Godwin, were of the generation affected by the general retrenchment and disillusionment of the late 1790s, a period when – as E. P. Thompson has said – it was difficult 'for men to hold on to aspirations long after there appear[ed] to be no hope of inserting them into "the real world which is the world of all of us"' (Thompson, 1969, p. 174). Less generously than Thompson, perhaps, in 1817 Shelley identifies Wordsworth's dissent as too easily reconcilable with 'servility, and dependence' (Shelley, 1954, p. 309). Two years later, in the *Dedication* to *Peter Bell the Third*, Shelley damns Wordsworth for accepting 'this world which is . . . the world of all of us, *and where / We find our happiness, or not at all'*.

In January of 1812, however, Shelley seems to have admired Wordsworth's ability to see historical reality *without* acquiescing to it. He singled out the first two stanzas of *A Poet's Epitaph* for praise, and these stanzas focus not so much on the solitary poet for whom the epitaph is written as on social and political realities. This brings me back to the point Shelley makes about his own poem in 1812, a record not only of a mind in motion uncontaminated by custom, but also a record wherein, as Shelley presents it, the 'facts are real ... literally true' (Shelley, 1964, I, pp. 223–4). This is, on one level, a curious statement from the author of *Alastor*, a poem the *British Critic* in 1816 saw as 'nonsense which ... spurns the earth, and all its dull realities' (Hayden, 1976, p. 379). Despite this contemporary judgement, the Preface to *Alastor* is intended to instruct 'actual men', it may be said, because the literal reality depicted is one of the 'situations of the human mind' (Steinman, 1978, pp. 255–69). However, in the earlier poem – significantly entitled *A Tale of Society as it is from facts 1811* in the *Esdaile Notebook* – the literal reality to which Shelley appeals is not so easily reconciled with the mental reality he equally insists informs the poem.[1]

Indeed, the poem seems a curious echo and revision of Wordsworth's early tale of Margaret in *The Ruined Cottage*, curious in that Shelley insists less than Wordsworth does on the act of perception and more on the facts perceived. Shelley did not, of course, read Wordsworth's revised version of Margaret's tale in *The Excursion* until 1814, at which point Mary Shelley records the family's judgement on its author: 'He is a slave' (Marshall, 1889, pp. 80–1). Nonetheless, as E. P. Thompson argues, the story is related in Wordsworth to passages from Southey's *Joan of Arc* on Madelon and Arnaud or on the death of a common soldier who leaves behind a wife 'tortur'd with vain hope' and perhaps to Coleridge's *Religious Musings*, where Coleridge writes: 'O thou poor widow, who in dreams dost view/Thy husband's mangled corse, and from short doze/Start'st with a shriek' (Thompson, 1969, p. 151; Southey, 1894, pp. 8, 84; Coleridge, 1912, p. 120). Thus, while Shelley could not yet have read *The Excursion* in 1812, these two earlier poems or perhaps, as Kenneth Neill Cameron suggests, Wordsworth's own even earlier poem, *The Female Vagrant*, which was published in 1798, could easily have been in Shelley's mind (Cameron, 1974, p. 208). He had after all just returned from visiting the author of *Joan of Arc*, and still hoped to meet the authors of *Religious Musings* and *The Female Vagrant*, whose works he presumably discussed with Southey in 1811. We know he discussed politics with Southey; this was the source of Shelley's disappointment. What likelier source, then, for *A Tale of Society as it is from facts 1811*?

Shelley's aged woman, like Wordsworth's Margaret, or the Soldier's Widow in *The Female Vagrant*, or the other unnamed women mentioned by Southey and Coleridge, has a loved one (in Shelley's tale, a son) taken from her by war. She lives in solitude with the 'proofs of an unspeaking sorrow . . ./Within her ghastly hollowness of eye' (quotations from the poem are taken from the version found in Shelley, 1964, I, pp. 224–6). Unlike the women in the other tales, however, Shelley's has her family restored to her, only to die with her son because they cannot support themselves and refuse the mercy of the parish: *'the insolent stare*/With which law loves to rend the poor mans [sic] soul'. On 'this scene of legal misery', Shelley's poem closes. Southey's, Wordsworth's and Coleridge's poems are texts against war, but to some degree war is an ill so mixed with supernatural or natural disasters, as indicated by Coleridge's gothic mannerisms or Wordsworth's mention of bad harvests, that it is presented as an impersonal, almost extra-human force. There is nothing to be done about war, a point emphasised in each poem by the fact that hope or vision is seen as devastating. For example, Coleridge's widow is only tortured by her dream vision; Southey's woman, like the male vagrant's wife in *The Female Vagrant*, has a 'dim eye', and we are told what hope each has is 'vain' (Southey, 1894, p. 84; Wordsworth, 1977a, pp. 137, 121, 127); Wordsworth describes Margaret's eye as 'busy in the distance, shaping things', feeding a hope that is only 'torturing' (Wordsworth, 1977b, pp. 65–6). Wordsworth in fact explicitly describes the causes of war as if they are quite beyond human control: 'It pleased Heaven to add/. . . the plague of war' (Wordsworth, 1977b, p. 55).

Shelley's poem, on the other hand, emphasises the 'tyrants' who draft common soldiers and the 'Power' – that is, political power – that ruins common people. Further, the hopes of Shelley's aged woman are fulfilled with the return of her son, and the misfortunes that are visited on the reunited family are those of English law, as Shelley echoes the images of sight or vision in the Lake Poets, and shifts the source of devastation from the deluded hopes of the sufferers to the 'insolent stare' of the law at the sufferers. My point, first, is that because of the exchange among the Lake Poets, to respond to one poet would be (even if inadvertently) to enter into a conversation already in progress. Second, I wish to underline Shelley's political position, which is in pointed contrast to the stance implicit in the poems by the other Lake Poets, even as it draws on the stanzas Shelley admired, and had in mind, from Wordsworth's *A Poet's Epitaph*. Shelley's point is that there can and should be legal reform. Moreover, his poem does not view its subjects paternalistically. While the widows in Coleridge's and Southey's poems remain shadowy, anonymous figures, Shelley allows his family some autonomy, as he emphasises in his intro- ductory remarks that he has not put words in their mouths and that he respects their desire for dignity and independence.

Ironically, this is just the same way in which E. P. Thompson argues that Wordsworth, in *The Ruined Cottage*, revised Coleridge's and Southey's poems (Thompson, 1969, pp. 151–2). That is, Shel- ley's poem might be said to set itself in opposition not only to Coleridge's and Southey's poems, but also to Southey himself, the man Shelley saw contaminated by custom, and so proleptically to the Wordsworth Shelley would soon describe in comparable terms as slavish or allied with servitude in Book I of *The Excursion*. At the same time, we can see that far from revising Wordsworth, Shelley follows in the footsteps of the early Wordsworth by humanising the tale of woe recounted, and setting his poetry against that of Coleridge and Southey. It may be a further irony of history that it was Wordsworth, engaged in rewriting the *The Ruined Cottage*, who was the true revisionist and opposer of his own earlier self, that self whose poetic stance Shelley mirrored, and in effect re-enacted, in 1812.

By 1814 Shelley was far more aware of how much of early Words- worth's mind he could see in himself, which must have caused him some dismay given his view of the later Wordsworth, especially if he recalled Southey's words in 1812: – 'Ah! when you are as old as I am you will think with me' (Shelley, 1964, I, p. 223). This is not so clearly the case, however, in 1812, although by then Shelley had already found his two major thematic concerns – the self, including the poetic self, and politics, or social change – and he was self- consciously aware that his thoughts on these subjects were articu- lated through his exchanges with the Lake Poets. The language in which Shelley in 1812 describes Wordsworth, Southey and his own enterprises also indicates Shelley's desire to connect his various concerns: the mind in flux and historical facts, the growth or habituation of men and poets, the moral and the political.

Shelley's interest in what might most generally be called the moral and the political, and his acknowledgement that they are not easily combined, are also shown in his letter to his bookseller towards the end of 1812, where he writes:

> I am determined to apply myself to a study that is hateful & disgusting to my very soul, but which is above all studies necessary for him who would be listened to as a mender of antiquated abuses. – I mean that record of crimes & miseries – History. You see that the metaphysical works to which my heart hankers, are not numerous in this list. (Shelley, 1964, I, p. 340).

This uneasy mixture remains a constant in Shelley's life; by 1816 he was reading Gibbon and Rousseau; by 1818, Herodotus and Plato. Already in 1812, the study of history, linked with political activity, is juxtaposed to the study of metaphysics, linked in Shelley's earlier letter with more introspective study and in the letter just quoted with personal desire.

With this portrait of Shelley from 1812 in mind, I would like to turn to a second moment in Shelley's life, and in particular to focus on two of the poems in his 1816 volume. The *Alastor* volume shows, first, Shelley's continued awareness of the Lake Poets. Critics have commented at length about the allusions to Wordsworth found in *Alastor*, while *To* – ('Oh! there are spirits of the air') is a poem Mary Shelley says was addressed to Coleridge.[2] Finally, *To Wordsworth* is explicit about its subject, and we know that four years earlier Shelley had ordered and probably read the 1800 edition of the *Lyrical Ballads* as well as Wordsworth's 1807 *Poems in Two Volumes*, while in 1814 he had brought home a copy of *The Excursion*.[3] Shelley also sent a copy of his *Alastor* volume to Southey.

By 1816, Shelley's view of Southey was more charitable than it had been in 1812. Shelley says that he trusts that both poets can forget 'how widely in *moral and political* opinions [they] disagree', and that both can 'attribute that difference to better motives than the multitudes are disposed to allege as the cause of dissent from their institutions' (Shelley, 1964, I, p. 462, emphasis added). Shelley no longer identifies Southey's moral or political opinions with that inner state (or set of motives) from which they arise. This may be due to the fact that, by the time of this letter, Shelley was personally and painfully aware of the way in which motives could be misread. The years between 1812 and 1816 had included Shelley's Irish activism, his move to and flight from Wales, his flight with Mary Wollstonecraft Godwin, surveillance by the government following his political activities in Devon, and constant financial worry. The generally negative public response to *Queen Mab* and *A Refutation of Deism* had clearly also affected Shelley.

Concern with the moral, the political and the literary community similarly informs *To Wordsworth*, a poem written in 1814 or 1815, and published with *Alastor* in 1816. On first reading, the sonnet seems to be Shelley's recast version of *A Poet's Epitaph*, in that it reads as an elegy. The poem on which *To Wordsworth* most obviously draws, one of Wordsworth's political sonnets, *London, 1802*, is itself addressed to an earlier poet, Milton. Wordsworth writes that England needs Milton because she has forfeited 'inward happiness' – presumably the paradise within that Michael promises Adam (*Paradise Lost* XII.587) – and become, as Wordsworth says using the language Milton uses to describe Hell, 'a fen/Of stagnant waters' (Wordsworth, 1977a, pp. 579–80; see *Paradise Lost*, II.621). England's hell-like condition is a reference to both an inner and an outer state; similarly the freedom mentioned in the sonnet's list of what England needs is carefully placed between and thus connected with both the private and the public realms: 'give us manners, virtue, freedom, power'. Like Milton's diagnosis, however, Wordsworth's ultimately concentrates on an internal condition rather than on larger social structures. 'We are selfish men', Wordsworth concludes, although he adds that lack of selfishness is what allows social sympathy, as Milton is said to have travelled unselfishly 'on life's *common* way' – that is, with others, as a man in society, even as he also looked inward: 'and yet thy heart/ The lowliest duties on herself did lay' (emphasis added).

By implication, it is the minds of selfish men that have made England what it has become, and Wordsworth thus alludes to Satan's vaunt in *Paradise Lost* that the mind makes heavens and hells with the added proviso that, unlike Satan, Milton served duty and God (*Paradise Lost*, I.254–5). These themes are echoed in Shelley's reading of Wordsworth. Just as Wordsworth hails Milton as one whose 'soul was like a Star, and dwelt apart', so too Shelley describes Wordsworth as having been a star or refuge, and as one whose poetry – 'consecrate to truth and liberty' – like Milton's, according to Wordsworth, was in the service of freedom. Yet while the end of Shelley's elegiac poem finds that Wordsworth has deserted the cause and so ceased to be a guiding light, the beginning of the sonnet emphasises a somewhat different Wordsworth – the poet of nature, the author of *Ode: Intimations of Immortality* more than the author of those tales of society which Shelley reportedly admired (Medwin, 1913, p. 251) and which, like *A Poet's Epitaph*, are most clearly characterised as songs of 'truth and liberty'. Moreover, if Wordsworth follows Milton by suggesting that public good will rest on private conscience, Shelley's poem raises questions about the relationship between the Wordsworth who deserted the cause and the poet who 'wept to know/That things depart which never may return:/Childhood and youth, friendship and love's first glow'. Interestingly, these questions again have Shelley entering a dialogue already established between Coleridge and Wordsworth, and again following in Wordsworth's footsteps. Furthermore, as in *Alastor*, and as in the letter to Southey, Shelley seems to be paying attention to the motives behind opinions and feelings, which becomes a way of viewing, though not of denying the problematic nature of, the relationship between morals and politics, as well as as between metaphysics and history.

Wordsworth, we know, wrote the first four stanzas of his ode in 1802, the same year in which is sonnet invoked Milton. The ode as it stood in 1802 ended with the fourth stanza, in which the poet views the natural world and proclaims, 'I feel – I feel it all', while still reading out of nature what is lost: 'the visionary gleam . . . the glory and the dream' (Wordsworth, 1977a, pp. 523–9). More precisely, the poem ended with a series of questions: where have these things gone? As Coleridge's reply in his 1802 *Dejection: An Ode* helps us see, the beginning of Wordsworth's ode has no reference to the process of ageing; it is simply about the loss of 'a glory from the earth'. The headnote about the child being father to the man was not added until 1815 (see Levinson, 1986b, pp. 84–99). And in answer to the 1802 ode's question of where that glory has gone, Coleridge provides a half reply, namely that an *inner* light has failed: 'I may not hope from outward forms to win/The passion and the life, whose fountains are within'; Coleridge adds that 'the soul itself must issue forth/A light, a glory'.[4] The end of Wordsworth's poem continues this conversation with the response that the soul itself – 'our life's Star' – is not our own; it comes 'from afar', and as we age – significantly imaged as a process by which the soul finds that 'custom lie[s] upon [her] with a weight' – vision fades 'into the light of common day'. The compensation, Wordsworth insists, is a 'philosophic mind' and an abiding 'primal sympathy'.

Shelley, then, enters this exchange in To Wordsworth. He writes of Wordsworth's sense of loss ('These common woes I feel'), thus underlining his own act of sympathetic imagination and echoing Wordsworth's insistence on commonality both in the sonnet to Milton and in the ode's description of how vision fades into and informs the light of common day. Shelley thus resists Coleridge's point of view. For Wordsworth, the loss of vision is necessary but not fatal to social sympathies; for Coleridge, since nature lives only in our vision of her, the loss of vision prevents the imagination from turning outward.

At the same time, Shelley borrows some of Coleridge's criticisms of Wordsworth. Echoing Wordsworth's claim to feel the joy of spring despite his loss of what the second part of the ode will identify as 'our life's Star', Coleridge portrays himself looking at the stars as follows: 'I see them all so excellently fair, / I see, not feel, how beautiful they are.' Shelley returns to this point in his statement that Wordsworth's loss of his former self is something the older poet 'feels', that is experiences, but does not 'feel' in the sense of emotionally responding, as Shelley in deploring the loss of Wordsworth does feel. Sympathetic feeling is here linked with maintaining some vision of what is lost (for Wordsworth, childhood and youth; for Shelley, especially in 1814–16, friendship and Wordsworth), as Shelley relates Wordsworth's inability to maintain his frustrating vision of loss to Wordsworth's desertion of truth and liberty.

This, in any event, seems a promising way to understand the connection between the two apparently diverse images of Wordsworth (beloved nature poet and political defector) in Shelley's sonnet, and Shelley's reported comment that Wordsworth 'always broke down when he attempted [an ode]' (Medwin, 1913, p. 251). In other words, as with the Wordsworthian narrator of Alastor, Wordsworth's problem is implicitly for Shelley that he has accepted the inevitability of imaginative failure; no longer weeping for what is lost, he sees in the world only thoughts 'too deep for tears' and thus ends with 'pale despair and cold tranquillity' (Wordsworth, 1977a, p. 529; Shelley, 1977, p. 87).

There is another way by which Shelley seems to repeat

Coleridge's criticism of Wordsworth in *To Wordsworth*. Coleridge argues (taking a stand reminiscent of Shelley's response to Southey in 1812) that age does not necessitate a change in the sense of leading to a capitulation to custom, and that the visionary gleam, which Wordsworth claims has set like a star, is in fact merely a projection of inner light. Shelley's image of Wordsworth as a star seems to make the same point, namely that Wordsworth was himself a star; the light he shed was his own. The end of Shelley's poem similarly recasts Wordsworth's understanding of the loss of vision by seeming to suggest it is not that vision has deserted Wordsworth, but that Wordsworth is a deserter. Such a reading however, does not do justice to the turns in Shelley's deceptively straightforward looking poem. If Shelley's charge were simply that Wordsworth should have known that his mind was the source of imaginative vision and that Wordsworth should not have betrayed his inner light, we would have to accuse Shelley of repeating the error, since the poetic voice in *To Wordsworth* equally looks outside of the self, to Wordsworth, and equally claims that a guiding light *from outside* has departed. Shelley's insistence on Wordsworth as a guiding light seems quite consciously to seek an externalised object of desire in the figure of the earlier poet.

As G. Kim Blank points out, Wordsworth is one of the things that have departed for Shelley (Blank, 1988, pp. 48, 63). Blank further notes (p. 49) that if this is so, we are left with the problem of whether Shelley would have condemned Wordsworth's attempt to feel a connection with his environment. I have argued above that Shelley himself in part ties imaginative desire to the natural world. Blank, who argues that Shelley condemns Wordsworth for just this act, bases his argument on a reading of *To —* ('Oh! there are spirits of the air') as a poem about a Wordsworthian poet who built his hope on 'the false earth's inconstancy' (Blank, 1988, p. 49; quotations from *To —* are from Shelley, 1970, p. 525). While such an interpretation is in many ways persuasive, it ignores Mary Shelley's opinion that *To —* was addressed to Coleridge, as does Wasserman's reading of the poem, which he footnotes by saying that reading the poem as an address to Coleridge 'contributes nothing to the meaning' (Wasserman, 1971, p. 8). This seems to be worth questioning.

Shelley often explored irreconcilable viewpoints by writing dialogues in the sceptical tradition (Wasserman, 1971, pp. 3–83). The title of the poem *To —* not only mirrors the title of *To Wordsworth*, but thematically the two poems again repeat the argument between Wordsworth's and Coleridge's odes. 'Oh! there are spirits' echoes the imagery in Coleridge's ode, referring to thwarted love, to the image of the blank eye viewing the stars and the old moon, and to Coleridge's statement that his 'spirits fail'. Shelley writes of 'spirits of the air', and of how the 'glory of the moon is dead'. In *To Wordsworth*, in part just because it is an attempt to correct Wordsworth, Shelley tacitly explores the need to keep one's eyes on some mortal embodiment of an ideal – Wordsworth 'as a lone star' – and not to desert what nonetheless will depart. In contrast, *To —* seems to take Coleridge's point of view, imaging the earth, that which is external, as 'faithless', and focusing, like Coleridge, on the imaginative self: 'Did thine own mind afford no scope / Of love, or moving thoughts to thee?'

However, we cannot take Shelley's poem as wholly affirming Coleridge's understanding of the loss of vision, since *To —* points out that Coleridge's dejection is itself imaginatively colouring the world. If 'dreams have now departed', says Shelley, 'Thine own soul still is true to thee, / But changed to a foul fiend through misery.' Like the visionary in *Alastor*, the person addressed in *To —* finds the self still bound to the world it finds inadequate, but to a world now informed by a 'ghastly presence' or sense of its inadequacy. Moreover, in his essay *On Life*, Shelley cautions that the source of life is probably not similar to mind, since mind can only perceive. Any internalised quest occasioned by the proposition that the object of imaginative desire lies within the self is doomed in just the way that the quest of the visionary in *Alastor* is doomed and in just the way that the Coleridgean figure in *To —* is told that to pursue his dream would be a 'mad endeavour' (Steinman, 1978, pp. 262–7). Finally, and perhaps most persuasively, Shelley proposes that the view given voice in *Dejection: An Ode* entails reaching a dead end as surely as does frustration in the face of the earth's inconstancy; *To —* ends: 'Be as thou art. Thy settled fate, / Dark as it is, all change would aggravate.' It seems that Shelley wants, on the one hand, not to despair of either political change or the mental activity by virtue of which political change is envisioned and, on the other hand, to remain constant in *not* yielding to change of the sort Wordsworth and Southey (one implicitly, one explicitly) predict. Put another way, one might say that Wordsworth and Coleridge pose for Shelley the problem of leaving open the gap between aspiration and disillusionment, a gap that is equally closed, as Shelley sees it, by Wordsworth's repudiation of politics or his fixation on the natural world, and by Coleridge's fixation on the self, which for Shelley may come to the same thing. Shelley's earlier questions about morals and politics, self and history, then resurface as questions about the nature and ends of imaginative activity. It is just such questions that are addressed in the paired poems to Wordsworth and Coleridge. *To Wordsworth* insists on imaginative desire and its frustrations as the necessary basis of moral sympathies even as *To—* suggests that to seek to know the origins or true nature of the desiring self may be madness.

In the same vein, Shelley's essay *On Love*, written three years after the poems I have been examining, posits that love 'is that powerful attraction towards all that we conceive, or fear, or hope beyond ourselves, when we find within our own thoughts the chasm of an insufficient void and seek to awaken in all things that are a community with what we experience within ourselves' (Shelley, 1954, p. 170). Shelley's point seems to be that when we find a vacancy within the self we turn to the world ('all things that are'), and attempt to call forth a like-minded community. The difficult syntax of Shelley's sentence does not rule out the idea that the community thus awakened will share an inner experience primarily characterised as a vacancy or absence, although as the essay proceeds Shelley posits an inner presence that not only 'thirsts after its likeness' but also is an inner ideal or 'anti-type' (Shelley, 1954, p. 170). This view seems to inform Shelley's 1814 portrait of the early Wordsworth, whose own experience of loss in *Ode: Intimations of Immortality* led him to see images of that loss in the world, and so to form a bond of sympathy with the world. For Shelley, too, it is within the gap between what we want and what we do not have that we experience love, which is thus a result of our unfulfilled aspirations.

Yet the essay *On Love* further concludes that as 'soon as this want or power is dead, man becomes the living sepulchre of himself, and what yet survives is the mere husk of what once he was (Shelley, 1954, p. 171), a more negative image surely also informed by Shelley's portraits of Wordsworth and Southey, who are not as they were. The essay thus suggests Shelley's self-consciousness about the difficulties of his relationship to the earlier poets he admired. In *To Wordsworth*, for example, the image of the early Wordsworth functions, in effect, as an ideal for Shelley, that is (to use Shelley's terms) as a mirrored reflection of Shelley's own anti-type or desires. Yet to see Wordsworth as a figure of imaginative desire is also a problem. Once having claimed the early Wordsworth as a figure of imaginative desire, Shelley cannot easily dismiss the older poet, since to give up on Wordsworth is to some degree to risk, on the one hand, becoming like him a man who no longer aspires to change the world or, on the other hand, becoming like Coleridge a man whose aspirations are no longer directed towards the world and so equally a man without love, without community. The tone with which Shelley then wrote to Peacock about Wordsworth in 1818, saying 'That such a man should be such a poet!', is thus not solely dismay that an admired poet had written the *Address to the Freeholders of Westmorland*, but that imaginative desire could become so thoroughly divorced from a sympathetic imagining of historical and political good (Shelley, 1964, II, p. 26).

In 1816, then, Shelley clearly worried about how to connect the poetic self with human society and with history. For instance, he wrote to Byron suggesting that negative worldly opinion ought not to prevent Byron from acting on the 'pure, and simple' motive of wishing 'to express [his] own thoughts; to address [him]self to the sympathy of those who might think with [him]'; Shelley also mentions that Byron might consider writing an epic poem on the French Revolution (Shelley, 1964, I, pp. 507–8). Finally, Shelley adds that Byron should not aspire to fame, although he assures his friend that fame follows 'those whom it is unworthy to lead' (Shelley, 1964, I, p. 507). The references to both fame and epic certainly involve Shelley's thoughts on his own place in literary history. The letter may also be understood in relation to Shelley's concern about poetry and history more literally conceived, as in his 1817 preface to *The Revolt of Islam*, where he similarly refers to the French Revolution, addresses himself to those sympathetic to the reform movement, and attempts to place himself in the canon, in part by claiming to be motivated by the spirit of the age (Shelley, 1970, pp. 32–7).

Speaking of *The Revolt of Islam*, Kenneth Neill Cameron points out that Shelley's belief in the possible efficacy of an epic on the French Revolution is ironically the same belief 'Coleridge had urged upon Wordsworth some eighteen years before' (Cameron, 1974, p. 315). But on Shelley's own account of the spirit of the age, this irony is not mere coincidence. As he wrote, responding to an

1819 *Quarterly Review* article (which he thought Southey had written and in which Shelley was accused of imitating and perverting Wordsworth), there is a 'certain similarity all the best writers of any particular age inevitably are marked with, from the spirit of that age acting on all' (Shelley, 1964, II, p. 127). For Shelley, a poet earns a place in literary history in part by his or her engagement with actual history, although to set out only to achieve literary fame is, as Shelley says to Byron, unworthy. This is not to say that Shelley did not struggle with unworthy motives; an 1819 letter asks Leigh Hunt to print *Julian and Maddalo* anonymously: 'I would not put my name to it – I leave you to judge whether it is best to throw it into the fire, or to publish it – So much for self – *self*, that burr that will stick to one. I can't get it off yet' (Shelley, 1964, II, pp. 108–9). It is to say, first, that Shelley would have reacted quite negatively to the very first page of Wordsworth's *Peter Bell*, which begins asking 'What's in a *Name*?' and which goes on to present Wordsworth's stated goal as being primarily to earn himself a permanent 'station, however humble, in the Literature of our Country' (Wordsworth, 1977a, p. 315).[5] That is, Shelley would have found fault with Wordsworth's ostensible aspirations and motives given Wordsworth's unintended use of the same language Shelley had been using to question himself, as well as with Wordsworth's apparent self-centredness. Second, Shelley's appeal to the spirit of the age is not simply a way of declaring his originality, but perhaps more centrally a way of reaffirming his moral and political beliefs. Yet, at the same time, there are again implications to Shelley's insistence that he and Wordsworth followed the same path because of the spirit of the age, which Shelley would not have wanted to embrace; in particular, Shelley could hardly have given assent to Wordsworth's account of the effects of ageing on the poetic imagination of the age, even as those effects were presented in *Ode: Intimations of Immortality*, let alone as evidenced in *The Excursion* or proclaimed by Southey. In other words, to argue that poets of active imagination resembled one another by default, as it were, was not an argument Shelley – given his judgement on Wordsworth and Southey as defaulters and his discomfort with Wordsworth's views on poetic development – could wholly sustain. Nor was it an argument he could avoid, and it seems that *Peter Bell the Third* is where Shelley most starkly records his recognition of this fact. If the poem reveals Shelley's ambivalence about Wordsworth (Blank, 1988, pp. 63–71), it also records Shelley's self-doubt, not so much about his feelings towards Wordsworth as about his own endeavour and about his career as a re-enactment of Wordsworth's (Keach, 1984, pp. 95–6). The writing of *Peter Bell the Third*, then, marks the third moment in Shelley's dialogue with Wordsworth and the Lake Poets that I will, briefly, address here.

Mary Jacobus notes that, despite its opening address to Southey in the 1819 revision, Wordsworth began *Peter Bell* in 1798 as a response to Coleridge after his failed attempt to collaborate with Coleridge on *The Ancient Mariner*; specifically Wordsworth seems to have been responding to Coleridge's accusation (as reported by Hazlitt) that Wordsworth was too matter-of-fact (Jacobus, 1976, pp. 262–3). Indeed, the 1798 poem begins the exchange continued in *Ode: Intimations of Immortality* and *Dejection: An Ode*, as Wordsworth questions 'imaginative activity that is also a retreat from reality' and 'restates the redemption-theme of *The Ancient Mariner* in terms that are not merely anti-supernatural, but emphatically humane' (Jacobus, 1976, pp. 263–5). Reading Wordsworth's 1819 poem, Shelley once again re-opens the earlier exchange between the older poets, and follows the earlier Wordsworth by rejecting Coleridge's retreat and by addressing himself to contemporary reality, transposing hell 'into contemporary industrial society' (Curran, 1975, pp. 148, 143). At the same time, Shelley proposes that Wordsworth fulfils Satan's prescription for the self as hell (*Paradise Lost*, IV.75), having 'sold himself to the devil in order to save himself from . . . uncertainties' (Curran, 1975, p. 145). It might be added that Shelley presumably introduces Wordsworth as Proteus not so much to point to the older poet's unnerving change *per se* as to underscore how, like Proteus, Wordsworth changed to avoid facing questions. Finally, even as Shelley focuses on and deplores Wordsworth's resulting 'loss of compassion', *Peter Bell the Third*, 'the form of the poem itself – its genre, its methods, its tone – uncomfortably reflects the very vices Shelley would castigate. . . . There is "Small justice shown, and still less pity"' (Curran, 1975, pp. 150–1).

That Shelley's poem should seem ungenerous is not surprising if we compare Shelley's earlier voiced admiration for epic poetry with his introductory statements, however satirically they are meant, on *Peter Bell the Third* as mock epic. Shelley enters his poem as the latest in a 'series of cyclic poems which have already been candidates for bestowing immortality upon, at the same time that they receive it from, [Peter Bell's] character and adventures'. To deplore Wordsworth's insertion of himself within literary history by appeal to Southey's fame as poet laureate is one thing. But to describe his own highest aspirations by way of reaction as an historian of Fudges is potentially to doom himself to the cycle he deplores; if Shelley's satire does not accept what is, it still closes the gap between what is and what should be, much as Shelley saw Wordsworth doing. The point is one Shelley himself makes implicitly a few months later, in December 1819, when he writes:

> Towards whatsoever we regard as perfect, undoubtedly it is no less our duty than it is our nature to press forward; this is the generous enthusiasm which accomplishes not indeed the consummation after which it aspires, but one which approaches it in a degree far nearer than if the whole powers had not been developed by a delusion. It is in politics rather than in religion that faith is meritorious.   (Shelley, 1954, p. 256)

This is Shelley's reaffirmation of faith. As P. M. S. Dawson says, it 'cannot be easy to maintain the necessary commitment when one knows that it is to a "delusion" ' (Dawson, 1980, p. 5). Shelley's and Dawson's remarks are about politics, specifically about resisting both expediency and utopian fantasy in the face of the political unrest of 1819. Yet the statement holds true of Shelley's view of the poetic as well as the political imagination, which indeed, as Shelley argues, seem in this light inseparable. To avoid the error of demanding that one's ideals be embodied, without abandoning either the body of the world or ideals, is not easily accomplished either in poetry or politics.

It is in his encounter with Wordsworth in 1819 that Shelley seems first fully to recognise the implications for himself of the fact that – to return to the 1822 letter about love with which I began – although 'one is always in love with something or other[,] the error . . . consists in seeking in a mortal image the likeness of what is perhaps eternal' (Shelley, 1964, II, p. 434). In light of this explicit caution against seeking the likeness of one's ideals in a single image, it is not surprising to find Rousseau substituting for Wordsworth as Shelley's literary father in The Triumph of Life. Still, it should also be said that the ways in which The Triumph of Life opens a space between heaven and hell, and suggests how poetic vision succeeds in the course of failing to achieve what it wants, reveal what Shelley learned from Wordsworth (see Steinman, 1983, pp. 32–3). That is, Shelley retraces in his last poem the lesson already figured in the delicately modulated rhetoric of commonality and separation found in the lines from *To Wordsworth*: 'These common woes I feel. One loss is mine / Which thou too feel'st.' It is in his repeated enactments of both commonality and separation that Shelley writes cyclic poems that most seriously become 'candidates for bestowing immortality upon, at the same time that they receive it from', his predecessors.

Part II

Readings

5

The Web of Human Things: Narrative and Identity in *Alastor*

Tilottama Rajan

Labyrinths, weavings and related figures are ubiquitous in Shelley's texts, whether they are used to characterise language or other ways of grasping the world, such as thought, vision or emotion. Thus in *Prometheus Unbound* language 'rules with Daedal harmony a throng/Of thoughts and forms' whose complexity it does not so much eliminate as contain within its own labyrinthine structure (IV.416–17). In an essay on imagery, Shelley describes the mind as 'a wilderness of intricate paths . . . a world within a world' (Shelley, 1911, II, p. 102). Perhaps the most famous of such images occurs in *The Revolt of Islam*, where Cythna describes the tracing of signs on the sand to range

> These woofs, as they were woven of my thought:
> Clear elemental shapes, whose smallest change
> A subtler language within langue wrought
> (VII.xxxii)

Like the epipsyche which is 'a soul within our soul' (Shelley, 1977, p. 474), language in this account seems implicated in intricacies and involutions that promise not difference but a grasping of identity. But on closer inspection we can see that the passage describes reference as displacement rather than *epoche*. For it seems that the process of articulation generates a secondary discourse by which the clear elemental shapes with which we begin are subtly shifted, and that representation is a recursive activity, a turning inwards which is not so much the finding of a centre as an act of self-reflection. Taken together, these images suggest that Shelley senses in language a disseminative potential, and that the representation of desire, its embodiment in language, will prove to be a mirror stage that discloses hidden articulations and fragmentations within the elemental shapes projected on the plane of the imaginary.

That there is this potential in language is registered from the beginning in Shelley's poetic practice, which manifests in its syntax as well as its imagery that tendency condemned by Leavis to 'forget the status' of the initiating metaphor or proposition and 'to assume an autonomy and a right to propagate' (Leavis, 1936, p. 206). Shelley himself describes this tendency more positively when he defines imagination as a non-synthetic productivity that composes from its initiating thoughts 'as from elements, other thoughts, each containing within itself the principle of its own integrity' (Shelley, 1977, p. 480). But the way Shelley's language works is frequently at odds with what he seems to desire for the creative process in metafictional texts like *Alastor*, and the history of his poems is thus the history of their gradual alignment with the mode of functioning of their discourse. This alignment takes form as an increasing acceptance of lyric as (dis)placed within more extensive structures like narrative. For in so far as genre can be considered phenomenologically as representing the desire, though not necessarily the possibility, for a certain kind of language, lyric resists those differences that emerge in more dialogical forms of utterance like narrative and drama. Traditionally Romanticism has been associated with the lyric and with the 'lyricisation' of various other forms such as epic, drama and quest-narrative (Rajan, 1985b, pp. 194–207). Lyricisation, in turn, has been a metaphor for 'internalisation', for a retreat away from history or temporality and into the visionary or the transcendental. Emulating the inscription of lyric as transcendence that he associated with Wordsworth, Shelley in *Alastor* also thematises lyric by bringing it into an uneasy dialogue with narrative, so as to make both modes an object of reflection within the text.

I shall approach *Alastor* not at the mimetic level, as a poem about a visionary who seeks for his ideal in nature and then defers it to an after-life, but at the level of the signifier, as a text which presents the process by which the Narrator tries to represent the Poet and discloses to himself the inevitable functioning of language as difference. Through the Poet, Shelley presents a thematic nexus which he had inherited from Wordsworth and which he was to elaborate in *Adonais*: that of a vocation that is visionary rather than ordinary, invested in a special being whose life and death are understood only by nature, and whose memory becomes for his or her survivors the site of a bitter separation between the public and private realms. The Narrator tries to idealise the Poet and present him as an epipsyche who stands in relation to him as the veiled woman does to the Poet himself. But as has been widely recognised, his sentimentalisation of the Poet is haunted by doubts he is barely able to repress about the value of the visionary life (Rajan, 1980, pp. 75–82). We can attribute this ambivalent attitude to a 'Wordsworth' who is himself a construction of Shelley's desire and to the latter's re-visionary position in relation to his precursor. Inheriting the Wordsworthian myth in the second generation,[1] Shelley inherits it as a set of symbols. Moreover he departs from the Wordsworth of the Lucy poems by conveying the myth through elegiac narrative rather than lyric. Representing himself as a narrator, Shelley encounters in the process of representation, and specifically in the problematic of genre, a kind of mirror stage in which the search for a unified self-representation is enacted and called into question. As the Narrator, who represents himself in the form of a lyric poet, finds his lyricism subtly displaced by the pressures of narrative, so too 'Shelley' finds a language within his language. He discovers that narrative is not simply a more ambitious version of lyric, an extensive rather than intensive totality in Lukács's terms,[2] but a deconstruction of lyric totality. *Alastor*, in short, is more about the process of its production than about the product of that process: the figure of the Poet. For one of the curious things about the poem is that its main figure never comes alive, speaking only once and reverting at the end to an 'image, silent, cold, and motionless' (661). Summoned up from a realm of 'incommunicable dream, / And twilight phantasms' (39–40), the Poet seems an archetype or more properly a semiotype in the Narrator's consciousness. He is less a person than a textual figure: a sign that has no objective referent, being rather the sign of a desire, a desire for a Romantic ideology of vision that remains still (to be) born. The poem of which he is the nominal subject is thus a poem about itself: about the process of making figures true, and about whether it is possible to find a mode of language that will confer identity on the Poet and thus on his author, the Narrator.

As narcissistic narrative *Alastor* thus defers its referent from the mimetic to the discursive level so as to make its subject the signification of a visionary ideology. This movement from the sublime to the hermeneutic brought about through a displacement of interest from the signified to the signifier is connected to another phenomenon: the unwilling transposition of the visionary theme from the lyric to the narrative mode. The pre-text for *Alastor* is the Wordsworthian motif of the visionary self: the sensitive soul who, like Lucy or the Boy of Winander (or somewhat differently Margaret), dies young. Thus the Narrator's initial 'There was a Poet' (50) recalls Wordsworth's *There was a boy*. The depiction of the Poet as unrecognised except by nature recalls Lucy, who dwelt by the untrodden ways and whose death made a difference only to Wordsworth. And the final re-absorption of the Poet by nature resembles, though more nihilistically, Lucy 'Rolled round in earth's diurnal course / With rocks and stones and trees' (*A slumber did my spirit seal*, 7–8). The figure of the sensitive soul is by no means uncomplicated in Wordsworth. For even in its simplest inscription as the visionary child it is rendered ambiguous by the child's death, which seals it in an identity with its essence yet denies it any being in the world, as though in some sense it has not been, and yet as though by not having been it has not *yet* been. But in those pre-texts which comprise for Shelley's Narrator an ideal limit, the figure of the beautiful soul is sealed against any probing of its liminality by being re-called in the mode of lyric rather than narrative. Lyric thus becomes for the Narrator the mode in which he can best approximate a discourse that will make the figure of the poet identical with itself. For the autonomous (as opposed to the intertextual) lyric comes as close as is possible in language to the forgetting of difference. Lyric concentrates on a single spot of time: on someone like Lucy seen in a single moment, and not in a series of situations in which she might appear differently. In reducing time to a moment, it also selects the moment that most expresses the essence of the subject's life: the moment that is, like the epipsyche, a 'soul within our soul'. Unfolding as voice rather than narrative, lyric does not posit a narrator different from the subject of his story or caught in relationships of (non)-identity with characters who displace him from his desire. Finally lyric, as Frye points out, is overheard rather than heard (Frye, 1957, p. 249). By forgetting its reader, or at least by eliding its reader as someone different from the author, it simulates a hermeneutics of identity that confirms the oneness of the speaker with his subject.

The lyricisation of the beautiful soul is thus part of the Romantic attempt to embody it in a language that will not displace it. By and large the Romantics conceive of the lyrical consciousness as one that is present to itself, able to bypass the reflective and therefore reflexive mode of language in song, or at least to make language the true voice of feeling. There are later deconstructions of lyric and music, such as those of Schopenhauer and Nietzsche, who see feeling as itself a mobile army of metaphors, and 'mood', that quintessentially lyric attunement, as a conflictual site.[3] But representations of lyric in terms of nightingales and Aeolian harps largely ignore this association of music with the subconscious and the will, and thus with the trace of non-identity. Instead they make art identical with nature, while conceiving of nature immediately as song and not reflexively as the book of nature. If lyric functions in terms of a semiotics of presence, it also involves a suppression of temporality. Lyric compression, as Sharon Cameron points out, produces an abridgement of time: a concentration on the moment rather than the sequence which has the effect of exempting the self from action, from involvement in the complex intertexture of events (Cameron, 1976, pp. 204, 250), and thus from a reading that would situate its values. Often focusing on experiences of loss or death that seem to confirm the triumph of a life that thwarts the desires of the subject, lyric protects the subject's interiority from what is merely exterior through an idealism that sublates material circumstance into its rhetorical figuration. Lyrics, as Cameron suggests, 'oppose speech to the action from which it exempts itself, oppose voice as it rises momentarily from the enthusiasms of temporal advance to the flow of time that ultimately rushes over and drowns it' (Cameron, 1976, p. 23). Or, as Adorno puts it, lyric is a 'self-forgetting in which the subject submerges in language' (Adorno, 1974, p. 62).

Narrative, by contrast, is the insertion of the subject into a temporal and historical world: into a space populated by other people and no longer defined purely by the subject. If *Alastor*, which is concerned with only one character, is in this respect an ellipsis of the mode, the pressure of narrative is still felt in the presence of figures like the Arab maiden and the veiled woman, whose unreality renders interiority symptomatically as an effacement of, rather than an exemption from, being-in-the-world. The chronotope of narrative, its configuration of space as something inhabited by others and of time as something that continues beyond the moment of speech, necessarily generates a more complex hermeneutic than that of lyric. The fact that the narrator is telling the story *of* someone other than himself reminds us that he is telling it *to* someone other than himself, a fact emphasised in more complex narratives by the presence of characters telling each other things. Equally important in *Alastor*, as in most narratives, is that the time of the poem is not identical with the time of the Poet's story, still less with a moment of that story expressive of a single mood. *There was a boy* in its form as an autonomous lyric ends with the epiphanic absorption of the boy in nature. The time of the poem is the time of the poet's memory, and the poem ceases when he stops speaking.[4] In *Alastor* the Narrator survives the Poet, reflecting on his death not for two lines but at length, and thus breaking whatever mood he has created. Inserting the past into the present, the format of narrative as a story told *to* someone necessarily implicates it in a future in which the story may be retold, re-visioned. The time of narrative is a space that others will come to inhabit, as the text recognises in the gesture of a preface: a preface, moreover, whose uncertainty as to whether it should idealise or didactically dismiss the Poet uneasily anticipates a division in the poem's audience.

The vulnerability of narrative to a hermeneutics of difference is corroborated by other features of the mode. Narrative is both psychoanalytically and structurally a mode of difference at odds with unmediated vision. That texts like *Alastor* are not narratives in the way that novels are, and seem closer to the lyric in making the main character a version of the speaker, is not crucial. For if they interiorise narrative so as to conserve lyric identity, that identity is now articulated in terms of a splitting of the subject. Subjective narratives of the sort the Romantics write project the self in the form of an *alter ego* who is then inside and outside the narrative voice. Where the lyric poet is undivided and speaks in *propria persona*, the Narrator of *Alastor* projects himself as the Poet, seeking to identify with a visionary ideology that he also constructs through someone he is not. Endemic to such narrative is a structure of repetition, a doubling of the subject into narrator and character, author and narrator, by which the self is repeated as something outside itself and displaced from itself. Put differently, narrative is also the displacement of the self into an objective world that will disclose it as other than itself. The events of the Poet's life, the path followed by the Narrator's (poetic) desire in the actual world, divide him from this desire and force him to know (however reluctantly) its gaps and inadequacies. Narrative is, in this sense, the mirror stage of lyric. Even as it promises the subject an identity in the objective world, it also marks the unsettling insertion of the imaginary ego both into what Lacan calls the symbolic and into what Kristeva calls the semiotic order.[5]

If from a psychological point of view narrative is a process in which the self discloses its difference from itself, on a structural level its very length creates in it complications elided by the brevity of the lyric and by the hermeneutics of the lyric mode, which elicits unreflective reading. For narratives contain characters and episodes which are linked to each other in relations of connection and difference. The intratextual complexity of narrative is inevitably the source of hermeneutic difference, since the various characters provide more than one perspective from which the reader can view the project of the protagonist. Moreover, the elements of a narrative are interimplicated, present within each other, in such a way that no element exists in and of itself. A narrative thus forms an intratextual network of differences much like that of language or the text as Derrida describes it:

> The play of differences supposes, in effect, syntheses and
> referrals which forbid at any moment, or in any sense, that a
> simple element be *present* in and of itself, referring only to itself
> ... no element can function like a sign without referring to
> another element which itself is not simply present. This inter-
> weaving results in each 'element' ... being constituted on the
> basis of the trace within it of other elements of the chain or
> system. (Derrida, 1981, p. 26)

To put it another way, the syntagmatic arrangement of events in a plot is suspended by paradigmatic relations between these events that render the reading of plot recursive rather than progressive. Thus the Poet in his wanderings through lands whose foreignness registers his self-estrangement seems to proceed from the Middle East to India, cradle of the human race, in a Hegelian journey towards greater inwardness that should bring him closer to cultural identity. But the vacancy that follows his vision of the veiled maid recalls the similar vacancy of his mind in Ethiopia, and makes us wonder whether the second episode does not contain traces of the first, where inspiration is asserted but not described, so that it seems to reproduce the vacancy it replaces (106–28).

Shelley himself speaks of difference in representation in *A*

Defence of Poetry when he contrasts the semiotics of language with that of other artistic media:

> language is arbitrarily produced by the Imagination and has relation to thoughts alone; but all other materials, instruments and conditions of art, have relations among each other, which limit and interpose between conception and expression. The former is as a mirror which reflects, the latter as a cloud which enfeebles, the light of which both are mediums of communication.   (Shelley, 1977, p. 483)

A word directly evokes its referent, whereas a painting distracts us from using it mimetically by allowing us to be caught up in the interplay between its parts, between its forms and its colours. But if Shelley at this point allows words to exist in and of themselves, he later complicates the opposition between language and other forms of art by conceding that 'Sounds as well as thoughts have relation both between each other and towards that which they represent' (Shelley, 1977, p. 484). His hesitations about narrative in the *Defence* may be due, among other things, to a distrust of forms that fail to abstract the poetical 'parts of a composition' from the 'intertexture' produced when the hermeneutic whole conceived by inspiration is executed in parts that develop relations among each other as well as towards the whole they are supposed to create (Shelley, 1977, pp. 485, 504).

That intertexture is troubling on grounds that are semantic as well as syntactic. Distinguishing narrative from poetry (presumably lyric), Shelley criticises the 'story of particular facts' for failing to idealise that 'which is distorted' (Shelley, 1977, p. 485), for failing to omit those elements of chronology and circumstance whose interference prevents the text from being 'a mirror whose surface reflects only the forms of purity and brightness' (Shelley, 1977, p. 474). Moreover, as a 'catalogue of detached facts' (Shelley, 1977, p. 485), narrative strikes Shelley as episodic rather than epipsychic. It introduces scenes, and thus considerations, at odds with a causality that would make plot into the text's self-explanation, and it thus inhibits the closure that allows narrative to refer directly to what it represents. Telling the story of the Poet chronologically rather than according to principles of retrospective selection that would make each episode a stage in an argument, the Narrator includes in it an encounter with an Arab maid who plays no further part in the poem. The episodic character of her appearance is visually marked by her insertion into an unusually short verse-paragraph that is simply dropped into the poem, unintegrated with anything else. We can read her as constellating a phase in the phenomenology of the Poet's mind, and can thus absorb her into the poem's causal structure as a shadowy material type of the more spiritual veiled maid. But some of the questions she raises – about the Poet's metaphysical quest as an evasion of his existence in the material world – challenge the phenomenology she is supposed to subserve. Moreover these questions (repeated in the Preface) do not recur in the poem, which raises epistemological but not ethical doubts about the Poet's quest. Rather they are symptomatic of the narrative's tendency to generate complications that it is not always able to integrate into a more complex unity: sub-plots that contain within themselves the principle of their own integrity.

From the invocation where the Narrator describes himself as a 'long-forgotten lyre' (42) and asks nature to favour his 'solemn song' (18), to the end where the dead Poet is described as a 'lute' and the Narrator refers to his own poem as a 'simple strain' (667, 706), lyric and not narrative is the desired mode of *Alastor*. But curiously the Narrator describes his own previous history as given over to narration, though he tries to view this stage as merely a prelude to vision:

> I have made my bed
> In charnels and on coffins, where black death
> Keeps record of the trophies won from thee.
> Hoping to still these obstinate questionings
> Of thee and thine, by forcing some lone ghost,
> Thy messenger, to render up the tale
> Of what we are.
>
> (23–9)

Narrative is pictured psychoanalytically as a search for identity in language, but one that yields only inadequate self-representations: a mirror stage that discloses the specular structure of any identity between Narrator and text. Proclaiming that he has had enough of 'twilight phantasms' (39–40), the Narrator sees himself as about to emerge from the temporalising and deferral of identity endemic to narrative through a resumption of his long-forgotten lyre. But what he constructs is another narrative in which the Poet's failure to find his ideal reproduces the Narrator's failure to create a figure that will render up the tale of what he is. The poem, in other words, is the story of the Narrator's failure to write his text as lyric. Moreover, if lyric ideally is a transcendence of narrative, its belatedness in the Narrator's career suggests that it has no more than a liminal status, as a desire produced by what it seeks to forget. It is interesting that the Narrator describes the music produced by his Aeolian lyre as a 'woven' hymn (48), suggesting that he cannot really conceive of a form of expression which points single-mindedly outwards to a referent or source or affective state, rather than inwards to its own intratextual complications. Images of weaving are the site of a crossing in Shelley's aesthetics from an essentialist to a differential concept of language. In *The Revolt of Islam* it is arguable that the subtler language within language produced by the woof of thought is meant to be like that soul within a soul defined as the epipsyche, more identical with itself as it becomes more refined and complex. But increasingly weaving becomes a figure for the autonomous complexity of language and other forms of mediation as something that displaces and produces rather than simply signifies thought.

The (un)weaving of lyric desire is thematised in the poem's most important episode: the scene of the Poet's own creative origination in which he sees the veiled maid in the vale of Cashmir. It is well known that she develops from simple to complex as she is unveiled, that her ideality turns out to contain a darker subtext, and that the attempt to articulate concretely what begins as a dreamy abstraction discloses what seems spiritual and pure as partly material. The intense physicality of what the Poet projects as a Platonic form, so troubling that he swoons rather than consummate his love, enacts the embodiment of vision: the linguistic process by which the Idea is given a body in words that do not exist by themselves but inevitably refer to other elements in the chain or system. To begin with, the veiled woman is characterised in terms of allegorical abstractions that allow her song (or that of the Poet who projects her as Muse) to bear a direct relation to transcendental referents:

> Knowledge and truth and virtue were her theme,
> And lofty hopes of divine liberty,
> Thoughts the most dear to him, and poesy,
> Herself a poet.
>
> (158–61)

Yet the multiplication of these referents makes us wonder if she is indeed simple in essence: whether knowledge, truth and virtue are the same thing, and whether there lies beneath these simple terms what Nietzsche calls a philosophic mythology, which makes these concepts into figures in a series of stories and family romances. This diffusion of reference is linked to the presence of the woman's body, or rather to the body of her emotions: her 'tremulous sobs', 'beating . . . heart', and her 'pure mind' which is confusingly experienced only through her body, kindling 'through all her frame / A permeating fire' (161–72). The body has been linked by Nietzsche and more recently by Kristeva to the problem of representation. The female body is for Kristeva the site of pulsions that disturb the order of both the symbolic and the imaginary – of what cannot be said or imagined and thus of something felt in language only in terms of gaps and absences.[6] Resisting logical representation, the body of the veiled woman disrupts the Poet's attempt to link her to a transcendental signified or to make the music she sings the vehicle of a disembodied and simple lyricism.

The multivocality of the veiled woman corresponds to her profound ambiguity as a figure for poetry and for a lyricism linked not just to the feelings but de-idealised and complicated by the association of feeling itself with the female body. The veiled woman is both epipsyche and Muse, 'Herself a poet' who plays upon a harp. As lyric poet, she produces a Wagnerian music strangely lacking in lyric serenity: 'wild numbers then / She raised, with voice stifled in tremulous sobs' (163–4). Her music, moreover, tells an 'ineffable tale' (168), a tale curiously like the poem itself in that it cannot be interpreted so as to render up the tale of what we are. Describing it as ineffable rather than obscure, the Narrator tries to etherealise its disruptiveness. Yet even as he transforms narrative into music by figuring its silences as unheard melodies, the song he creates in his mind is 'intermitted' (172), full of gaps and absences, as if there is more to be told about this woman who never becomes present in the song she sings and must be pursued beyond the 'realms of dream' (206) if the Poet is to discover to what the song refers. As a *mise-en-abîme* of the larger poem, the vision of the veiled woman thus deconstructs lyric as the epipsyche of narrative. Lyric is not so much the antitype of narrative as a sublimation maintained only by the absence of narrative. As the withholding of narrative, the woman's song is present only as the absence of something which the Poet must recover if the song is to be fully self-present, but which paradoxically might deconstruct its identity as song.

That lyric is no more than the absence of narrative, constituted on the trace of what it does not tell, is suggested by the fact that the woman's song is associated with weaving. We shall return again to this image, which is Shelley's image for the differential texture of language. At the end of the poem 'the web of human things' becomes an image for everything that the Poet, in imagining the epipsyche, seeks to forget: for 'Nature's vast frame . . . / Birth and the grave' (719–20), and thus for the complex intertexture of existence in which nothing is present without its opposite. As a mode which tells of life from birth to the grave, narrative inevitably recreates this intertexture. By contrast, lyric, as the attempt to abstract a single moment and thus a single referent from life, brackets the interconnections between this and other moments so as to reduce existence to some simple essence. But it is precisely this simplicity that the Poet fails to find through the veiled woman, who seems a natural rather than transcendental Muse (associated with 'streams and breezes' – 155), and whose voice thus creates no single mood:

> Her voice was like the voice of his own soul
> Heard in the calm of thought; its music long,
> Like woven sounds of streams and breezes, held
> His inmost sense suspended in its web
> Of many-coloured woof and shifting hues.
>   (153–7)

As already observed, images of weaving are the site of an unfolding complication in Shelley's aesthetics, in which the very notion of lyric as an *epoche* achieved through interiorisation is here implicated. Associated with interiority and thus with the promise of a deep truth, they reveal the Poet's inmost sense not as a centre but as a place of dissemination. As used in *The Triumph of Life*, where the place in which the Shape all Light appears is 'filled with many sounds woven into one / Oblivious melody' (340–1), weaving is explicitly presented as the creation of an illusory unity: of something which seems a single fabric only because we are oblivious to how it is woven of multiple strands. As weaving, lyric is thus no more than the illusory unification of that web of differences which unravels in more extensive structures like narrative.

*   *   *

The development of the poem as a web of differences is everywhere apparent, most obviously in the fact that the Narrator tells
the story of the Poet's journey towards death twice, but also in the
syntax and texture of the poem. This unravelling of the poem's
identity may be ascribed to the tendency of extended structures to
organise themselves in terms of repetition. It is in the nature of
language to repeat along different axes: to illustrate concepts
through figures or fables, or conversely to reduce symbols or
narratives to conceptual paraphrases. These textual repetitions
combine in larger forms of utterance with doublings of characters
and repetitions of similar episodes. While repetition may be
intended to confirm and emphasise, it also produces differences
and functions as part of the economy of the supplement. We do
not repeat something in different words if we mean to say exactly
the same thing. If we do repeat something it is because what we
said is not sufficient: because there is also something else to say.

Let us consider the passage which follows the Poet's futile
attempt to pursue the veiled woman beyond the 'realms of dream'.
What exactly this passage says is crucial to determining the Poet's
choice of death, and whether it is legitimised by the existence of a
transcendent realm:

> Does the dark gate of death
> Conduct to thy mysterious paradise,
> O Sleep? Does the bright arch of rainbow clouds,
> And pendent mountains seen in the calm lake,
> Lead only to a black and watery depth,
> While death's blue vault, with loathliest vapours hung,
> Where every shade which the foul grave exhales
> Hides its dead eye from the detested day,
> Conduct, O Sleep, to thy delightful realms?
>
> (211–19)

Logic tells us to interpret the second question as a gloss on the first.
In that case the speaker begins with the paradox of something
apparently negative yielding its opposite: the dark gate of death
leading to the paradise of sleep. He then expands on this view of
life as operating through a system of paradoxes by asking if the
apparently negative paradox of appearance and reality does not
conceal its own reversal into a positive paradox. Does the possibility that the promise of the rainbow clouds seen in the lake may

hide the reality of death by drowning, yield in turn to the possibility that this ugly and dark appearance may hide the more positive reality of sleep? Logic tells us also that the expansion of the first question is designed to valorise the transcendent over the natural realm. For it is nature which tricks us with the appearance of beauty only to reveal the clouds in the lake as an atmospheric illusion, while the reality of ugliness ceases to be a reality as soon as we move beyond the merely material world. But this reading is far from easy to extract from the passage, for its syntax blocks or at least retards our attempts at paraphrase. The problem is the labyrinthine complexity of the second question, which introduces a long and not clearly subordinate clause between the subject 'death's blue vault' and the main verb 'conduct'. This syntactic detour allows various other grammatical possibilities to come into play, and while they may not finally prevail, the paraphrase suggested is destabilised by the presence within it of these other alternatives. Initially it seems that the first three lines of the second question provide an alternative to the first question, and that the Narrator, having suggested that death may lead to the positive condition of sleep, raises the possibility that what seems beneficent may hide something threatening. The very next line makes it clear that this is not his intention, and that the Narrator means to overturn the negative alternative with a further positive paradox. But the positive alternative is a long time in coming, and the depressing description of 'death's blue vault' seems to take over the sentence. This is all the more true because the subordinate clause on death contains a further subordinate clause ('Where every shade which the foul grave exhales'). The effect is to convert the larger subordinate clause into a main clause in relation to the subordinate clause which it contains, and thus to give it a certain autonomy in relation to the main sentence in which it is contained. It is not immediately clear where the second question ends and whether the verb 'hides' or the verb 'conduct' is the main verb of the sentence. To put it differently, if the aim of the text is to subordinate the negative concessions in this second question to an affirmative suggestion, the subordination is disrupted, and we are made aware of how each suggestion is diacritically constituted on the trace of what it does not say. Syntax is not the only source of complications in this sentence. The second question is organised around an opposition between the deceptive paradoxes of nature and the saving paradoxes of transcendence. But the image of death's blue vault uneasily recalls the earlier sky image of rainbow clouds in the lake. It reminds us, even as we hope death's vault will prove an exit to something better, that all constructions of hope may lead 'only to a black and watery depth', and that the Poet's deferral of his ideal to the after-life may also be futile.

This microscopic analysis has been directed to a larger point about the way extended systems of representation function. Their very extensiveness brings into play the differential potential of language. For the more elaborate the structure, the more our attention becomes riveted on the interrelations of its parts, and the more parts there are to generate such interrelations. Such relations often disrupt on the connotative axis the relationship of individual signifiers to their referents on the denotative axis. We saw, for instance, how the subtextual resonance of the earlier sky image in 'death's blue vault' unsettled the ability of those lines to convey the superiority of death to life, how the intratextual relations between images interposed between conception and expression. The 'inter-texture' of an elaborate structure, to borrow Shelley's word, creates detours in the movement of a narrative to its conclusion. Though the passage in question is not a narrative, as the lengthening out of what begins as a simple question, it functions as a paradigm for the process of extension and repetition at the heart of narrative. It does not simply pose a philosophic question using concepts like sleep and death. It goes on to narrate the relation of sleep and death, by replacing them with figures which not only embody their relation but also unfold its complexities and create a subtler language within language.

The differential repetition which pervades the texture of the poem is similarly present in its macrostructure. One of the curious things about this poem is the doubling of the narration, whether because the Narrator actually tells the Poet's story twice, or because he has him go through a similar sequence of events twice in a vain attempt to construct his life as a history with a beginning, a middle and an end.[7] It is as though in the course of the initial narration the Narrator has discovered gaps and possibilities that make it necessary to weave the strands differently, so as to achieve a closure that will again be impossible because the re-enactment of the Poet's life simply displaces the gaps in the first version. The doubling of the narration makes it clear that the poem is involved in a kind of autosignification. It does not so much give us a finished product in the form of the Poet's story as manifest the process of narrative as (dis)articulation. Very briefly the Poet sees the veiled woman (140ff.), and having failed to find her again, is seized by a daemonic passion that rouses him from his couch 'As an eagle grasped/In folds of the green serpent' (227ff.). The futility of his quest leads him to waste away (245ff.), until at the end of his journey he arrives in a nook, nature's 'cradle, and his sepulchre' (430). But now, when we expect him to die, he again sees a feminine spirit (469ff.), is roused from his couch by a 'joyous madness' (518), ages in a ghastly way (531ff.), and again arrives in a cove where he expires (571ff.). The repetition of the story undoes the Narrator's attempt at mimesis, giving the Poet's life a phantasmatic quality. As Hillis Miller has pointed out, repetition can function in a Nietzschean way, creating a world of 'simulacra' or 'phantasms', a series of 'ungrounded doublings which arise from differential interrelations among elements which are all on the same plane' (Miller, 1982, p. 6).

It is impossible to separate neatly the different figurative intentions behind the two versions of the Poet's life, since these intentions are largely swallowed up in the intratextual complications of the poem. But the crucial problem in the text is clearly the significance of the Poet's life and death, and one of the more awkward aspects of the text is thus the repetition and deferral of a climax that would retrospectively confer value on the Poet's life. Although the Narrator, in the conventionalised opening and closing of the poem, seems to idealise the Poet, his postponement of the latter's death some two hundred and fifty lines beyond its announcement, and his seemingly endless protraction of the narrative, manifest an emergent doubt as to whether the death is indeed a climactic event. This doubt is augmented by the fact that narrative proves to be a hermeneutic rather than a mimetic process. The Narrator has no clear view of what the Poet's story 'means', and thus he produces accounts which try to determine this meaning as they work themselves out, and which tacitly re-read themselves as they proceed. Thus one way of viewing the first account is to say that in it the Narrator sees the Poet's vision as having some external sanction which legitimises his pursuit of it beyond the realm of life. Correspondingly he tries to see the Poet's life as having come full circle, bringing him to a sepulchre that is also the cradle of his mother nature, an end which is an origin. But in this positive figuration of the Poet there are numerous gaps. For one thing it is never clear whether he is in sympathy with nature or at odds with her, and thus it is never clear whether the benediction of circularity that the Narrator has her confer on the Poet's death is an empty formula. Even at the beginning of the poem, where there are no 'human hands' to build the Poet's 'untimely tomb', the pyramid of mouldering leaves that shelters his remains seems assembled more by the random movements of the wind than by design (50–4). Then at the end, although the Poet's blood is described as having beaten in 'mystic sympathy/With nature's ebb and flow', heaven remains 'Utterly black' at the moment of his death (651–60). Moreover it is unclear whether there is any reality beyond death where the mirage of the veiled woman can be found again. Nor is it clear that she is anything but a narcissistic projection. Her voice is, after all, like the voice 'of his own soul/ Heard in the calm of thought' (153–4).

Because of the many questions that the first narration raises, we can speculate that the Narrator recasts the Poet's death as the conscious pursuit of an interior ideal. This time the scene of his encounter with the female spirit is overtly narcissistic. She appears immediately after he has seen his reflection in a well and is without links to the transcendent or to nature:

> clothed in no bright robes
> Of shadowy silver or enshrining light,
> Borrowed from aught the visible world affords . . .
>   (480–2)

When he follows her it is in obedience to 'the light/That shone within his soul' (492–3), and thereafter he consciously interiorises the landscape by seeing it as an image of his life (502–8), exploring whether meaning can be found in the landscape of the self, when it cannot be found outside or above the self. Finally, according to this version, he dies at peace with himself, having made the mind its own place: 'Yet the grey precipice and solemn pine/And torrent, were not all; – one silent nook/Was there' (571–3). But this account, while it resolves some of the contradictions in the previous one, is not without its complications, for it does not follow that the landscape of the self is any less labyrinthine than that of nature. Nor do we ever make contact with the Poet's self, except as displaced from itself into some specular image, reflected in the water in the form of a 'treacherous likeness' (474). Even the closing

description of the nook in which the Poet peacefully dies, begins,
on closer inspection, to unravel:

> Even on the edge of that vast mountain,
> Upheld by knotty roots and fallen rocks,
> It overlooked in its serenity
> The dark earth, and the bending vault of stars.
> It was a tranquil spot, that seemed to smile
> Even in the lap of horror.
>
> (573–8)

The spatial position of the nook is ambiguous. It is described, on
the one hand, as overlooking the dark earth, as though its serenity
comes from its having transcended the complications of life; on the
other hand, it is described as being in the '*lap* of horror', as though
it is surrounded by what it seeks to forget, to overlook. What the
repetition of the story makes clear is that narrative is a potentially
endless process: not a closed structure, but a proliferating web of
complexities.

This is not, however, the way that the Narrator would like to
conceive of narrative. At least at the level of desire, narrative is for
him a supplement to lyric. In deferring lyric as a way of achieving
identity with his text, he casts his poem as quest narrative: the quest
of the Poet for the epipsyche and of the Narrator for the essential
meaning of the Poet's life. In troping narrative as quest, he
assumes that he can fulfil the goals of lyric by a more circuitous
path, like the one modelled in Hegelian phenomenology, where
the subject must become alienated from himself in order to achieve
an identity that is not simply unreflective. Through the self-repeti-
tion of himself as the Poet, the Narrator thus tries to gain access to
himself, to construct himself to himself, so as to find an *alter ego*
who will no longer make a ghost of the self but will render up the
tale of what we are. This *alter ego* must be a unity; it must not be
different from itself if it is to tell its tale clearly. But from the
beginning the attempt to achieve such identity is accompanied by
difficulties, for no representation of the Poet succeeds in making
him present to us, or making the Narrator's conception fully
present to him. Since the Poet is rarely represented as speaking,
we know him only from the outside, like the pyramids among
which he wanders in search of meaning, which similarly present
an exterior that baffles penetration and perhaps conceals an

absence. His mind is repeatedly described as 'vacant' (126,191), and though we are once told that 'meaning' flashed on it 'like strong inspiration' (126–8), we have no sense of what that meaning is and infer from the parenthetical way in which the claim is made that it may be simply a trick of light. On to this empty schema the Narrator projects different and contradictory interpretations that constantly unravel each other.

In *Alastor* Shelley for the first time faced the sense that there might be no ground behind language, a possibility to which he returns very differently in Asia's visit to the Cave of Demogorgon. At a structural level the doubled narration can seem to evaporate the poem as a vicarious achievement of identity for the Narrator, because it shows him assembling and disassembling an identity for the Poet. But even at the textual level the vanishing ground of the poem is constantly felt in its blurred and tangled descriptions. There is, for instance, the passage in which the Poet embarks in the death-boat:

> Following his eager soul, the wanderer
> Leaped in the boat, he spread his cloak aloft
> On the bare mast, and took his lonely seat,
> And felt the boat speed o'er the tranquil sea
> Like a torn cloud before the hurricane.
>
> As one that in a silver vision floats
> Obedient to the sweep of odorous winds
> Upon resplendent clouds, so rapidly
> Upon the dark and ruffled waters fled
> The straining boat.
>   (311–20)

Here it is unclear whether the weather – both physical and emotional – is calm or stormy. The sea is tranquil, yet the boat proceeds as if driven by a hurricane. The Poet floats in a silver dream, yet he moves rapidly along the dark waters. On the one hand he seems at peace with himself, masterfully in control of his destiny as he stands at the 'steady helm' (333), having chosen freely to embrace death in the pursuit of his ideal. On the other hand he appears a harried figure, a victim of forces without and within which push him helplessly towards destruction. The radical con-tradictions that occur in the space of a few lines make it seem that

his identity is an arbitrary linguistic construct, so that the Narrator
is left with the failure of his attempt to make figures true, to make
the Poet more than a textual figure.

*   *   *

The Narrator's failure can be seen as a failure of narrative as well as
lyric. Unable to make the Poet credible as a character, the Narrator
is also unable to give his life the status of fact, of something that
has happened. But it is just as possible to say that the contradictions that haunt the figure of the Poet arise precisely from his being
the subject of a narrative, and that the narrative process generates
a series of differences: differences between the narrator and a
character who is other than him, differences between the narrator
and a reader whose presence dialogises the narrator's relationship
to his protagonist. In so far as he is committed to a model of
narrative as *mimesis* and interpretive closure, in other words as
plot, the Narrator resists those elements in its structure and
reception that make it a dialogical mode. This resistance manifests
itself in a nostalgia for lyric and in a concluding attempt to bring
back lyric as elegy. Yet the opposition between lyric and narrative
does not simply function to the detriment of the latter. In writing
the beautiful soul into the form of narrative, Shelley seeks to give it
what it lacks in Wordsworth: namely the dimension of being-in-
the-world. *Adonais* and *Alastor* are longer than Wordsworth's *She
dwelt among the untrodden ways* because Shelley wants to claim for
his visionaries a status that Wordsworth does not claim for the
reclusive, almost invisible Lucy. Given no voice and scarcely
spoken of in a poem whose brevity feels language to be a
profanation, Lucy exists only as an unheard melody. The figure of
genius in *Alastor* is similarly silent but his Narrator is not. In
describing the life of the Poet at such great length, the poem
presses beyond the modesty of the Lucy poems, with their
concession that Lucy's death makes no difference except to Wordsworth. Similarly in describing his displaced wanderings through
various foreign cultures, the Narrator pleads – albeit by negation –
for the Poet's place in his own culture. In speaking about the Poet
and trying to create a cultural context for him, the Narrator
inevitably opens the figure of the Poet to an ideological contesta-
tion that is symptomatically present in his own inability to sustain
a uniformly idealised portrayal of the Poet. Narrative, in other
words, is not simply a deconstruction but also an expansion of

lyric, a mode that embodies desire in the world. At the same time it removes this desire from the protection of a self-contained subject and requires us to view it from more than one perspective. We wonder whether the Poet's life is to be deemed a success according to his own criteria or a failure according to the standards of others. We wonder whether his ideal is an illusion and whether or not that matters. We also ask whether his wanderings through cultures associated with the infancy of the world mark the visionary ideology he (dis)embodies as outdated, though this response is divided by our sense of him as closer to lost origins than we are. The diacritical structure of narrative, in other words, makes it profoundly self-critical.

As a moment in the history of Romantic attitudes towards narrative, Shelley's poem is thus something much more complex than an elegy for the death of lyric consciousness. The Narrator can no more abstract lyric from narrative than the Poet can achieve an *epoche* that will bracket the body of the veiled maid and give him access only to her soul. Narrative, as a form that gives vision a history, is precisely the (re)visionary Narrator's means of access to history: to the readers to whom he tells his story and to a future that may see beyond the death of the Poet. Writing the Poet into a narrative, he enables him to survive, if only as a sign of something still (to be) born. The Narrator, in other words, does not simply fail to be a lyric poet. He also chooses to write his text as narrative. The double structure of narrative as promise and risk, as an embodiment of visionary intention that also complicates it, is something that Shelley accepts in *Prometheus Unbound*. In writing a lyrical drama he transposes a relatively private vision of the Promethean age into the public domain, recognising at the same time that the emplotment of this vision in terms of characters who enact it and events that bring it about inevitably discloses aporias in the Promethean ideology (Rajan, 1984, pp. 317–38). The Narrator of *Alastor*, however, never really resolves his discomfort with the web of narrative, which prevents us from reducing the text to a single strand without recognising how one possibility is interwoven with others. At the end he abandons narrative for elegy. Through elegy he appeals to his readers to re-member the Poet, and yet seals his subject against further reading by leaving us with the reproach of the Poet's death, which would make any questioning of his life a profanation. Mourning the departure of a 'Spirit' whose death leaves the world empty, the Narrator renounces 'Art and eloquence' as inadequate (710ff.). As a silencing of the reader, elegy attempts to restore the hermeneutics of lyric, but in a form whose assumption of a public voice conflicts with the enforced privacy of its grief, and which is thus infiltrated by the very dialogism it resists. A similar avoidance of ambivalence is evident in the Preface, where the writer seeks to simplify narrative by suggesting that the Poet's life is a picture 'not barren of instruction to actual men' and that it is 'allegorical of one of the most interesting situations of the human mind' (Shelley, 1977, p. 69). Replacing lyric sympathy with allegorical didacticism, the Preface-writer tries to restore the direct relation between language and referent disrupted by the narrative process, which through the introduction of multiple characters generates different perspectives from which to view the protagonist. But paradoxically he supports his allegory by providing an account of the Poet's career: a narrative which divides his attempt to assume a position outside the Poet's life, by requiring him also to see that life from the perspective of the Poet.

This uneasiness with a mode to which he keeps returning has its roots in a more fundamental ambivalence on the part of the Narrator towards the functioning of language as difference. It may be apparent that I have said two somewhat different things here, perhaps because Shelley at this stage does not clearly distinguish between the two. First, I have described narrative as an intertexture in which the process of representation does not simply translate conception into expression, but also produces autonomous and destabilising meanings which are non-synthetically incorporated into the pattern of the fabric and displaced further. These displacements do not call into question the value of telling stories; they comprise the conditions under which narratives are transmitted and survive. By disclosing gaps within the telling of a story, they open narrative to what Ricoeur (1985, p. 160) calls 'refiguration' – a concept which means that the 'work of narrative does not conclude with the closure of emplotment but continues into the reception of the work by the reader' (Harpham, 1987, pp. 84–5). Second, I have suggested, in descriptions of how the Narrator assembles and disassembles the character of the Poet, that language produces figures upon a vacant ground. The web of language is not quite the same thing as the abyss of language, though some contemporary theory tacitly identifies the two. These two images, drawn from Shelley himself, define the parameters within which his perception of the disarticulating potential of language moves.

The web or tissue is a favourite image among current theorists for what Barthes calls a 'text' as opposed to a 'work' (Barthes, 1977, pp. 155–64), because unlike other forms of aesthetic construction it can be unravelled. Indeed, a weaving is potentially endless, its apparent centres functioning also as points of dissemination, its individual strands more confusingly woven into and underneath each other than appears to the superficial eye. But for all this the process of weaving creates something, though it is complicated and problematic. Moreover the web expresses not only the differential relations between elements of a text, but also their connectedness. Because it is the image with which *Alastor* concludes, it is not unfair to see it as a de-idealised version of the image with which the poem begins: that of the 'brotherhood' of the elements (1). In this poem the complications of (self)-representation produce a fear that what underlies language may be an abyss of meaning. As the poem veers philosophically between faith in a transcendental realm and a nihilistic materialism, so too it oscillates between positing a transcendental signified accessible through lyric or allegory and seeing language as subtended only by a vacancy. This sense that the intertexture of language conceals something destructive is apparent in the way the Narrator associates it with a spider's web. The music of the veiled woman's voice, we are told, holds the Poet 'suspended in its web / Of many-coloured woof and shifting hues' (156–7). The Poet cannot live in what at the end is described as 'the web of human things, / Birth and the grave'. That perhaps is why he rarely speaks.[8] The Narrator, though he speaks at length and lives in a world where everything is constituted on the trace of its opposite, cannot reconcile himself to it. Whether one can find meaning in the web of differences and displacements that constitutes speech, life, and all systems of representation, is a question that preoccupies Shelley for the remainder of his career.

6

Shelley as Revisionist: Power and Belief in *Mont Blanc*

Jerrold E. Hogle

A recurrent problem for serious readers of Shelley (as in Bloom, 1976b , pp. 83–111; Leighton, 1984; and Blank, 1988) is his oscillation between strongly rejecting and constantly repeating Wordsworth and Coleridge. On the one hand, despite his clear indebtedness to both of them (noted by his friend Peacock, 1970, p. 43), he comes to regard these immediate precursors as reactionary 'slaves' and systematisers, especially in their later writings. In his eyes they turn their 'natural pieties', because of the 'one Life' they find 'within us and abroad' (to quote Coleridge's *Eolian Harp*, 26), to the service of monotheistic religions, social hierarchies centred on one dictating figure or class, and German idealisms positing internal and eternal Absolutes,[1] all of which Shelley wants to put in question. The younger poet therefore reworks the sceptical empiricism of David Hume, William Godwin and Sir William Drummond partly to counter the absolutism that, more and more, seems to dominate the so-called 'first generation' of English Romantics.[2] In answer to Wordsworth and Coleridge (among others) and in support of all things existing only as perceived, Shelley decides that all 'causes' and points of origin are late suppositions retroactively assumed by thought to explain why one thought – or remembered perception – repeatedly precedes or succeeds another. According to Shelley's brief essay *On Life*, 'cause is only a word expressing a certain state of the human mind with regard to the manner in which two thoughts are apprehended to be related to each other' (Shelley, 1977, p. 478). Causes are thus the effects of their own effects, of thought-combinations being 'read' and interpreted ('apprehended') by other thoughts, not necessarily the pre-existent and dominant sources of what the psyche beholds and interrelates.

One consequence of this stance is the daring and difficult lyric *Mont Blanc*, that 1816 challenge to *Tintern Abbey*[3] and the Coleridge *Hymn Before Sun-rise*, the latter of which (as first noted thoroughly in Bloom, 1959, pp. 10–19) addresses the same face of the same mountain from the same vale of Chamouni. Here Shelley redefines what Coleridge terms the 'mighty voice' of 'God' commanding the cascades (*Hymn*, 51, 58) and what Wordsworth intuits as the underlying 'presence' that 'impels ... all objects of all thought, / And rolls through all things' (*Tintern Abbey*, 100–2). Shelley names the force behind the rolling cascades 'the Power', recalling the way Drummond defines that very word as an impetus projected by present thoughts into the receding (though immediate) past of certain successive perceptions (Drummond, 1805, pp. 169–216). Shelley's Power consequently becomes a largely invisible *natura naturans* that is assumed only because the speaker perceives a series of impressions, a 'com[ing] down' of ice turning to water 'in likeness of the Arve' (*Mont Blanc*, 16), and only because *that* descent is observed as emanating from 'ice gulphs' above it (17) which also appear to have been formed by some earlier process. Such an impetus, as something that differs from what is visible yet operates through it, need not be an anthropomorphic supremacy nor be known as an 'essence' at one with itself nor even be contained in what appear to be its products. This 'presence', once proposed in so rebellious a fashion, actually helps 'repeal' such monarchical 'codes of fraud and woe', unsettling the most established Western beliefs (80–1), mainly because it is presented as a process being left behind even as it becomes different from itself in what it seems to rule and produce. 'The Power' in this poem, after all, 'dwells apart', altogether 'remote' and 'inaccessible' (96–7) above or behind the 'coming down'. It resides, if it exists, in silent removal from the roaring activity of its 'likenesses', and so speaks in a sound that cannot strictly be called its own – nor be regarded as God's own – by any means.

On the other hand, this self-retracting force is still attached to some key images in the poetry that Shelley wants to refute. The Power's withdrawal pointedly alludes to the 'something far more deeply interfused, / Whose dwelling is the light of setting suns' in *Tintern Abbey* (96–7). Indeed, when Shelley writes of any 'power of strong controul' manifested by an alpine cataract, he is more or less quoting line 352 from Wordsworth's *Descriptive Sketches* of 1793 (Wordsworth, 1984, p. 72). In addition, by opening *Mont Blanc* as he does with the whole perceived 'universe' as initially an Arve-like turbulence flowing around and 'through the mind', the poet is refashioning, among other images, the many Coleridgean thoughts 'uncall'd and undetain'd that fluidly 'Traverse [the partly] passive brain' in *The Eolian Harp* (38–40). Consequently the commanding voice of Coleridge's 'Soul of each, and God of all' in the traversing motion (48) is almost impossible for Shelley to avoid. The repeal of the tyrannical codes, he writes, is ordered by the 'voice' of the 'great Mountain' (*Mont Blanc*, 80), perhaps from an oracular point hidden behind and beyond the highest ice-gulphs.

The Shelley of *Mont Blanc* must oppose what he takes to be the philosophies of his immediate predecessors by employing many of the exact figural patterns in which those philosophies are advanced, even to the point of seeming to repeat the blank verse of both *Tintern Abbey* and the *Hymn* along with the structure of five verse-paragraphs by which *Tintern Abbey* is organised. Hence, much as he tries to desanctify, depersonify and displace a kingly Ruler of nature and thought, Shelley gives us so much of an ice-bound 'throne' in *Mont Blanc* (17) – and then so much of an authored Primal Movement manifesting itself in a descent towards a sort of Moses approaching Mount Sinai – that we can still hear the speaker in the *Hymn Before Sun-rise* claiming that the torrents and the 'ice-falls' of the mountain serve chiefly to 'echo God!/ God!' and so to make the 'dilating Soul' swell 'vast to Heaven!' (*Hymn*, 49, 59–60, 19 and 24). How can we account for such a seemingly double stance? How can we say that Shelley is subverting a version of what Jacques Derrida has called the 'metaphysics of presence' when the poet pursues that aim by forcefully re-emphasising the metaphors that have helped re-establish that same metaphysic in the lyrics of Wordsworth and Coleridge?

My aim here is to suggest some possible new answers to these questions and hence to reveal the precise kind of revisionary iconoclasm practises in Shelley's poetry. In particular, I want to expose the methods by which and the precise reasons why he 'breaks the icons' re-established by Coleridge and Wordsworth and does so in a poetic process that deliberately repeats those forms so as to draw out something other than what is supposed to be in them. This disruptive effort is especially visible throughout *Mont Blanc* in the ways this poem redefines the 'something more deeply interfused', in the self-questioning image-patterns by which the piece urges a half-sceptical attitude towards religious belief, and in the revisionist modes of allusion, versification and address through which this meditative lyric works out its new understandings of causality and faith.

After all, the most current answers to the questions I ask above are, in my view, not sensitive enough to what Shelley's revisions actually face and do when they respond to previous texts. The later Harold Bloom and his progeny[4] may be accurate up to a point when they picture Shelley striving wilfully to internalise and then conquer his own belatedness and the external tyranny of supposedly 'authoritative' verse. Shelley does, as Bloom maintains, redirect existing tropes, or sometimes fails to do so, in an effort to seem a more commanding voice newly enthroned within the turns of language attempted by his predecessors. Yet Bloom, I think, is wrong to insist (as he does most directly in 1976a) that the figures initially read by Shelley, or other 'strong' poets, offer only an *ethos* of ordered and limited relationships and are made to 'swerve' only when the poet hyperbolically wrests them into a *pathos* of deviant reinscriptions. Shelley, by his own account, confronts more than a centred and framed-off system whenever he takes on those existing texts that attract him in spite of the ideologies that appear to govern them. In the final paragraph of the *Defence of Poetry*, a passage highly valued by Bloom himself (1976b, p. 110), the reigning and older Romantic poets reveal an 'accumulation of . . . power' (the 'spirit of the age') for Shelley, not in what they manifestly assume and encourage, but in 'words which express what they understand not' – or rather in an 'electric life which burns within their words' without their being entirely aware of it (Shelley, 1977, p. 508). What most attracts Shelley to their poems is a galvanic motion in their language which they contact but do not will, a crossing of charged energy from point to point, analogous to the basic movement of electricity, that forces even the poets themselves to feel 'astonished at its manifestations' (508). Because something like that mobility is already operative in the works of his precursors, Shelley can make figures swerve in different directions; this is, as Shelley writes in his *Defence* (1977, p. 508), 'the Power . . . seated upon the throne of their own [poetic] soul' – the force which enables them to propose what they call 'the Power', even though they claim otherwise. Bloom is almost onto this motion in *Poetry and Repression* (again at 83–111), where he points to Shelley's compulsion to rework the *Merkabah* or Divine Chariot, that age-old Hebraic figure of 'transumption' which has usually been depicted in the process of transfiguring its own features even as it passes from moment to moment or heaven to earth. However, Bloom never quite argues for what I find to be the actual basis of Shelley's revisionism. He never shows, first, how Shelley really uncovers a subliminal transumptive process underwriting the movements between his precursors' words and, second, how Shelley's poetry brings that drive forward in the face of his precursors' attempts to contain its transformative energy.

Shelley approaches his predecessors' texts, especially after he rereads them in 1814–15,[5] first as a semi-Freudian pre-psychoanalyst and then as a kind of pre-Derridean 'deconstructor'. He starts by probing the suggestive verbal patterns in Wordsworth and Coleridge that seem to pull him towards 'something far more deeply' at work. In these figures he discovers the basic *Übertragung* or mental 'carrying over' that Freud will later define (in 1965, pp. 571–88) as the activity behind all subsequent forms of transference and identity-construction.[6] Especially in a *Tintern Abbey* or a *Frost at Midnight*, where objects recently observed are drawn by present interpretation towards memories of additional forms perceived at other times or different places, the younger poet finds that every apparent 'object of thought' is always 'a thought upon which [an]other thought is employed' in a process whereby the latter relates the former to 'a train of [further] thoughts' also resulting from previous observation, in the words of the essay *On Life* (Shelley, 1977, pp. 477–8). Wordsworth and Coleridge turn out to be offering readings of their memories from already later perspectives that change and displace the previous nature and significance of their recollections before both poets can specify – though both of them *do* finally specify – exactly what is being remembered (as in *Tintern Abbey*, 58–111, and *Frost at Midnight*, 24–43). They persistently 'carry their memories over'; they transfer them towards and into images/thoughts from once-different contexts, both in order to possess and in order to keep from facing directly (since direct recontact is impossible) a sense of what their pasts might have actually been or meant. This crossing is a fundamental aspect of the 'electricity' in their lines, yet Shelley encounters repressive attempts in both poets to wrench that decentred action into seeming a 'motion and a spirit' which gives perceived nature an absolute centre, thus making nature an 'anchor [for one's] purest thoughts' (*Tintern Abbey*, 100, 109). Shelley, like an analyst responding to the words of his patients, has to draw out from their discourses what Wordsworth and Coleridge 'deny and abjure' (Shelley, 1977, p. 508): the primacy of subliminal transference in the poetic impulses which led to their writing.

At that point, though, Shelley must also remember that these precursors could not even have worked out their basic transfigurations were that continual cross-over not inherent in the language they employ, in the words that really 'create' and shape 'thought' according to Shelley's Asia in *Prometheus Unbound* (II.iv.72).[7] Consequently the 'second-generation' poet must turn into a deconstructor and 'aim', as Derrida aims in his 'task' of reading, 'at a certain relationship, unperceived by the [earlier] writer, between what he commands and what he does not command of the patterns of the language that he uses' (Derrida, 1976, p. 158). The younger aspirant must expose the partial failure of any precursor-poet's attempt to dominate the existing symbolic systems from which all new figures and relations between figures must be composed. He must show that all poets, even himself, are subject to the perpetual recasting of one verbal unit by a different one, to the activity in existing texts, basic to discourse, by which each sound, letter, word or phrase swerves towards others in order to mitigate its lack of meaning-within-itself by finding that meaning in some other place. In his own work Shelley must therefore reach into and through the rhetoric of his elders to expose and recover the most basic – indeed, the older – shifts from figure to figure that his predecessors look back to and try to control at the same time. Only in that way can Shelley come close to re-articulating the self-transforming process that engenders the 'electric life' he so values in older poets. Shelley revises the poetic patterns he takes on by releasing from repression the subliminal movement of transference in thought and language, usually after it has been covered over by writers who depend on it yet who try to ground it in a higher Absolute supposedly at one with itself.

Nowhere is this procedure more manifest than it is in the striking re-visions offered throughout *Mont Blanc*, and these shocks, at least to readers of Coleridge and Wordsworth, begin as early as Shelley's opening verse-paragraph. This Coleridgean beginning dares to fail in its attempt to counter religious orthodoxy by boldly presenting a kind of genesis, a vision of what may have produced existence as we perceive it. Yet, in proposing different answers to some of the questions that Coleridge asks in his *Hymn* (such as 'Who gave you [wild torrents] your invulnerable life [?]', 44), Shelley offers no more than a movement of transfers between differences that has no one original point of departure and recalls no singular author. If we can suppose a basic construction of the 'universe', it turns out to be an 'everlasting' (not originated) process which has been and remains but a mutable onslaught that simply 'flows through' the perceiving 'mind' (1–2). It is a sheer cascade, a blur of liquid motion, until 'rapid waves' appear to distinguish themselves in the rush by glancing away from and towards one another (2–4). This genesis is a motion, then a differentiation, then a turning of the differences, once perceived, towards both clearer distinctions and increased interconnections between themselves. The waves thus emerge as 'dark' or 'glittering' in aspect, threatening to resemble God's separation of darkness from light in the biblical Genesis, yet only as waves are found to be 'reflecting gloom' from or 'lending splendour' to other waves (3–4).

Mont Blanc plainly denies Coleridge's vision of what empowers the basic 'traversing' of thought, in part by transferring his concept, beyond where Coleridge seems to leave it, towards Wordsworth's more hydraulic sense of perception's foundations. Shelley's first sentence – especially when the 'source of human thought its tribute brings' to the cascade from 'secret springs' within the overall flow (4–5) – half-echoes the dawn of personal thought as it is dimly remembered in the *Ode* on 'Intimations of Immortality', where the mind is originally a liquid result of and a tributary to the 'mighty waters' of an 'eternal sea' flowing inland (*Ode*, 162–7). Shelley is even recalling Wordsworth's later turning of the mind into an 'ebbing and flowing' place both open to receive the influx of perceptions and inclined to project that confluence on to high 'mountain-steeps and summits' (*The Excursion*, II, 848; note also Blank, 1988, pp. 176–7). The recovery of interacting 'waves' without an origin from within tyrannical assertions of an origin that is finally God is made possible for Shelley, on one level, by a transfer of elements between two God-based visions, ones made to revise their former assumptions precisely because this new set of lines has forced echoes of Wordsworth and Coleridge to 'lend' and 'reflect' images back and forth. Shelley's transfer-based procedure, in other words, both creates and is the revisionary awareness at the start of this poem, particularly as he shows the interactions of his figures to be potentially there in the poems he recalls.

Indeed, the opening of *Mont Blanc* even goes so far as to suggest why such a potential is present in the images borrowed from Wordsworth and Coleridge. Not content with simply performing a transfer among images that his predecessors do not attempt themselves, Shelley draws their conceptions back towards what he thinks has made those notions possible initially, a centreless and non-Christian metaphysic – with a particular sense of language – which both his precursors depend upon yet refuse to acknowledge. His first verse-paragraph alludes, almost in the way he alludes in a letter of January 1811 (Shelley, 1964, I, pp. 44–5),[8] to the hydraulic cascade of globules or droplets which forms existence and even mind in *De rerum natura* by Lucretius (II. 80–221).[9] After all, in the words of the Preface to Shelley's *Laon and Cythna* (1817), Lucretius has given us 'that poem whose doctrines are yet the basis', though often the forgotten basis, 'of our metaphysical knowledge' (Shelley, 1975, p. 105). The inclination of a thought towards another thought, a thought towards a supposed object, remembered objects towards other memories, or parts of perceived nature towards other parts – none of these can even be conceived of by Wordsworth and Coleridge, in Shelley's view, without their first subliminally accepting two movements that Lucretius posits as generators of all that has ever existed: the separation of an initial and basic cascade into relatable parts *and* the wave-like swerving of those parts (their *clinamen*) towards different ones to form whorls of transfers set apart from, though always in relationships with, other whorls. Shelley therefore pulls figures from Wordsworth and Coleridge 'back to basics' by opening *Mont Blanc* with a 'rolling' of myriad waves or swerves that produces the combinatory activity leading to perceptible 'things'; that generates the flow of 'mind' as one stream among many, yet one able to interpret the others by flowing towards and across them; and that makes the object–subject relationship so much an interplay of connected differences that 'objects' should not be completely distinguished from 'thoughts' (all things existing only as they are perceived). All strictly dichotomous and hierarchical 'codes of fraud and woe', in Shelley's eyes, now stand 'repealed' by an exposure of the actual movement underwriting and 'flowing through' the world we observe.

This return to a Lucretian base is pulled enough in the direction of Wordsworth and Coleridge that *Mont Blanc* must downplay the specific units of matter that swerve in *De rerum*, the 'atoms' that

fascinated the adolescent Shelley from the time he first read
Lucretius until the year he finished *Queen Mab* (1812–13).[10] This
alteration only forces the Shelley of 1816 to make each 'element'
more of a swerve or 'rolling wave' from the start. Each must now
be a de-forming form perpetually turning aside and crossing away
from its present condition. It must carry out a drive of desire both
harkening towards the future interplays it may join and taking
flight from past relationships (or contexts) that are always receding. Shelley grants the *clinamen*, the transfer initiating all orders for
Lucretius, *the* supreme and eternal generative role in the formation
of thought and the world it perceives. By eschewing the atom, he
actually gives the movement of transference more primacy than it
has in the Lucretian passage on the descent and diversion of
globules. Shelley's opening lines even show differences and then
their interrelations in a series of phrases that call attention to the
movement (or swerve) from one verbal unit to another: 'Now dark
– now glittering – now reflecting gloom – /Now lending
splendour' (3–4). *Mont Blanc* thereby points us to the cross-over
between already crossing figures of language that must be under-
way before the very words of this poem (or any other verbal
construct) can be drawn together. Shelley, in fact, reminds us, if
we have read Lucretius, that *De rerum natura* cannot de-scribe (or
'write out') how different atomic forms converge to produce an
organised mass unless the poet offers the analogy (*De rerum*,
II.688–94) of different letters gravitating towards others to produce
his words and then different words seeking other words to
produce additional interconnections.[11] To bring about his concept
of how all things begin – however much he derives it from
Democritus and Epicurus – Lucretius must look back to what
Derrida has called the basic 'differing and deferring' movement in
sign-relations, thus exposing the transference demanded of words
by language as what really 'originates' *De rerum natura* and the
concepts within it. Shelley makes the same move in *Mont Blanc* by
pulling his echoes of Wordsworth and Coleridge back to the verbal
and conceptual *clinamen* from which they develop their work even
as they 'deny and abjure' it. Now, just as we can no longer say
that 'causes' precede interpretations of effects or that subjects
dominate their objects (or vice-versa), we cannot still maintain a
simple priority of personal thought over the drives in interpersonal
language, nor can we dogmatically believe in any point or element
– or any enthroned being – already at one with itself prior

to an interplay of verbal and perceptual differences in which such an object might later be sought. Anticipating Derrida (1976, pp. 61–5) and Michael Ryan (1982), Shelley reminds us that no sense of that oneness could even exist without a prior relationship between signifiers that can be interpreted, after it appears, as pointing to some non-differentiated 'other'.

All these reversals, of course, lead to additional transformations in Shelley's revisionary notion of 'Power', making that drive more than just a causality projected by thought as it 'reads' successive effects to be signs of something else. Now the Power, as what we suppose once we have seen *clinamen* after *clinamen* and as what seems to be the impetus behind and within each *clinamen* whenever it 'comes down in likeness', takes on the qualities of the transference that Shelley has found moving between the thoughts and words of his predecessors. Instead of being a presence strictly at one with itself, the Power is a sheer 'becoming other' or a going out of itself in self-extensions of its 'electric life', especially when it 'Burst[s] through' what the senses observe 'like the flame / Of lightning through the tempest' (*Mont Blanc*, 18–19). It fulfils its nature, as each 'rapid wave' does, by 'carrying [its drive] over' into a form or set of relationships different from the forms or states of even a moment ago. That is why, as perception succeeds perception in *Mont Blanc*, the Power 'comes down' in a manner that appears to produce ice-gulphs while already turning the ingredients of those into the gush of unfrozen torrents further down. Even the 'voice' of the 'Mountain' partakes of and is 'grounded' in this 'becoming other'. Now there is an outpouring of sound from Mont Blanc only in so far as what withdraws into silence makes itself different from itself in cascading 'likenesses', each of which allows its sound to be amplified by the 'caverns echoing to the Arve's commotion' (30). These amplifiers, in turn, along with the flow of perceiving thought bringing the 'tribute' of an added 'sound [that is at least] half its own', transfigure what has already been transfigured, continuing the transference that is now clearly prior to and at the foundations of the 'voice' that we hear. Indeed, it is only to the extent as we recognise such an 'origin' for the voice that it can help 'repeal ... [the hegemonic] codes' now confining our thoughts (80–1).

Moreover, if the observer tries to penetrate this process with a gaze that looks back through that succession for some 'deeper cause', what can be found – and then only as a vision projected by the viewer into a distant level that cannot be seen directly – is another movement of transference bringing differences into relationships and then changing the relationships as other elements are brought into the process. When Shelley's speaker finally tries to picture what it is like at the very high level where 'the power [supposedly] is' (127), the power at that height, unless it is repressively turned into a God, has to emerge as no more than a composition 'of many sights, / And many sounds, and much of life and death' (128–9), as a dynamic in which numerous differences, like snowflakes descending (131) or words starting to interact, are impelled to cross towards and into each other or to break up relationships for the sake of forming others, leaving the vestiges of the older ones for dead. 'The secret strength of things / Which governs thought' and is perceived to 'inhabit' the highest reaches of Mont Blanc, it turns out (139–41), is simply what is forming at that level 'when the flakes burn in the sinking sun, / Or the star-beams dart through them' or 'Winds contend' to the point of 'heap[ing] the snow' – sometimes in an icy 'city of death' (105) – in places different from those where the flakes interacted with the sun- and star-beams (133–5). After all, the 'human mind's imaginings' (143) cannot project a primal impulse into the invisible depths or heights of what can be seen unless the projection takes with it the most basic movement of thought, the subliminal transference, that both empowers such projections and allows impressions (or words) to interrelate enough so that causes can be proposed as the foundations of thoughts-relating-to-thoughts. Transference is the 'cause' behind constructions of causality, in other words, being itself 'the secret strength of things / Which governs thought', and Shelley releases that fact from its repression in Wordsworth, Coleridge and others by making that energy the 'Power', thereby overthrowing any idea of a Oneness which can be viewed as commanding all transformations from a position completely beyond them.[12]

Still, Shelley's revision of 'Power', by continuing the quiet withdrawal of Wordsworth's 'something deep', remains admirably responsive to the tendency in observers and readers to look back through 'comings down' or signs so as to locate a primal impulse that is genuinely 'other'. *Mont Blanc* may deny that a conventional deity is the primal force behind perceptions of nature, but it does acknowledge the call of successive transformations, at least as we 'read' them, towards a different point, apparently behind or above them, to which they seem to refer. Yet the reason for this apparent concession still lies in the movement of transference which the Power now enacts. Just in the way a *clinamen* in Lucretius is as much a swerve *away* from a receding past as it is a shift *towards* a future relationship, a transfer in thought or the language that 'creates' thought is always Janus-faced, harkening back towards what is behind or prior to it in a succession (as does any word in a discourse) even while deferring ahead to a connection yet to arise. Although they repressively see their Oneness as common to past and present thoughts, even Wordsworth and Coleridge suggest this much in their senses of how and what we remember. Hence the 'Power' in *Mont Blanc* can 'come down in likeness' only if each simulacrum leaves something truly 'elsewhere' or 'otherwise' behind. This latter version of the Power must be supposed as so completely different from the turbulent and roaring cascade that any 'adverting mind' (literally a mind 'turning towards') must seem drawn back through the visible level (100) towards a distant state that is 'Remote, serene, and inaccessible' as opposed to near, tumultuous, and apprehensible (97). Such a process, Shelley is even suggesting, is the basis of how people, and especially religious poets, arrive at a sense of infinite or even sacred depths or heights in nature (see Rieder, 1981). There is no awareness of a deep, immobile, mysterious, 'unsculptured image' on the moun-tainside seemingly 'veil[ed]' by what is taken to be an 'etherial waterfall' (26–7) unless there is first the 'sweep' of the falling waters from one position to another and the crossing of that swerve by 'earthly rainbows' (25), all of which composes a series of mutable and semi-transparent layers calling on the observer to look through such veils towards something 'far more deep' and much more immutable. By analogy, then, the rising of 'a remoter world' above and beyond Shelley's speaker and the visible mountain (49) comes from a series of 'comings down' trailing the otherness they also continue and compelling the awe of the responding 'spirit' to climb back up the descent, to feel 'Driven [towards some Other] like a homeless cloud from steep to steep' without feeling able to arrive completely at any highest or final referent (57–8). The sublimity of an up-rising landscape in the 'natural piety' of Wordsworth and Coleridge, we now discover, comes from a viewer's response to transference's most backward-tending motion once that retrogression is seen as still looking back, again and again and again, from whatever earlier or higher position is reached by

the gaze of the perceiver. That tendency must be felt and appreciated just as much as the outward flow of the same motion so that
the attraction of the 'remote' and 'serene' can be truly understood
alongside the appeal of the increasingly fluid 'comings down' that
change a 'city of death' into streams of life-giving water.

What Shelley is promoting, we should remember, is an attitude
in his readers – and in any observer of such a scene potentially or
actually infected by absolutist perspectives – that rejects all
submission to a projected natural Father at one with Himself on
high, yet does not lose the quasi-religious wonder that leads us out
of ourselves towards a greater and more multiple 'thou' able to
help expand the range and reach of our perceptions (see Bloom,
1959, pp. 19–35). As I read him in *Mont Blanc*, this poet is drawing
forth the Janus-faced motion of transference from images that have
repressed its primacy so that we can realise *both* how longings for
the sacred can and should come about *and* how we must avoid
restricting those passions to one monarchical target of desire and
celebrate instead the metamorphic 'becoming other' in whatever
we seem to take in or project. We should listen, in the words of the
poem, to the 'mysterious tongue' of withdrawing silence and
outpouring sound 'Which teaches awful doubt, or faith so mild, /
So solemn, so serene, that [humankind] may be / But for such faith
with nature reconciled' (77–9). With the Power redefined as it now
is, the awe it calls forth can be kept from becoming abject worship
by doubts as to whether there is an absolute at one with itself, even
with the name 'Power', at the level of serene withdrawal.

Faith, too, though it may believe only in the transformability of
the Power into and within 'All [perceived] things that . . . revolve,
subside and swell' (94–5), can be rendered 'mild' and thus peaceful
in its solemnity, instead of fanatical and oppressive, by refusing to
affirm the unqualified or complete adequacy of any one 'likeness'
(such as the word 'God') in which the Power has 'come down'. The
transfer-process that begets our sense of Power and so acts
through and within it is too other than itself and too inclined to
shift towards appearing as something else at any moment for any
attitude other than a sceptical idealism to be a match for its
instability and its continual production of 'likenesses' veiling
deeper levels. In so far as this poem puts any set of figures in the
position of the Judeo-Christian deity, it draws that set back, not
just to the Lord that seems to descend towards the chosen people
on Mount Sinai, but to the very ancient, pre-Christian hebraic

sense, still visible in the Book of Exodus (particularly at 19:9, 16 and 18), of Yahweh as an always alien and self-alienating force – a transference – that perpetually comes concealed in 'thick clouds' of 'likeness' and so ought never to be confined within any one system of figures or projections (see Schneidau, 1976, pp. 1–49). Shelley finally asks us to be wary even of the Wordsworthian and Coleridgean effort to craft imaginary bridges between humanity and nature that 'reconcile' the two in a familial relationship because they supposedly have the same Father, the 'One life within us and abroad'. Though one draft of 'Mont Blanc' (noted especially well in Chernaik, 1972, p. 291) uses 'In such a faith with Nature reconciled' instead of the 'But for such faith' that Shelley approved for publication, the late change he made prevents any easy amalgamation of different entities into manifestations of the same Essence. As much as the line beginning 'But for' can perhaps mean 'only through such faith are people and nature brought into a healthy relationship', the possibility that 'humankind and nature may be reconciled *if it were not for* a sceptical idealism' cannot be rejected by readers out of hand (as the skilful Shelley must have realised in making this choice).[13] Belief is here being reconstituted from 'natural piety' into an outpouring of desire for a beneficial interchange between 'I' and 'thou' yet a cautious resistance, at every turn, to a relationship that might subsume both its entities under a Master Figure.

Hence this double attitude is suggested repeatedly throughout the finished poem in patterns of allusion, rhyme and apostrophe, all of which strive to promote such a delicate balance by acting out aspects of the transference on which the doubts and longings of 'mild faith' are based. When the 'likenesses' of the Power seem to draw Shelley's speaker towards seeing them as 'gleams of a remoter world' (49), he darts at once among many different, even incompatible, mythological explanations for that attraction. He wonders if he 'lie[s] in dream' while the 'mightier world of sleep/ Spread[s] . . . Its circles' towards him (54–7), as though he were subject to the 'god of sleep' in Ovid's *Metamorphoses* (XI. 610–15). Yet very soon the same speaker asks, 'Is this the scene/Where the old Earthquake-dæmon taught her young/Ruin?' (71–3). Now he steers between scientific theories which see the formation of great mountains as resulting from a series of earthquakes and Persian legends of such dark gods as the violent Ahriman, who raised up 'deadly glaciers' as 'the proofs and symbols of his reign' (as Shelley wrote to Peacock upon viewing Mont Blanc in his *Letters*, 1964, I, p. 449).[14] Shelley, of course, is not allowing his speaker (or readers) to affirm any one of these statements as an article of faith, only to keep shifting from older perspective to older perspective so that the call in the 'coming down' towards a level apparently above it will not catch the sceptical speaker in a commitment to any final explanation, despite his acknowledgement that he is drawn towards explanatory systems. The series of 'likenesses' in the 'coming down' are quite literally responded to in kind – are interpreted with a transference between and across several different ideologies – so that the 'becoming other' is redeemed from fixed 'codes of fraud and woe' in an intertextual sequence of responses that is as unsettled and decentring as it is desirous of an ultimate centre.

A similar disruption, meanwhile, is attempted in the general verse-pattern (or lack of it) in *Mont Blanc*. Shelley violates our expectations even of blank verse, whether it be the Miltonic type in *Tintern Abbey* or the end-stopped variety in the *Hymn Before Sun-rise*. As William Keach has pointed out, the Shelley of this poem crosses 'extended blank-verse enjambment with irregular rhyme', some of it 'internal', to a point where 'every resolution' into some definite scheme gives way to 'at least an undertow of dissolution' (Keach, 1984, pp. 195–7). Witness this sequence of lines from the fourth verse-paragraph on the mutability of what the Power produces in existence as we perceive it:

> The fields, the lakes, the forests, and the streams,
> Ocean, and all the living things that dwell
> Within the daedal earth; lightning, and rain,
> Earthquake, and fiery flood, and hurricane,
> The torpor of the year when feeble dreams
> Visit the hidden buds, or dreamless sleep
> Holds every future leaf and flower; – the bound
> With which from that detested trance they leap;
> The works and ways of man, their death and birth,
> And that of him and all that his may be;
> All things that move and breathe with toil and sound
> Are born and die; revolve, subside, and swell.
>
> (84–95)

Here, as in all acts of transference crossing between points and then looking both backwards and ahead, the tug-of-war between finding resemblances and maintaining differences never ends. Each entity in this sequence is initially and finally distinct from the others, with even the most related realms ('lakes' and 'streams' or 'rain' and 'flood') kept distant from their counterparts. All this while, though, the sequence is trying to conflate these differences into 'all the living things' that have a common motion in them. That attempt is apparently aided, not just by the speed of the shifts from area to area, but by recurrent sounds creating links between what seems separate ('streams' and 'dreams', 'dwell' and 'swell', 'sleep' and 'leap', 'earth' and 'birth'). Still, none of these echoes occur in the same pattern of rhyme. One happens after three lines, another after nine, another after only one, and yet another at the end of the ninth line as it picks up a sound from the mid-point of the third. The more the sequence goes on, the more its recurrences assert their near-randomness, their refusal to synchronise their repetitions according to a principle of unity that allows us to predict future patterns of rhyme. The Power that is transference and 'comes down' by way of its own 'becoming other' thus cannot be viewed legitimately as an immutable Essence lending an exact and repeatable pattern to whatever it generates. We have been drawn back again to a Lucretian process like the one at the start of the poem where waves swerve towards and away from other waves according to no predetermined mould. The result for the speaker and reader, it is hoped, remains a sceptical belief in such a Power underlying mutability, but that belief must also posit a mutability *within* the Power's operation that cannot be reduced to any one structure of figures that keeps reappearing in exactly the same way.

On top of all this, given a Power (and a basis for it) in which anything specified is already reappearing as something else in a different location, this poem cannot address any particular entity or being without soon being forced to address some other form or figure in an act of apostrophe, a 'turning away' (see Culler, 1977). So that the reader can be drawn towards that subliminal logic, in fact, Shelley repeatedly makes the speaker of *Mont Blanc* change addressees: from the speculative reader open to the initial vision of the everlasting flow (1–11), to the ravine of Arve in which that vision finds a visible analogue (12–48), to the speaker himself in his own rhetorical questions (53–7, 71–4), to the mountain and its ability to voice a repealing of codes (80–3), to the broad-minded reader able to see the mutabilities in perceived nature (84–126),

back to the speculative reader in so far as he or she is willing to
envision the hidden top of the mountain (127–39), and finally to
the heights of Mont Blanc themselves, where the interplay of the
opening lines reappears in a different state and place (139–44). One
revelation made by these shifts, of course, especially in the early
one that turns from the reader to the ravine, is the inability of the
mind's awareness to 'see itself, unless reflected upon that which it
resembles' (Shelley, 1977, p. 491). As Jacques Lacan has shown us
in his account of the 'mirror stage' (1977, pp. 1–10), the sense of
having thoughts in a self or of being able to envision thought's
wider context from within the self's own mind depends on that
vision's being 'made other', on its transfer-based combination of
elements being reflected in a perceptible counterpart that is itself a
site of transference. Then, too, the 'self' established in this exchange is revealed as having composed its 'identity' from a process
that is non-identical, an interplay of sharply differentiated elements. Any notion of identity in the self or what it sees is thereby
exposed as an illusion that should be deconstructed despite our
tendency to construct it. Every 'other' that seems to reflect an
identity should be exposed as itself referring to additional 'others'.
One later shift of address in this poem even helps to reinforce that
revisionary awareness by calling successively on different stances
in the reader – sight-seeing, on the one hand, and speculative, on
the other – as though the reader were really a heteroglossia of
several different interpretive modes that can be made to interact
but need not be subsumed under one restrictive way of seeing.[15] A
revision of what and how we believe cannot be entirely effective
unless the process of thought underlying belief is recovered from
repression and shown to include a capacity for crossing between
positions without an 'irritable reaching' for one absolute point of
view.[16]

Moreover, such shifts between types or points of focus in *Mont
Blanc*, even when the objects of address are technically unchanged,
modify a Shelleyan belief we have already noted: the interdepend-
ence of subject and object. When the 'I' gazes at the ravine it keeps
speaking to in the second verse-paragraph, it cannot help but
'muse on my own separate phantasy' as the 'human mind' appears
to 'receive . . . fast influencings' much in the way the vaginated bed
of the Arve takes in and directs the various 'comings down' of the
Power (36–8). Concurrently, however, the incoming 'thoughts'
have 'wings' that turn and 'float' back towards the ravine and even

'above' it, while perceptions that have become 'shadows' of their initial influx – and consequently objects of attention 'In the still cave of the witch Poesy' – attract the imagination to the extent that each is a 'shade' or 'faint image' of 'the breast/From which they [all] fled', the 'thou' on the outside still being addressed apparently from an inside at a distance from its opposite (41–8). Clearly this oxymoronic situation points to more than a subject-object interaction that is too continuous for either to be distinct from the other. Shelley is now suggesting an additional and ultimate retort to the poetic bridging of these poles as Wordsworth and Coleridge define it. After all, they too frequently view the relationship as one beween an actively masculine mind and a nourishing but passive feminine nature, wherein the phallic projection of thought towards its 'mother' finally draws the latter back towards her deeper or higher grounding in a masculine God, the all-encompassing (if hidden) 'Soul' animating both mind and its objects.

Shelley's retort is being worked out, at least implicitly, with every shift of attention in *Mont Blanc* from subject to object or vice-versa. But the most explicit statement appears in the 'interchange' between the ravine and the 'separate phantasy'. Here there seems to be at first little more than a restatement of the hierarchisation in Wordsworth and Coleridge, since the Power appears to 'come' down through the vaginal ravine from '*his* secret throne' above (17, my emphasis) and the projecting 'wild thoughts' are spoken of as 'wandering' erotically in a kind of foreplay over the 'darkness' of the vagina/ravine (41–2). Yet when the 'Ghosts' of what seems the Arve's descent arouse the 'phantasy' to 'Seek' something 'among the shadows' (45–6), what appears to call the shades back to their point of departure is a 'breast', and the mountain, so framed by this response to its features,[17] suddenly seems an enormous, flowing, milk-covered mammary gland, even at the level of the peak, which now seems as much a woman's nipple as it is a 'throne' of masculine ejaculations. All this time, too, the 'phantasy' that may be producing these transformations is as 'passively' receiving such 'influences' as it is phallically reaching out. It is also the container of a womb, the cave, which itself envelops a process of poetry-making, surely one 'source' of all we now behold, and that process is manifestly gendered as feminine (a 'witch') and seen as both receiving the signifiers of an other and actively constituting the search for that other's location.[18] Alongside and at the same levels as the Coleridgean response of an imaginative son to signs of an enthroned masculinity, we find feminine mental attractions, passive and active, to a feminine breast, an object which now seems to be a desirable source as much as the reaction in the cave/womb seems to be the source of the desire. Given the feminine nature of the poetic gestation that may have produced the forms of language 'creating' all these thoughts, it is possible that there is a feminine fore-language of 'render[ing] and receiv[ing]' (38) – another way of naming transference – that subliminally empowers the interrelation of subject with object. [19] Certainly she/it now seems the recovered motion that really 'gives birth' to the 'bridging' efforts of Wordsworth and Coleridge, even if those efforts work to repress it by subjecting the feminine to two male powers, the interpreting mind and the underwriting God.

Shelley's process of revision, then, thoroughly deconstructs the hierarchies of Wordsworth, Coleridge, and their forebears. *Mont Blanc* finds in relational movements never strictly at one with themselves, in the movements that his precursors have placed in secondary, receiving positions, the operations *underlying* what older thinkers regard as primary, causal and unified from the start. There cannot be a 'bridging' of thought and nature that even appears to show some Absolute at the heart of them unless there is first the sheer seeing of one in terms of the other and vice-versa in an interchange where no one 'side' (or gendered position) is primary or dominant and where differences are more partial resemblances than they are oppositions or subordinations. It is vital for Shelley, morally and politically, that such a realisation be 'deeply felt' by more and more people. Such a turn in thinking, especially since it is a re-turn of the truly primal and now suppressed, will undermine the claims to priority trumpeted by the hierarchical myths and theologies that now uphold patriarchal/ monarchical systems of political control, even in the thinking of those being controlled. A newly relational way of seeing, too, can transform the grandeur of existence as perceived away from the fear-based sublimity of an Edmund Burke, for whom size and endurance are too simply set against weak mortality (another construct of male strength vs. feminine weakness, as in Burke, 1759, pp. 127–29, 210–12). Shelley offers a sense of nature and its observer as magnificently pouring transferential Love out from themselves towards each other, whether a mountain perceived as a large breast gushes with nourishment for the valleys it feeds with rivers, or a womb of witch-like imagination reaches out towards that breast with its benevolent transformations of the 'shadows' it observes.

There remains only the question of whether this transfiguration of standard thought will be read for what it is and embraced for what it says by enough of 'the wise, and great, and good' open to such an understanding. This question, of course, persists even today as we continue to approach Shelley's poetry, particularly *Mont Blanc*. How we choose to interpret this kind of iconoclastic writing is really part of what is being asked about in the final rhetorical question that Shelley's speaker addresses to the mountain as he closes the poem:

> And what were thou, and earth, and stars, and sea,
> If to the human mind's imaginings,
> Silence and solitude were vacancy?
>
> (142–4)

Are we going to give in to the temptation, to which many have indeed succumbed,[20] that leads us to read these lines in a Wordsworthian or Coleridgean way? Are we going to assume that these words refer to the quasi-phallic ability of the mind or poetry to infuse life, figures and significance into a possibly empty waste on the highest, most icy slopes? Or are we going to decide that there is no 'vacancy' because there simply is a God-like Power atop a frozen 'throne'? Or will we read Shelley to be as genuinely revolutionary and revisionist as he claimed to be? Will we see that, in the context of the final verse-paragraph of *Mont Blanc*, this question refers *both* to the quiet intertransference among snow-flakes and star-beams at the peak that recalls the opening interplay of waves *and* to the interaction of perceived natural transformations with imaginative projections into levels beyond human sight, the interaction required before we can even envision the snows and beams descending where 'none beholds them'? Will we see that there is no vacancy and that there is a relationship to be celebrated between mountains, valleys, stars and seas because there is always already a subliminal transference in the way we perceive and in the methods by which language helps 'create' such thoughts-about-thoughts? The choices we make in answering such questions will determine, for us, whether our new approaches to Shelley can recover his true presuppositions, and will decide, for him, if we are able to perceive and imagine a brave new world at last.

7

Julian and Maddalo as Revisionary Conversation Poem

Charles J. Rzepka

Shelley's *Julian and Maddalo: A Conversation* has challenged formal interpretation for many years, and for good reason. Consisting of a madman's soliloquy framed by a first-person narrative that comprises both scenic description and dialogue, the poem has been variously characterised as a test of the reader's self-knowledge (Wasserman, 1971, p. 61), a 'psychodrama' (Newey, 1982, p. 74), a 'dramatic monologue' (Hirsch, 1978, p. 14), a 'fragment poem' (Levinson, 1986a, pp. 150–6), and an 'eclogue' (Curran, 1986, p. 110). Oddly enough, no one has yet thought to ask whether *Julian and Maddalo*, as its subtitle implies, might be generically indebted to the Coleridgean 'conversation poem'. This may be because, as Ronald Tetreault has recently noted, it so little resembles Coleridge's monologues (Tetreault, 1987, p. 149). Generic indebtedness, however, need not imply generic emulation. As I hope to show, Shelley's particular hybridisation of lyric, dialogue and narrative – an inclusive form similar to the pastoral eclogue – constitutes less an instance of or an experiment with traditional poetic genres than it does a specific generic anti-type, namely a critique of the essentially pastoral vision of social and cosmic harmony informing the first-generation Romantic conversation poem. In general, as Tetreault also observes (1987, p. 121), *Julian and Maddalo* reflects Shelley's growing uneasiness, during his first year in Italy, with the impassioned and highly personal lyric form as a means of establishing a true community of minds by which to potentiate social change.

Julian and Maddalo builds on an actual event: a conversation between Shelley and Byron ('Julian' and 'Maddalo') during their ride along the Lido on the afternoon of Shelley's arrival in Venice on 23 August 1818.[1] This event inspired the first 120 lines of Julian's description of his and Maddalo's 'descant[]' of 'God, freewill and destiny' (46, 42), the view of the sunset over Venice, and the continuation of the discussion on the way back to Venice in a gondola. When the argument resumes the next morning, the two friends agree that observing a madman of Maddalo's acquaintance, the inmate of an asylum sighted from the lagoon the evening before, will decide the issue (121–299). The Maniac's soliloquy, overheard by Julian and Maddalo, takes up the next 200 lines (300–510), followed by Julian's description of the inconclusive aftermath of the debate, his departure for England, and his learning the Maniac's fate from Maddalo's daughter on his return several years later (511–617).

The poem's initial 'conversation', which begins on the Lido and is continued the next day, addresses the question of whether or not one is responsible for one's own despair in the face of ill-usage or misfortune. Are we finally helpless to overcome evil, or does evil prevail because we assume ourselves to be helpless? Julian argues 'against despondency', while Maddalo 'take[s] the darker side' (48–9), maintaining that the human soul is incapable of self-transformation. 'It is our will,' insists Julian at one point, 'That thus enchains us to permitted ill' (170–1):

> 'We might be otherwise – we might be all
> We dream of happy, high, majestical.
> Where is the love, beauty and truth we seek
> But in our mind? and if we were not weak
> Should we be less in deed than in desire?'
> 'Ay, if we were not weak – and we aspire
> How vainly to be strong!' said Maddalo;
> 'You talk Utopia.'
>
> (172–9)

This 'conversation' has an important bearing on Shelley's revolutionary poetics. For if, as the poet argues in *A Defence of Poetry*, 'all things exist as they are perceived: at least in relation to the percipient' (Shelley, 1977, p. 505), and all perception is informed by the human imagination, then evil must prevail when the imagination is enfeebled by despondency, what Julian calls our 'own willful ill' (211). If the poet can correct our errant view of individual potential by encouraging the growth of our power to envision as

real possibilities 'the love, beauty and truth we seek', to 'imagine'
in the world around us 'that which we know' only as an abstract
idea (Shelley, 1977, p. 505), then the apocalyptic eradication of evil
must follow.

In *Julian and Maddalo*, however, this positive vision is qualified by
the visionary Julian's own tendencies towards solipsism and abstraction. Seeking refuge from the bustle of society in 'all waste/
And solitary places; where we taste/The pleasure of believing
what we see/Is boundless, as we wish our souls to be' (14–17),
Julian projects his own soul's millenial desires on forms of earth,
sea and sky so blended by the sunset over Venice that the city
itself, the locus of social change, is not so much transformed as
encircled and swallowed up by them, 'Dissolved into one lake of
fire' (81). Julian's sunset apocalypse is visually sublime, but
grandiose and, finally, sentimental. These qualities become especially apparent if we contrast it to the detailed vignettes of a
transfigured society offered in the nearly contemporaneous *Prometheus Unbound* (III. iv. 33–85; 98–204), where, in addition, human
agony and its 'wilful ill' are made to appear in their true shapes,
the better to show us how such evils are to be overcome.

The spuriousness of Julian's vision is further indicated by
Shelley's allusion to that Miltonic 'lake of fire' from which Satan's
new city, Pandemonium, arises in Book III of *Paradise Lost*. This
imagistic reference is anticipated by Julian's comparison of his and
Maddalo's 'talk' to that which 'the devils held within the dales of
Hell' (41) and his apostrophe to Italy as a 'Paradise of exiles' (57).
The combined effect is to turn Julian's visionary Venice into a
shimmering mirage that flatters his otherwise thwarted hopes and
ambitions, a proud outcast's surrogate for that true Heavenly City
towards which the poet would have impelled England by action
and example had he not, like Julian and his friend, been prevented
by self-exile (see Curran 1975, pp. 137–8).

Maddalo challenges Julian's millenial self-delusions by taking
him to 'a better station' (87) from which to view the sunset:

> 'Look, Julian, on the West, and listen well
> If you hear not a deep and heavy bell.'
> I looked, and saw between us and the sun
> A building on an island; such a one
> As age to age might add, for uses vile,
> A windowless, deformed and dreary pile;

> And on the top an open tower, where hung
> A bell, which in the radiance swayed and swung;
> We could just hear its hoarse and iron tongue:
> The broad sun sunk behind it, and it tolled
> In strong and black relief. – 'What we behold
> Shall be the madhouse and its belfry tower,'
> Said Maddalo, 'and ever at this hour
> Those who may cross the water, hear that bell,
> Which calls the maniacs each one from his cell
> To vespers . . .
> And such, '– he cried, 'is our mortality
> And this must be the emblem and the sign
> Of what should be eternal and divine! –
> And, like that black and dreary bell, the soul,
> Hung in a heaven-illumined tower, must toll
> Our thoughts and our desires to meet below
> Round the rent heart and pray – as madmen do
> For what? they know not . . .'
> (96–127)

Maddalo's choice of 'emblem' for the incoherent and isolated human soul will be realised the next day in the person of the asylum's chief inmate, the Maniac.

Following immediately upon Julian's enthusiastic sunset vision of cosmic and social unity, the madhouse bell is not only a striking indictment of millenial ambitions, but also, considered in its specific scenic context and as part of a poem explicitly subtitled 'A Conversation', oddly reminiscent of a famous 'conversational' precursor:

> My gentle-hearted Charles! when the last rook
> Beat its straight path along the dusky air
> Homewards, I blest it! deeming its black wing
> (Now a dim speck, now vanishing in light)
> Had cross'd the mighty Orb's dilated glory,
> While thou stood'st gazing; or, when all was still,
> Flew creaking o'er thy head, and had a charm
> For thee, my gentle-hearted Charles, to whom
> No sound is dissonant which tells of Life.
> (68–76)

The generic and scenic context of Maddalo's madhouse bell, as well as its discursive function (emphasised by the phrase 'hoarse and iron tongue'), suggest that its pointedly dissonant resemblance to Coleridge's pointedly *un*dissonant rook in *This Lime-Tree Bower My Prison* is not an accident.[2] Nor, as I shall demonstrate, is this image the only feature of the poem indebted to a Coleridgean antecedent. Rather, Shelley's allusions to Coleridge's example serve as integral clues to the generic intentions that helped shape *Julian and Maddalo*. In order to understand what these echoes mean, however, we must attend, first, to Shelley's representations of conversation in the poem and, second, to the manner in which conversation is represented in Coleridge's own conversation poems.

Two types of 'conversation' take place in *Julian and Maddalo*: the real one between the poem's eponymous friends, which is recounted in Julian's framing narrative, and the imaginary one between the Maniac and his absent lover, his 'spirit's mate' (337), whose abandonment apparently caused him to go insane. The second type of 'conversation', which is overheard by Julian and Maddalo, puts a stop to the first, in which they participate. Astonished and appalled by the Maniac's ravings, says Julian, 'our argument was quite forgot' (520). The encounter with the Maniac not only makes painfully clear, by stark contrast, the Utopian sentimentality and abstraction of Julian's millenial hopes, but also – and surprisingly, in light of Shelley's poetic practice in general – calls into question the power of suffering to move its compassionate beholders beyond a merely spectacular relationship to it. The discourse of individual suffering, which Shelley calls in his 'Preface' to the poem a 'sufficient comment for the text of every heart' that overhears it (Shelley, 1977, p. 113), turns out to impede rather than encourage philosophical reflection and dialogue. It interferes with that dialectical submission of heart-'texts' to mutual 'comment' that is both the beginning of all self-knowledge and the only firm basis of all concerted public action, whether for reform or revolution.

Shelley's rigidly disjunctive representation of imaginary and real conversation stands in marked contrast to the rhetorical assumptions informing the first-generation Romantic conversation poem, namely that an overheard soliloquy (the sincerest verbal register of the individual mind and soul) and conversation (the form of discourse upon which human community fundamentally depends) could be conflated into a 'conversational soliloquy' that would offer a transparent medium by which to register and affirm the solidarity of otherwise disparate minds. In Shelley's poem, however, the conversational soliloquist is apparently insane, and this anomalous rhetorical hybrid is shown to be utterly destructive of true community, not only discouraging real conversation among those who overhear it, but also paralysing any impulse to approach and respond to the soliloquist as a speaking subject.

Instead, the Maniac's audience relates to him either scientifically, as a specimen (his case will decide their debate), or voyeuristically, as a spectacle (they watch his ravings and weep for, but not with him).[3] But as G. M. Matthews points out, it is difficult to see how merely observing the Maniac can resolve the question of his responsibility for his suffering (1963, pp. 72–3). As for whether or not his despondency can be corrected, that clearly depends on inductive rather than deductive logic: some attempt must first be made to correct it. In lieu of such an attempt, it still 'remains to know', as Julian originally put the case, 'how strong the chains are which our spirit bind;/Brittle perchance as straw' (179–82). It also remains to know what Shelley wished to demonstrate by staging this sanitary encounter with the discourse of suffering.

I. ETHOS AND PATHOS: THE MANIAC AS LYRIC POET

Julian and Maddalo's verbal disengagement, both from the spectacle of madness and from each other's reaction to it, is not an indication of moral failure on their part so much as a necessary consequence of Shelley's generic aim, which is to explore the 'conversational' limitations of lyric expression, its suitability, or unsuitability, as an instrument of persuasion and social change. Like the Maniac's ravings, but unlike real conversation, lyric elevates passion over reason, spontaneity over deliberation, expression over communication, and passive identification over active participation.

Richard Cronin, in his comments on the poem, has summarised these differences by resorting to the ancient rhetorical distinction between *pathos* and *ethos*: roughly, affective as opposed to argumentative means of persuasion. Citing the contagion of Byron's enthusiasm for eighteenth-century poets, and Shelley's own use of the Horatian phrase '*sermo pedestris*' to characterise his new poem (Shelley, 1964, II, p. 196), Cronin contends that *Julian and Maddalo* recasts the classical generic differences between *pathos* and *ethos* in terms of the contrasting rhetorical orientations of Augustan and Romantic poetry: the ethical or 'conversational' speaker, like Julian or Maddalo, or like Pope and the Augustans in general, seeks the reader's accession to an argumentative position with which the speaker identifies or to which the speaker is personally committed, while the pathetic or expressionistic speaker, like the Maniac, or like Shelley and the Romantics in general, seeks the reader's largely uncritical identification with the thoughts and feelings expressed by the speaker, or by an adopted *persona* or character (Cronin, 1981, pp. 110–32).

In general, the English Romantics were skilful at distinguishing between ethical and pathetic writing, and at elaborating each form's unique features and functions. Wordsworth and De Quincey, for example, identified ethical or moral writing with the literature of 'knowledge', pathetic or empathic, with that of 'power'. For Keats, ethical truth was the goal of the philosopher, and could be grasped only by means of 'consequitive reasoning', while pathetic truth was the goal of the imaginatively prehensile, self-annihilating 'camelion Poet', and could be grasped only by 'Negative Capability' (Rollins, 1958, I, pp. 185, 387, 193). Indeed, precisely in so far as pathetic writing moves us towards Keatsian self-annihilation, it militates against the kind of commitment to a particular point of view that is implied by the very term 'ethical'. 'What shocks the virtuous philosopher,' says Keats, 'delights the camelion Poet', who has 'as much delight in conceiving an Iago as an Imogen'. The 'poetical character', apparently, 'has no Identity' of its own, but takes pleasure in 'filling some other Body' (Rollins, 1958, I, p. 387).

Ethical writing, in short, is necessarily referential as well as representational. Unlike the 'poetical character', the ethical writer is understood to have defined himself or herself as a particular social and historical being, a person, in and by the act of writing, and to have conveyed not just a way of envisioning and experiencing the world, but a way of living in the world so envisioned and experienced. For this reason, empathic identification encouraged purely for its own sake, as Keats realised, cannot succeed if contaminated by ethical intentions. Of Wordsworth's later, aggressively philosophical work he exclaimed, 'For the sake of a few fine imaginative or domestic passages, are we to be bullied into a certain Philosophy engendered in the whims of an Egotist ... We hate poetry that has a palpable design upon us' (Rollins, 1958, I, p. 223).

While *ethos* seems fatal to the amoral exhilaration of chameleon *pathos*, the reverse does not necessarily hold true. An ethical writer trying to change an audience's moral understanding and behaviour can, obviously, use empathy for that purpose. Indeed, the classical rhetoricians believed that *pathos* should serve precisely such ends, and so, apparently, did Shelley. In his work, personal suffering and political intent, lyric and polemic, usually take one and the same discursive path, and Shelley often represents himself in his private torment much as the Maniac does: 'as a nerve o'er which do creep / The else unfelt oppressions of this earth' (449–50). In the productions of his *annus mirabilis*, where the polemics of *Song to the Men of England* and *The Masque of Anarchy* provide a hortatory supplement to the visionary theatre of *Prometheus Unbound* and the dark despair of *The Cenci*, and where *Ode to the West Wind* brilliantly integrates both pathetic and ethical impulses, Shelley was clearly attempting to change both hearts *and* minds, to enlarge empathy as well as to incite action. *Julian and Maddalo*, however, differs markedly from these more integrated works, for here *pathos* – passive identification with others – is clearly represented as precluding rather than intensifying *ethos* – active personal engagement with others.

One explanation for this divergence of ethical and pathetic impulses may be found in the emotional turmoil of Shelley's life soon after his arrival in Venice. The Maniac's soliloquy can be seen to reflect Shelley's own secret agony over Mary's estrangement of affection following the death of their daughter Clara on the day the family joined him. Mary apparently blamed Clara's death on Percy's insistence that the girl make the journey despite her illness (see Cameron, 1974, pp. 261–6; Holmes 1975, pp. 439–47). The intimate origins of the Maniac's outpourings of grief partly help to explain Shelley's inability to integrate them firmly into a larger visionary or philosophical framework. Far from enabling the poet to distance himself from his torment and consider it in melioristic perspective, the introductory framing narrative is shattered by the impact of the violent and unexpected emotions that are given voice by the Maniac.

For whatever reason, the claims of the ethical and the pathetic directly conflict in *Julian and Maddalo* as they do not in any other poem by Shelley. Here, feeling comes in aid of feeling *at the expense of* both individual and concerted action, diluting the impulse to act by preventing the witnesses of 'our wilful ill' from reflecting on and discussing the larger issues raised by what they behold. The result is not reform, but palliation: Maddalo continues to pay for the luxurious appointments of the Maniac's cell without hope of curing him (252–8). Or worse, empathy substitutes for action altogether – Julian imagines he can cure the Maniac by merely watching him 'day by day', studying 'all the beatings of his heart / With zeal', and thereby 'find / An entrance to the caverns of his mind' (568–73). That this is in fact, as Julian himself suspects, a 'dream[] of baseless good' (578) becomes clear when he departs the very next day for London, 'urged by [his] affairs' (582).

A wholly abstract response to the Maniac as 'Exhibit A' is not the desideratum, of course, but neither is the wholly affective, spectacular response that replaces it. What would prevent the Maniac's being reduced to either a scientific specimen or a theatrical spectacle, and what is glaringly absent from Shelley's representation of Julian's and Maddalo's responses to the Maniac's plight, is direct personal engagement with the sufferer so as to bring him out of his discursive isolation and into the dialectical interplay of 'conversation'. What such an engagement would entail we can only imagine, but it is not at all unimaginable. Although the Maniac's speech is 'fragmented', the fragments are extended, motivically coherent, and thematically integrated – more like movements in an oratorio than unrelated puzzle pieces of some monstrous whole. Moreover, the *general* cause of the man's grief is not a mystery to his hearers: although their 'argument' about free will and evil is 'quite forgot', Julian and Maddalo still 'talk of [the Maniac] / And nothing else, till daylight ma[ke] stars dim' (520–4). In the process, they manage to 'guess' much of the cause of his woe (535).

Though frantic, then, the Maniac is not incoherent, and his discursive gaps and discontinuities are almost entirely the result of his 'conversing' with an imaginary interlocutor (his former lover) who supposedly already knows, intimately, the specific history of his lament. That history being closed to Julian and Maddalo, as well as to Shelley's later readers, they must fill in the blanks as best they can. But why, if the Maniac is not 'mad' by any conventional sense of the word, should Julian and Maddalo remain at a distance at all? It is almost as though, by invoking the descriptive category and deploying the stage machinery of 'madness', Shelley wished to establish a rationale for deliberately isolating the Maniac's auditors, for making them, in effect, 'readers' of the Maniac rather than 'interlocutors'. As a result, what Julian and Maddalo (and we as actual readers) are forced to 'guess' at becomes less a speaking subject who shares our discursive universe than a speaking 'text' or poetic persona that must be interpreted – and responded to – in silence.

Shelley registers his intentions to textualise the Maniac's suffering when he has Julian characterise the 'wild language of [the Maniac's] grief' as 'high, / Such as in measure were called poetry' (541–2), and Maddalo replies, 'Most wretched men / Are cradled into poetry by wrong, / They learn in suffering what they teach in song' (544–6). This 'poetry' or 'song' is specifically meant to be apprehended as though it were something being read as well as heard. The Maniac is described as speaking 'sometimes as one who wrote and thought / His words might move some heart that heeded not / If sent to distant lands' (286–8). He calls his own speech a 'sad writing' (340), and indicates that even as he speaks, 'from [his] pen the words flow as [he] write[s], / Dazzling [his] eyes with scalding tears.' 'My sight,' he continues, 'Is dim to *see* that *charactered* in vain / On this unfeeling *leaf* which burns the brain / And eats into it . . . *blotting* all things fair / And wise and good which time had *written* there' (476–81; my italics). Even the madhouse bell, emblem of the Maniac's soliloquial soul, is cast 'in strong and black relief' against the sun, like a word on the printed page (see Blank 1988, pp. 115, 120–1).

While critics have attributed such inconsistencies in the representation of the Maniac's speech to Shelley's carelessness in transcribing the verses he wrote to express his feelings about Mary's emotional withdrawal, this does justice neither to Shelley's craftsmanship nor to what Stuart Curran calls the poem's quite 'finished' effect, in support of which he cites the 'evidence of careful structuring and thoughtful revision' in its drafts (1975, p. 137). That the references to writing were deliberately retained in the final version suggests that Shelley meant the Maniac's speech to be apprehended as the written text of an interiorised, mental 'conversation' – or, to be more specific, a conversation poem – etched, as with burning acid, into his brain.

II. THE AMBIGUOUS FORM OF THE CONVERSATION POEM

What is represented in the confrontation with the Maniac is less an encounter with human suffering than a silent 'reading' of the text of that suffering. This text is specifically informed by the narrative assumptions of the first-generation Romantic conversation poem, a genre that combines features of dramatic monologue, apostrophe and soliloquy, but strangely enough, like the Maniac's imaginary conversation with his absent 'spirit's mate', includes no representation of conversation in its ordinary sense.

The phrase 'conversation poem' was not employed as a critical term until 1925, when George McLean Harper drew on the subtitle of Coleridge's *The Nightingale: A Conversation Poem* to describe generically related poems like *The Eolian Harp*, *Reflections on having left a Place of Retirement*, *This Lime-Tree Bower My Prison*, and *Frost at Midnight*. The generic similarities among these poems, however, were recognised at least as early as the composition of Wordsworth's *Tintern Abbey*, which, as Paul Magnuson has demonstrated at considerable length, is heavily influenced by Coleridge's 'conversational' examples (Magnuson, 1988, pp. 139–76). The area of overlap among groups of lyrics classified as 'conversation poems' by Harper and later Coleridgeans like Humphry House and Albert Gerard, includes *The Eolian Harp*, *This Lime-Tree Bower My Prison*, *Frost at Midnight*, *The Nightingale*, and *Dejection: An Ode*. What these five works have in common – along with *Tintern Abbey* – is some representation of the physical situation in which they are to be imagined as spoken and some rhetorical orientation towards a specific auditor or auditors understood to be, if not entirely alert or immediately present, then at least located in the world represented and referred to by the text itself. Generally, the conversation poem seems to alternate between interior reflection and direct address, teetering precariously between the dramatically analogous forms of soliloquy – that is, a speaking overheard by others but directed to oneself – and dramatic monologue in its strictest sense – that is, a speaking overheard by others but directed at a specific implied auditor.

The expressive and empathic ambiguities of this hybrid form that is both lyrical soliloquy and dramatic monologue by turns, and neither *in toto*, can be clarified if we observe the particular kind of discursive desire the form makes manifest. Far from displaying, as its name implies, the objectivity we normally associate with the drama's inclusion or acknowledgement of differing points of view, the conversation poem expresses the lyrical *nostalgia* for otherness that is characteristic of the traditional apostrophe, namely a longing for the confirmation of private speculations, feelings and assumptions *about* others that only the real, responsive presence *of* others can make possible. This longing is nostalgic (that is, inauthentic and sentimental) because, like the longing of apostrophe, the otherness it seeks is denied its voice by the generic perspectival constraints of lyric form, in which the entire text by which otherness is to be represented must be understood as spoken by the poet alone.

Unlike the typical apostrophe, however, which makes no claim to dialogical engagement and, indeed, wears its wishful heart on its sleeve, the conversation poem conveys the impression that the speaker has in fact secured the agreement or shaped the thoughts of his otherwise unresponsive – or even absent – auditor, and that a true communion or identity of minds has thereby been established, without such an expression of faith having ever received an explicit or implicit reply. (*The Eolian Harp*, as will become evident in a moment, is the glaring exception that proves the rule.) Thus we are left, at the end of *This Lime-Tree Bower*, with the poet's clearly expressed conviction that the joys he has 'lift[ed] the soul' to 'contemplate' with his own 'lively joy' were actually experienced by his 'gentle-hearted Charles' in the manner the poet described; or that in *Frost at Midnight* the poet's 'Dear Babe, that sleepe[th] cradled' by his side *shall* 'see and hear / The lovely shapes and sounds intelligible / Of that eternal language, which thy God / utters' (44, 54, 57–61), exactly as the poet, the child's own 'Great universal Teacher', decrees in the present lyrical moment (64); or that in *The Nightingale* the speaker's intimate audience – his friend, Wordsworth, and his friend's sister, Dorothy – resting on 'this old mossy bridge' (4), *do* end up sharing his untoward reinterpretation of the nightingale's melancholy song as 'full of love / And joyance' (42–3). Because these speculative assumptions of empathy and agreement encounter no expressions of resistance from their objects, they seem to impress the speaker (and often the reader!) as intersubjectively confirmed.

If the conversation poem differs from true apostrophe in its spurious establishment of otherness as a source of self-confirmation, it differs as well from true dramatic monologue, where the speaker's utterance is nearly always shown to be influenced, often in ways he or she seems unable to recognise, by the real possibility of a negative response – the expression, for example, of doubt, denial, anger, alarm, or derision. This reaction to or anticipation of a negative interlocutory response is what makes the dramatic monologue, strictly speaking, 'dramatic', as even a cursory examination of Browning's definitive works in the genre, such as *My Last Duchess* or *Fra Lippo Lippi*, demonstrates. It is also, I might add, what makes *The Eolian Harp*, alone among the group commonly called 'conversation poems', a true 'dramatic monologue'. Here, dialogic resistance to the speaker's seductive philosophical speculations is manifested in the very utterance that would shape the other's thoughts, by the speaker's remarking not only the 'mild reproof' darted by Sara's 'more serious eye', but also her 'bidd[ing]' him to walk humbly with his God, and her 'holily disprais[ing] / These shapings' of his 'unregenerate mind' (49, 52, 54, 55).

In the other conversation poems, no such overt negative response from the addressee, whether experienced or anticipated, is ever registered by the speaker, even though it is apparently potentiated throughout his utterance by the implied dynamic of 'conversation'. Instead, confirmation is in each case presumed. What, then, is the point of giving the silent interlocutor of the conversation poem – present or absent, awake or asleep – a local habitation and a pronomen? I believe it is to reinforce the impression of the poem's referentiality, our sense that the poem documents a real occasion of empathy, without exposing that occasion to the interpretive threat imposed by true conversation.

As I have argued elsewhere at length, the mute interlocutors of the conversation poems serve as others *manqué*, enlisted in an attempt to get the reader to suspend his or her disbelief in the communal status of utterly private empathic assumptions. In that readerly suspension, the Romantic poet sought assurance that the radical ambiguity overtaking discourse at the end of the Enlightenment would not, after all, establish an insuperable barrier between mind and mind, soul and soul (See Rzepka, 1986, pp. 114–32). The conversation poem thus enacts a self-redemptive, and simultaneously self-mystifying, gesture towards the realm of the historical Other, a realm where the abstract, disembodied characterisations of consciousness can, ordinarily, achieve realisation as a person. In the presence of a sympathetic – and apparently historical – intimate whose silence can be taken as perfectly mirroring his hopes rather than his fears, the Romantic poet would enact, as it were, his own historicity.[4]

As a gesture towards dialogical self-redemption, the conversation poem necessarily projects a biographical and historical referentiality that, since the advent of Modernism, we have been taught to discount. Nevertheless, the power of this implicit, if spurious, claim to referentiality has often made itself felt, even among the most knowledgeable and sophisticated Coleridgeans (see Magnuson, 1974, pp. 17–18; Curran, 1986, p. 110, and below). It was, in any case, a claim quite evident to the real-life counterpart of Coleridge's 'gentle-hearted Charles': 'For God's sake (I was never more serious)', wrote Charles Lamb on 6 August 1800, after having read *This Lime-Tree Bower* again in the second edition of *Lyrical Ballads*, 'don't make me ridiculous any more by terming me gentle-hearted in print, or do it in better verses ... I should be ashamed to think that you could think to gratify me by such praise, fit only to be a cordial to some green-sick sonneteer' (Marrs, 1975, I, pp. 217–18).

Citing the biographical fallacy, we can reject as wrong-headed Lamb's attempt to engage the speaker of *This Lime-Tree Bower* in a real conversation that would test that speaker's presumptions about Charles's gentle heart. But however mistaken Lamb's response may appear from a formal perspective, it does call attention to the poem's otherwise unexamined gestures towards referentiality and dialectical engagement, 'ethical' gestures that we must finally reject even as we recognise their self-redemptive intent. Lamb, like the 'pensive Sara' of *The Eolian Harp*, understood that monologic conversation is rhetorically co-optative, projecting the illusion of conversational dialectic in order to validate what could only be, were it indeed enacted, an imaginative appropriation of other minds. Conversational soliloquy offers a delusively transparent medium by which to establish a sense of emotional and intellectual community because it encounters no dialogical resistance.

III. *JULIAN AND MADDALO* AS ANTI-PASTORAL

The conversation poem, like autobiography, resists the drawing of formal distinctions between maker and speaker. Shaped by the poet's anxiety over his own historical reception, the one-sided 'conversation' of the typical conversation poem attempts to deploy the dynamic, without incurring the responsibility, of true conversation, which depends on each participant's willingness to subject himself or herself to the interpretive self-dispossession of another's articulated responses. *Julian and Maddalo*, however, is no more a conversation poem like *This Lime-Tree Bower* than it is a dramatic monologue like *The Eolian Harp*. It is, rather, a generic anti-type that demonstrates the fundamental unsuitability of lyrical or soliloquial *pathos* for ethical purposes by framing, within a represented conversation, what is ordinarily taken to be the Romantic lyric's most 'ethical' – that is, honest and engaged – form, a conversational soliloquy. In the process, the impulse behind the conversation poem's representation of otherness is revealed to be nostalgic – inauthentic and self-delusory – by Shelley's reducing that representation to its apostrophic essence: in *Julian and Maddalo* the relation of the monologic conversationalist to his interlocutor has become wholly – and clearly – imaginary.

Carlos Baker, the first Shelleyan to apply the term 'conversation poem' to *Julian and Maddalo*, used it loosely to refer to *Rosalind and Helen* and *The Cenci* as well (1948, pp. 119–53). The poem obviously shares some features with drama, incorporating, in the Maniac's speeches, material originally intended for a play on Torquato Tasso, and showing the influence of the poet's translation of *The Symposium* the previous summer. Its composition, moreover, coincided with that of the first three acts of *Prometheus Unbound*. But *Julian and Maddalo* has even stronger ties, as Stuart Curran points out, to the pastoral tradition of the 'eclogue', a genre that includes both dialogue and lyric, and one to which Shelley himself assigned *Rosalind and Helen* (Shelley, 1964, II, p. 109). Noting that the poem focuses on the question raised by Virgil's *Tenth Eclogue*, from which Shelley drew his motto ('What can a sympathetic poet offer to compensate for the grief of another's misfortune in love?'), Curran situates *Julian and Maddalo*, along with the first-generation conversation poem, firmly in the pastoral tradition. 'The underlying impulse' of both, he writes, 'the exemplification of conversation, natural interchange, is always the same': '"The one Life within us and abroad"', as Coleridge phrases it in the first of the poems in this mode, "The Eolian Harp" (26), is the essential principle of pastoral, and its consequence is necessarily song' (Curran, 1986, p. 110). Following interpretive tradition, Curran cites the image of the creaking rook that 'tells of Life' as it crosses the setting sun at the end of *This Lime-Tree Bower* as an example of Romantic trust in 'the one Life' as a means of uniting otherwise disparate, finite centres of thought and perception. An image like this, argues Curran, indicates a renewal of faith in the pastoral tradition. Curran sees the rook, usually associated with death, as 'virtually synonymous with the divine, forming the apex of a triangle linking the sequestered poet and his absent friends' and affirming pastoral community (1986, p. 110).

But can such faith be justified when the poet's presumption of empathy is not tested by real conversation? As Lamb's angry response to Coleridge's well-meant 'cordial' demonstrates, song, the 'necessary consequence' of pastoral faith in 'the one Life', is not conversation, and the use of song *as though it were* conversation does not indicate a renewed faith in the pastoral tradition of 'community, affection, art' (Curran, 1986, p. 121), but rather a profound suspicion of that tradition, of ordinary expressions of affection, and of the arts in general, as a means of fostering true community.

Shelley's ironic allusion to the creaking rook of *This Lime-Tree Bower My Prison* registers his scepticism towards the pastoral transparency of conversational soliloquy. Both the rook that 'tells of life' and the madhouse bell with its 'hoarse iron tongue' are shared objects of perception that seem to 'speak'. Coleridge's rook, however, 'tells' its otherwise sundered observers of that logoistic 'one Life' which, according to *Frost at Midnight*, utters the 'eternal language' of the book of nature and thereby 'doth teach / Himself in all, and all things in himself' (60–2). The madhouse bell, in stark contrast, obstinately blots out this presumed source of universal life and shared understanding. It is, instead, 'the emblem and the sign' of the discursive opacity of the fallen and isolated human soul, as exemplified by the Maniac. That the visionary Julian disagrees with the cynical conclusions Maddalo draws from this 'emblem' merely deepens the madhouse bell's allusive irony: as an object of interpretation, a topic of real conversation rather than of silent contemplation, the bell highlights the *differences* between Julian's and Maddalo's points of view, not their identity, while the rook functions in exactly the opposite manner with respect to the poet and his absent friend.

In larger terms, the opening scene of the framing narrative (1–140) altogether reverses the empathic narrative perspective of its conversational prototype by literalising the facetious metaphor of incarceration in its title, *This Lime-Tree Bower My Prison*: Shelley literally imprisons his apostrophising poet-figure on an island, completely isolating him, mentally as well as physically, from the thoughts and experiences of his potential friends as they admire the sunset. From the estranged visionary perspective of the poet /

Maniac's lucid alter-ego, the 'gentle-hearted' Julian, the world appears anything but imprisoning. It is, rather, boundless, undivided and evanescent, the sky, 'Dark purple at the zenith', growing 'Brighter than burning gold, even to the rent / Where the swift sun yet pause[s] in his descent' (72, 74–5), with the 'mountains towering as from waves of flame / Around the vaporous sun, from which there came / The inmost purple spirit of light, and made / Their very peaks transparent' (82–5). Thus Julian experiences the same kind of sunset epiphany as Coleridge's 'gentle-hearted Charles', 'struck with deep joy' and 'silent with swimming sense; yea, gazing round / On the wide landscape, gaz[ing] till all doth seem / Less gross than bodily; and of such hues / As veil the Almighty Spirit, when yet he makes / Spirits perceive his presence' (38–43). To the visionary eye of Shelley's optimistic narrator, the material world of separate objects and others seems similarly diaphanous, permeated by that 'inmost purple spirit of life' that peeks through the 'rent' clouds as through a torn veil. (Surely, the perverse echo of 'rent' in Maddalo's image of the tortured and enigmatic 'rent heart' cannot be accidental?) The claustrophobic and opaque madhouse – 'windowless, deformed and dreary' – and its 'hoarse' bell will soon challenge Julian's presumptions of unmediated cosmic and fraternal communion.

Other features of the opening scene also point to *This Lime-Tree Bower* as its most important conversational antecedent. Julian's delight in 'all waste / And solitary places', for instance, which is inspired by the dreary wasteland of the Lido – 'a bare strand . . . Matted with thistles and amphibious weeds, / Such as from earth's embrace the salt ooze breeds' (3–6) – ironically realises Coleridge's profession of faith that 'Nature ne'er deserts the wise and pure . . . No waste so vacant, but may well employ / Each faculty of sense, and keep the heart / Awake to Love and Beauty' (60–4). The circumstantial details of the Maniac's soliloquy, however, draw on still another conversational prototype, Coleridge's *Dejection: An Ode*. Thus, the Maniac's 'accents' are said to mingle with those of the 'envious wind' from the 'loud and gusty storm / Hiss[ing] through the window' (295–7), a tuneless parody of the 'dull sobbing draft, that moans and rakes / Upon the strings' of an 'Æolian lute' (6–7) resting, presumably, in a nearby window at the beginning of *Dejection*. In both poems, too, the gradually realised threat of an impending storm (*Dejection*, 1–6, 9–16; *Julian and Maddalo*, 141, 211–15) contributes to the climactic impression of rhetorical frenzy. Near the end of 'Dejection', this oncoming tempest transforms the aeolian harp's desultory melody into 'a scream/Of agony by torture lengthened out' (97–8), the 'rav[ing]' (99) and 'frenzy bold' (109) of a 'Mad Lutanist' (104) who is also a 'mighty Poet' (109).

The Maniac as solitary singer also ironically anticipates Shelley's portrait of the lyric poet in *A Defence of Poetry*, a portrait that is, in large part, indebted to still another Coleridgean conversational antecedent, the 'merry Nightingale' who would 'disburthen his full soul/Of all its music' in *The Nightingale: A Conversation Poem*. Shelley's ideal poet, like Coleridge's unselfconscious nightingale, 'sits in darkness and sings to cheer [his] own solitude with sweet sounds'. 'His auditors', meanwhile, like the narrator, 'Friend', and 'Sister' of Coleridge's poem, 'are as men entranced by the melody of an unseen musician, who feel that they are moved and softened, yet know not whence or why' (Shelley, 1977, p. 486).[5] The Maniac, appropriately, subverts the 'different lore' that Shelley's first-generation mentor would teach – i.e. "Tis the merry Nightingale' – and reverts to his melancholic Miltonic prototype in *Il Penseroso*: 'Most musical, most melancholy' (62). Perched 'on high' (220) behind the 'black bars' (223) of a cage gilded, as it were, with works of art and musical instruments purchased by Maddalo, and far removed from the innocent impulses of Nature, the Maniac sings in the night of his own soul in order to torment rather than delight himself, and his address to the absent Beloved, marked by doubt, despair and an explicit longing for self-affirmation, exposes the presumptuous nostalgia of the lyrical representation of 'otherness' in this poem's first-generation conversational antecedents. Meanwhile, the Maniac's listeners, counterparts to the nightingale-poet's eavesdropping audience in the *Defence*, stand aside, entranced and moved by the jarring discord but unwilling to confront and engage the Maniac in a true conversation.

The resemblances between Shelley's poet/Maniac and poet/nightingale go beyond the circumstantial, however, for the Maniac is not only eloquent, but literally musical as well. Succeeding and contrasting sharply with the 'clap of tortured hands,/Fierce yells and howlings and lamentings keen . . . Moans, shrieks and curses and blaspheming prayers' of the other inmates that greet Julian and Maddalo on their first approach to the madhouse, 'fragments of most touching melody' are suddenly 'heard on high', reports Julian: 'But looking up [I] saw not the singer there' (215–22). Like the poet/nightingale, or Shelley's sky-lark, the Maniac sings invisibly. Meanwhile, pressed against the barred windows of the central courtyard, his fellow inmates are 'on a sudden ... beguiled/Into strange silence, and look[] forth and smile[]/ Hearing sweet sounds' (226–8).

The Maniac's 'unconnected exclamations of ... agony' immediately following his fragmentary song, are similarly 'musical' in their effect on Julian and Maddalo, who go so far as to ensure that the Maniac will remain unconscious of their presence during his performance, like Shelley's nightingale/poet: 'Let us now visit him', urges Maddalo when the singing stops. 'After this strain/ He ever communes with himself again,/And sees nor hears not any' (268–70). In their quieting effect on their respective audiences, moreover, both song and speech recall the 'hoarse' music of the madhouse bell, which can gather together and quell, by summoning to prayer (a silent, introspective 'comment' on 'the text' of one's own heart), the inmates shrieking and jibbering below.[6]

By means of such extended analogies between tolling, song and lyric, Shelley highlights the purely musical – that is, the expressive and non-referential – features of all three forms of 'discourse': they do not so much convey to auditors and observers a clearly discernible message or coherent narrative as entrance and thereby paralyse them. Like his own music, but even more like the monotonous and wordless music of the bell, the Maniac's 'unmodulated, cold, expressionless' (292) speech has communal power to silence and pacify, but none, apparently, to inform or refer. His words belong to the 'literature of power', not 'knowledge'; they summon the 'thoughts and ... desires' of his listeners, sane as well as insane, 'to meet ... Round the rent heart and pray,' but 'For what? they know not'.

In the anti-pastoral universe of *Julian and Maddalo*, impassioned lyrical utterance, like a virtuoso musical performance, arrests conversation, creating a *communion* of hearts that can be maintained only in the momentary lapse of a *community* of conversationally individuated minds. Shelley's imprisoned nightingale/poet and his silent audience thus bear witness to the disintegration of a pastoral ideal of mutually compatible lyrical (transparent) and conversational (engaged) discourses, a disintegration anticipated, in turn, by the monologic 'conversations' of the first-generation conversation poems to which Shelley alludes throughout *Julian and Maddalo*.

If the Maniac is a version of Shelley, as has often been taken for granted,[7] then he is Shelley textualised, a portrait of the artist as monologic conversationalist, a voice that can be 'read', not engaged. As Kelvin Everest points out, the Maniac's discursive isolation corresponds to his maker's own sense, in 1818 and 1819, of spiritual 'exile' from the arena of critical and political discourse in England; the Maniac embodies the poet's frustration at his 'failure to achieve an audience' (Everest, 1983, p. 83). If we accept Everest's interpretation, then in the Maniac's situation Shelley seems to have anticipated precisely the sentimental, apolitical and disengaged response to his poetry that largely prevailed for the rest of the century, a period during which emotional communion with (or repugnance to) the poet's represented persona came to replace rather than reinforce conversational community. As a result, true dialectic, the critical resistance of soul to soul that tends to stabilise language as a tool for the achievement of common goals, became impossible. Shelley's ideas were long considered not worth the effort of such an engagement.

IV. CONCLUSION

The discursive scepticism evinced in *Julian and Maddalo* reflects one half of Shelley's profoundly divided attitude towards language as a means of liberation. On the one hand, as in *Prometheus Unbound* (e.g., II.iv.72–4; IV.415–17), the poet professes the belief that language is fundamentally constitutive of – and therefore, in an unfallen state, transparent to – thought. Language is *Logos*; words are, ideally, the Word. Moreover, since nothing exists except as it is perceived, the entire universe of perception and intellection could be posited as a function of language and a reflection of its degree of creative, transformative freedom. In a fallen world, however, this priority of language is apparently forgotten, and the universe of things, which is assumed to exist independent of perception, comes to restrict the ideational and referential range of language.[8] Language itself becomes a material thing, opaque rather than transparent to the now-alienated 'text' of world and heart. In *Julian and Maddalo* Shelley seems to be acknowledging the limitations of this fallen state, where language becomes a Jamesonian prison-house for the individual soul, and even the most sympathetic dialogue, such as that between Julian and Maddalo in the opening scene, must lead eventually to disunion and distinction, the heightening rather than erasure of contrasts in personality and outlook. Unlike the logoistic 'Life' of which Coleridge's creaking rook 'tells' poet and friend alike, ordinary words serve ultimately to differentiate rather than to identify mind and mind.

But precisely because they are material things, words provide the only real point of meeting between mind and mind, and therefore the only hope of transforming this fallen world into something at least approximating the ideal world envisioned by the poet's liberated imagination. Ronald Tetreault has argued that Shelley came to recognise the apocalyptic efficacy of fallen language when used as a dialectical tool, a communal construct making thoughts 'things' – material words with shared meanings (Tetreault, 1987, pp. 11–15). If so, then *Julian and Maddalo* registers the poet's critique of the Romantic lyrical circumvention of such dialectical engagements, his realisation that avoiding the resistance of another's speech impedes not only communication, but also self-understanding. Even Julian admits that, were he to stay in Venice, Maddalo's 'wit/And subtle talk would . . . make me know myself' (559–61), presumably as much because of as despite their points of intellectual disagreement.

Julian can, nonetheless, be so moved by the Maniac's overheard speech as to declare, in a poem celebrating his friendship with Maddalo, 'Never saw I one whom I could call/More willingly my friend' (576–7). In Julian's empathic instability, Shelley demonstrates the extent to which feelings of sympathy and solidarity remain wishful unless they are tested in the crucible of real discussion, with its give-and-take, its resistance to private interpretative appropriations. Quite at odds with first-generation assumptions that connectedness can be achieved simply through the expression of the poetic imagination and the affirmation of the 'one Life' in which that faculty partakes, Shelley seems to be suggesting, in *Julian and Maddalo*, that unselfconscious expression, which invites us to cast our own emotional shadows on the opaque surface of another's speech, is something distinct from true 'conversation', in which the object of our affection continually checks our tendency to appropriate his or her utterances in our impatient attempts to transcend individual differences. The apostrophic, one-sided 'conversation' of the conversation poems, meant to satisfy the Romantic poet's nostalgia for otherness, not only cannot roll away the stone of fallen language that obstructs the discourse of the millenium, but delays our recognition that the New Jerusalem is to be built upon that stubborn rock.

8

Self, Beauty and Horror: Shelley's Medusa Moment

William Hildebrand

Shelley's *On the Medusa of Leonardo da Vinci in the Florentine Gallery* has always been something of an odd-man-out among his poems. He probably drafted it at the end of 1819, but when he drowned two and a half years later he still had not bothered to fine-tune it and supply the two missing words. Mary, however, thought highly of it, and included it in her first collection of his works, *Posthumous Poems* (1824). At the time of its conception, the Shelleys were living in Florence and, having just finished *The Cenci* and, as he thought then, *Prometheus Unbound*, Shelley was much engrossed in the contemplation of classical sculpture, not of painting. He seems, indeed, never to have been deeply taken with Renaissance painting or sculpture. Given his keener responsiveness to sculpture, one would expect that the Florentine Medusa head most likely to catch his creative eye would be the one held by Cellini's beautiful *Perseo* in the Loggia dei Lanzi, too close to the Uffizi for Shelley to miss it, and too near in name not to chime in his ear. Yet it was the painting, then attributed to Leonardo, that inspired his finest pictorial poem.

The basilisk glare of its sensational subject fascinated Victorian aesthetes like Swinburne and Pater. In the 1930s, the poem prompted Mario Praz to declare it a 'manifesto' of the 'peculiar' Romantic 'conception of Beauty' (Praz, 1956, p. 26). One would think that its being bundled, forcibly or not, with nineteenth-century Decadents, and that its seamy reputation for expressing, in Douglas Bush's phrase, of 'many sadistic imaginings' (Bush, 1963, p. 135), would have increased its currency, but unlike some other fragments, it has never found a firm footing in the canon, being anthologised infrequently and available usually only in complete editions.

Whatever one might say of Praz's thesis that the Romantics

cultivated a dark sensibility in which the Horrid is an essential element in the Beautiful (Praz, 1956, p. 27), or of the implication that the poem is, in Shelley's own words in the poem, a celebration of 'the tempestuous loveliness of terror' (33), an exercise in aesthetic luxury, its validity can be vetted by comparing *Medusa* to his best-known statement on beauty, *Hymn to Intellectual Beauty*.[1] Despite obvious differences, the two works display certain common elements that give them a dialectical relation that opens an interesting perspective on some of Shelley's most compelling concerns in 1818–19, when the Should Be or May Be of dream was being threatened by the 'sad reality' of necessity: the problematic of self and of evil and the duplicity of consciousness. Indeed, that perspective, which I shall call the Medusa moment, argues forcefully for *Medusa* as one of Shelley's most subtle and powerful lyrics and as an essential work in understanding his poetry of reflexivity and the modalities of the self and evil.

In addition to sharing a striking number of key words and concepts (beauty, loveliness, shadow, shine, grace, light, hue, cave, poisonous, harmonious; music/strain, grave/death), both *Hymn* and *Medusa* centre on the perception of beauty, its nature and power. Moreover, both use musical images for the action of beauty and set the experience of beauty against similar contrasting backdrops of existential vacancy, gothic desolation, and midnight gloom, symbolic of what is at stake. In *Hymn* beauty is immortal, in *Medusa* it is profoundly mortal, and although awe figures in both poems, it is central to *Medusa* but only peripheral to *Hymn*. It is, however, the symbol of the shadow of beauty that is decisive in establishing the dialectic. *Hymn* represents the perception of beauty under the figure of a winged Spirit whose shadow floats 'unseen amongst us', its 'inconstant glance' illuminating 'each human heart and countenance' (2–7) with an ecstatic sense of the beauty, truth, and goodness of life. Only in moments of the presencing of ideal beauty to the self, when its shadow falls, as it once fell on Shelley's young self, is life not a 'dark reality' (48). Paradoxically, the overshadow figure is equally significant in *Medusa*, where 'Loveliness like a shadow' 'seems to lie' (5–6) on the eyelids and lips of the head of Medusa, giving it the 'grace' that hardens the gazer's spirit (9–10); the shadow is repeated in the second stanza in the image of the 'melodious hue of beauty', where 'hue' means phantasm or appearance.

Two differences stand out: the self's relation to the source of the

experience and the effect of the experience on the self. *Hymn* posits
the Spirit as above or outside consciousness. The overshadow is
metaphorical of beauty perceived as immanent and assumed to be
transcendent; this sudden sense of beauty impinging on consciousness is Shelley's aesthetic *analogia entis*, although such images as a
'train' of shadow-thoughts (41) smack more of Locke than of
Aquinas. (*Mont Blanc*, its epistemological and chronological companion poem, also treats the act of perception, albeit from a clearly
sceptical standpoint, and uses similar imagery of floating, bird-
winged shadow-thoughts, but its mode is essentially reflective and
its concern more epistemological than existential. *Hymn* represents
the passionate immediacy of an experience transmuted by imagination: trusting consciousness, the self hypostatises the perception
and assumes the truth of desire – that beauty has objective
existence.) In *Medusa*, however, the locus of critical concern is not
on beauty above human consciousness but on what is 'underneath'
(7) the shadow of beauty, within Medusa's head. The second
difference is in beauty's power. This is manifest in the word
Shelley uses in both poems to express the attractive point of
interface between self and beauty: grace. In *Hymn* grace conse-
crates life, lending it truth, enabling love, instilling hope, inducing
harmony; in *Medusa* it fascinates and petrifies the self. Thus *Hymn*
centres on the bleakness of the world without beauty's grace,
Medusa on the mortifying effect on the self of beauty's grace. These
differences suggest that *Medusa* is a kind of demonic mirror-image
of *Hymn*: Narcissus looking into the fountain and seeing Medusa
staring out at him.

Although Shelley often uses shadow figures in a loosely Platonic
sense, especially after his rediscovery of Plato via Peacock in 1817,
the overshadow in *Hymn* and *Medusa* most likely comes from the
traditional metaphor in Luke's account of the annunciation – 'The
Holy Ghost shall come upon thee,' Gabriel tells Mary, 'and the
power of the Highest shall overshadow thee' (Luke, 1.35) – which
Milton echoes in *Paradise Lost* (7.165). It is a variant of the Old
Testament formula for God's grace as living under the shadow of
His wings (e.g. Malachi, 4.2; Isaiah, 18.8, 18.1; Psalms, 17.8, 36.7,
etc.; Job, 17.8, 36.7). Although *Hymn* seems to be Shelley's first use
of the overshadow as emblematic of inspiration and presence, one
can see him moving by almost measured degrees towards it in his
earlier writings, especially in his letters to Elizabeth Hitchener and
Thomas Jefferson Hogg in 1811. Once found, it became an idol of

his thought, a constitutional symbol in such works as *The Revolt of Islam*, *To Constantia*, *Prometheus Unbound* and *Epipsychidion*, nearly always in relation to beauty and love, as in this *Revolt of Islam* variant of the opening of *Hymn*: 'the shadow which doth float unseen, / But not unfelt, o'er blind mortality' (2659–60). Its attraction for Shelley came in part from his sceptical epistemology, according to which the mind is passive relative to sensory experience, and in part from his sedulous cultivation *à la* Rousseau of the habit of autoerotic reverie, which is reflected in his pervasive formula of the ideal woman bending over her dreaming lover.

This habit, in which experience is dimmed by desire and volatilised by imagination, gave Shelley the substance of *Alastor*, where he explores the problematic of self-reflection through the Poet's vain pursuit of the 'bright shadow' of his 'lovely dream' (233). Throughout the poem Shelley uses 'shadow' and 'image' interchangeably, precisely as Ovid uses 'umbra' and 'imago' in the story of Narcissus (Vinge, 1967, pp. 12–13). But far more urgently than Ovid, whose story he adapts, Shelley touches the deeper, demonic registers of the theme, making the 'mighty Shadow' of Death (306) the medium by which the Poet hopes to find the Veiled Maiden's shadow, the pure image of self that came upon his sleep and evanesced in his embrace, leaving the world leached of meaning and value.

The Narcissus experience, the critical moment in self-reflection, arises when the self realises that the beautiful object of its desire means its death; that the desire to be at once pure, discarnate spirit and to see or know oneself as such (hence the image) is to love and be a nothing. This moment is characterised subjectively by absolute ambivalence, by feelings of sympathetic antipathy and antipathetic sympathy, and objectively by absolute ambiguity. We can observe the subjective element of this moment when the Poet of *Alastor*, delivered from the whirlpool in the Caucasus, comes to a bower where narcissi, the flowers planted on Enna to lure Persephone into the Land of Shadows, 'For ever gaze on their own drooping eyes' (407). In the bower but, significantly, under 'the gaze of noon' (468) – the biblical symbol of the sun of justice (*sol iustitiae*) which Milton uses for the temptation and fall in *Paradise Lost* – the Poet looks into the well:

> His eyes beheld
> Their own wan light through the reflected lines
> Of his thin hair, distinct in the dark depth

> Of that still fountain; as the human heart,
> Gazing in dreams over the gloomy grave,
> Sees its own treacherous likeness there.
>
> (469–74)

What should be a peripeteia passes, however, because the Poet chooses to obey 'the light' of his soul radiating from his own 'two starry eyes' mirrored in the well (490–3). Although the figure of the heart betraying itself to death by self-reflection and the instructional aim of the Preface indicate Shelley's trepidations about the self and desire, *Alastor* ultimately is an equivocal utterance: the concluding exaltation of the Poet hardly bears out the Preface's intention of warning 'actual men' against 'self-centered seclusion' (69); nor does the narrator's ranting in the poem at the 'worms / And beasts and men' who survive the Poet (691–2).

At this time, it seems, Shelley might apprehend some of the dangers in a headlong commitment of self to possibility, but he could not bring himself wholeheartedly to affirm or even accept actuality; nor is there any evidence that his vehement idealism would permit him to see, as Kierkegaard would somewhat later, the tension between the two as potentially positive. This predicament betrays an inner conflict within Shelley's attitude towards the self that he explores in subsequent poems through the triple figure of the shadow: the overshadow, the shadow-self, and the undershadow. All three are present embryonically in *Alastor* and appear in various guises in other poems that I shall mention for purposes of illustration rather than of systematic exposition.[2]

First, the Veiled Maiden represents the overshadow, the pure ideal of the self's desire for eternal love and beauty and the reflex of its negative judgement of actuality; she stands in the same spatial and ontological relation to and has the same decisive effect on the Poet as that of beauty to Shelley in *Hymn*. Her lineage includes Panthea, Asia, Emily, and the Shape all Light in *Triumph of Life*.

Second, the Poet's 'spectral form', the 'glare' of his 'wild eyes', from which infants shrink as from the evil eye (262–4), and his sensing a 'fair fiend' beside him (297) luring him towards death, constellate the shadow-self, the sense of the self as divided and haunted. This figure reflects the duplicity of consciousness which, like Narcissus' fountain, displays an ambiguous, irresistible image of a possible something that is an actual nothing. The shadow-self makes an interesting early appearance in *To—*, which Shelley published with *Alastor* and addressed presumably to himself: here the self is 'changed to a foul fiend' that haunts him like a 'shadow' (30–2) because, forsaking the ideal creations of his own mind, he built his 'hope/On the false earth's inconstancy' (19–20). But Shelley, without losing his conviction of the 'false earth's inconstancy', began to find it ever harder to keep afloat his faith in the ideal, especially after the train of personal calamities that rolled over him during his first year or so in Italy: the death of his daughter in September 1818, the growing estrangement of his wife, and the death of his son in July 1819, while he was writing *The Cenci*. Throughout this period the shadow-self appears frequently in poems both major (Jupiter is Prometheus' shadow) and minor (*Invocation to Misery*), often in the context of exploring the caverns of the mind or heart.

The final permutation of the shadow is the undershadow, which, broadly speaking, stands for the self's capacity to delude and destroy. Ideal beauty, which first fell as grace from above (*Hymn*), then turned into a tormenting shadow beside the self (the Maniac and his lady in *Julian and Maddalo*), now becomes the riveting medium of evil. *Alastor* anticipates the undershadow in the following description of the Poet's decision to seek death on the ocean in the hope of finding his dream:

> For sleep, he knew, kept most relentlessly
> Its precious charge, and silent death exposed,
> Faithless perhaps as sleep, a shadowy lure,
> With doubtful smile mocking its own strange charms.
> (292–5)

The 'strange charms' of the 'shadowy lure' of death, so resonant with Medusan forebodings, also adumbrate the antipathetic-sympathetic relation of the self to beauty and terror that Shelley observes in the Preface to *The Cenci* and dramatises in the evil eye pattern and the incestuous relations of father and daughter, and internalises in the person of the 'Fair and yet terrible' Beatrice (I.iii.166). Although the Preface affirms the ideal of self-knowledge as salvific, Shelley's real interest in the play is in the non-visionary self, specifically in the dynamic of the mode of self-reflection he calls self-anatomy, which leads to the dizzy brink of the abyss within: the undershadow.

The paradox of beauty and terror, especially their intriguing, interpenetrating relation, was on Shelley's mind earlier in 1819 when, writing to Peacock on 25 February after visiting the Sistine Chapel, he disparaged the depiction of Jesus in the 'Day of Judgement'. For want of a 'sense of beauty', Shelley writes, Michelangelo failed to reveal the 'calm severe awe-inspiring majesty', the 'terrible yet lovely' quality required by the subject: 'For what', he asks, 'is terror without a contrast with & a connection with loveliness?' Michelangelo's 'real sphere', he goes on, is 'Hell & Death', and Shelley's ensuing sketch of that portion of the great painting – the 'cavern' in the 'lofty rock' thronged with devils conveying spirits of the damned, the 'bloodred light of the fiery abyss', the doomed 'chained in all forms of agony by knotted serpents, & writhing on the crags in every variety of torture' (Shelley, 1964, II, pp. 80–1) – suggests that, in a spiritual even more than in an aesthetic sense, it was becoming Shelley's 'real sphere' also. His characterisation in *The Cenci* Preface of one mode of Protestant theology as 'a gloomy passion for penetrating the impenetrable mysteries of our being, which terrifies its possessor at the darkness of the abyss to the brink of which it has conducted him' (Shelley, 1977, p. 240) has some of the lineaments of a self-portrait.

Near year's end in Florence, the oddly hypnotic imagery of 'Hell & Death' in the 'Day of Judgement' – the cavern, the fiery light of the abyss, the writhing forms of agony and torture, the knotted serpents – arrested his eye again, this time in the decapitated head of Medusa. The coincidence of these horrific details in paintings about the day of Judgement and Medusa, bracketing as they did his exploration of the 'most dark and secret caverns of the human heart' in *The Cenci* (Shelley, 1977, p. 239), sharply refocused his attention on the demonic aspect of self-reflection concentrated in the tradition of the evil eye, which he had used in *The Cenci* to symbolise the contagion of evil.

Shelley's growing consciousness of the human costliness of his high idealism is a major source of the pressures impelling his brilliant probings of the problematic of self and desire during his early Italian period. To assess these costs with any measure of accuracy, we must recall that the personal calamities that befell him and his family in 1818–19 followed hard on the heels of several equally desolating occurrences earlier in England, principally his loss of parental rights to his children by Harriet after her suicide, a blow that plunged him into a 'deep agony' (Peacock, 1970, p. 68) of guilt and grief. His poetry during these Italian years reflects also his doubts about the dark side of the self-love in which his metaphysic was grounded. The self-affirmation and fulfilment of his idealism, especially in the erotic component so attractive to his ardent nature, means that personal human relations can only be transitional stages and can have only instrumental value for the desiring self, no matter how noble or high-minded its motives. For self-realisation is both means and end: the means are the goal, others merely means to the goal. (This arises from a prime assumption of idealism, the identification of subject and object.) In the electric circuitry of eros, the desiring self and the object of desire are ultimately one and the same. Thus a major burden of Shelley's poems about the 'sad reality' is his inability to find in actuality the ideal beauty that is also love, which means that each person he desires – a Harriet, a Mary, a Claire, and soon an Emilia – can only be but a brief embodiment of the eternal image forged in his passionate heart, a moment in his own self-actualisation. Hence the cadence of Shelley's life and poetry is one of rapture and regret, of the bliss of desire followed by the break of hearts.

What he had grasped intellectually and envisioned in *Alastor*, then, he was now coming painfully to face and suffer on a more immediate, existential level. The 'error' of his erotic history, he would confide to John Gisborne on 18 June 1822, in the bleak aftervacancy of the Emilia Viviani episode, 'consists in seeking in a mortal image the likeness of what is perhaps eternal' (Shelley, 1964, II, p. 434). To speak more generally, Shelley's awareness of the great gulf between ideality and actuality was making him acutely sensitive to the limitations of a predominantly aesthetic consciousness, which opposes a changeless world of pure images to a changing world of impure things. Witness his wistful apology in the Dedication to *The Cenci* to the effect that all his previous poetry was no more 'than visions' that impersonated his 'apprehensions of the beautiful and just' (Shelley, 1977, p. 237). The order of listing – first the beautiful, then the just – indicates the primacy of the aesthetic category over the ethical. The *Medusa* poem suggests that the increasing strain he was feeling between the counterpresses of possibility and necessity was cracking the 'frame of his conceptions' (Shelley, 1977, p. 69) and that the fault line was in his conception of beauty.

To take *Hymn* again as typical, the beauty he had experienced and conceptualised hitherto had, in its subjective value, been characterised by rapture, bliss and joy, as if the only face beauty had presented to his perception had been a gracious and beatific one. These qualities are, in the aesthetic consciousness, analogous to what Rudolph Otto identifies with the *fascinans* component in the experience of the religious numinous (Otto, 1967, *passim*). Although the beauty Shelley describes in *Hymn* and in *Medusa* is non-natural, there is good reason for resisting the temptation of categorical logic, which is to take the analogy a step further and conclude that *Medusa* represents an experience of the aesthetic sublime, which has a 'hidden kinship' with the religious numinous (Otto, 1967, p. 63). Rather, the inversion of subjective values we notice when moving from *Hymn* to *Medusa* indicates, among other things, the impotence of either the psychological or the aesthetic category to contain or account for the primordial experience Shelley struggles to express in *Medusa*. For what was rapture in *Hymn* becomes astonishment in *Medusa*; what was bliss becomes horror; what was grace becomes 'inextricable error' (35) – and all occurs under the aegis of 'divine' beauty (4).

These are some of the co-ordinates by which we can chart Shelley's passage from a set of aesthetically reflected natural feelings analogous to elements in the religious numinous – that is, from the aesthetic counterparts of the *mysterium fascinans*: rapture, bliss, grace – to the *mysterium tremendum*, which the poem calls 'horror' or 'terror'. What is at issue, however, is not the case of a set of natural or aesthetic feelings, like those that animated Shelley's gymnastic gothicising and ghost-hunting, changing by insensible degrees into religious ones. It is rather a case of his moving from one order of experience to an order of an entirely different kind. (This disarms alike the sensual aestheticism of Swinburne and Pater and the suave psychologism of Praz and Bush.) Nor is it so surprising that such a shift should take place, if we recall that *Hymn* is to a high degree a poem about the anguished religious strivings of a self that has categorically rejected religion and that his strivings are less with beauty's inconstancy than with its 'mystery' (13), its otherness.

In *Medusa* the critical term indicating this shift is the phrase 'inextricable error', which seems to refer back to the sudden identification of horror and beauty as 'the tempestuous loveliness of terror'. But, grammatical logic aside, this is an explanation that explains nothing. In this regard *Medusa* is a paradox about a paradox, for there is about certain key parts of it an overplus of passion and meaning, an urgent incommensurateness, an uncouth sense of straining to say something that must be said but cannot be said directly, just as the paradoxicalness of terror and beauty points beyond itself to something that must be faced but cannot be faced directly, only reflected or deflected; or, perhaps more to the point, it is something that must be resisted but cannot be.

The subtle strategies of *Medusa* are rooted in the duplicities common alike to consciousness and to art. *Medusa* replicates the process of self-involution in which subject turns to object: to gaze at it is somehow suddenly to be gazed at. It commences with a sense of self-duplicity: at first it seems in tone and diction to be simply a more carefully considered and crafted version of the *Notes on Sculpture and Painting*, of the epistolary impressions of the graphic arts Shelley mailed to Peacock in England during this period: a concentrated, imaginative re-creation of both a visual perception and human feeling. But in transit from the first to the second stanzas, we suddenly sense it becoming something else – a representation of the experience Perseus avoided only with the help of his mirror-shield and the amulet eye of the Graeciae, that of gazing directly at the beautiful, still image of the Medusa. Then we realise that what seemed at first to be the detached descriptive tone and measured syntax appropriate to a connoisseur's reflection is in fact the numbed reaction to a spell of dizziness. *Medusa* becomes, in other words, a vertiginous experience of something unreflected, unmediated, ultimate.

Three patterns of imagery and movement – light, reflection, and involution – organise each of the five stanzas: the 'fiery' and 'lurid' light (7) radiating from Medusa's eyes and lips is reflected by turns in its terrifying effect on the midnight sky, the gazer's spirit, the serpent-locks, the senseless bat startled from the cavern just cleft in the rock, and the surrounding air vaporised into a shifting mirror. Although only the second stanza engages the gazer's self explicitly, the action of the entire poem represents the working of his consciousness in its agony to make sense of what is before his stupefied eyes: the incommensurateness of the horror and the beauty, which it first perceives as discrete properties of Medusa's head but finally apprehends and identifies as one and the same. Shelley represents this movement of consciousness as the process of involution, as with growing urgency in each stanza the 'hideous light' (29) compels the gazer's attention to move from the divine beauty overshadowing Medusa's countenance to the divine horror within.

What the myth objectifies as action, Shelley internalises; it is not the life of the body that is at stake but that of the spirit or self. The dynamic of involution is in the second stanza:

> Yet it is less the horror than the grace
> Which turns the gazer's spirit into stone,
> Whereon the lineaments of that dead face
> Are graven, till the characters be grown
> Into itself, and thought no more can trace . . .
>   (9–13)

It is then repeated in the next stanza in the image of the 'unending involutions' of the viper-hairs interlocking (21). Shelley's perception of this meaning of the myth, which Ovid rationalises, prompts the speculation that he had looked closely at Cellini's bronze *Perseo* after all and, further, that he had observed the striking, mirror-like similarity of Perseus' curly head in profile to snake-haired Medusa's (Siebers, 1983, pp. 12–13), and that this had suggested to him the fissiparous process of self-reflection in the Medusa myth. Shelley treats the encounter with the Medusa head as the fatal moment in self-reflection, with the result that *Medusa* becomes something more than a study of the relation of beauty and terror or even of self-reflection.

The paradox of *Medusa*, as epitomised in the enigmatic 'inextricable error', suggests that the strange pleasure of gazing at the painting of Medusa's beautiful dead head, like the pleasure of contemplating the themes of incest and parricide in the Cenci story, reveals beauty to be the inner filiation between self and horror. It also suggests that the horror is death, for it is somehow the agony 'underneath' the beauty that engraves Medusa's features into the self mortified by 'grace', transfiguring it into its own deathly image.

Clearly, Shelley's attitude towards beauty here is far more complicated, even conflicted, than in *Hymn*, so much so as to be contradictory. This contradictoriness, however, is intrinsic to the nature of beauty as well as of love in idealistic thought, classical and modern. For, positively, ideal beauty means a perfect state of immortal being; negatively, the attainment of this state means extinction of the personal self, ideal beauty being by definition – as it certainly is for Shelley – impersonal beauty. Moreover, even if attainment of ideal beauty means liberation from existential grief, it is the individual self which measures grief by joy that is quenched and, with it, all personal joy as well as grief. Because of the self-circuitry of eros, the self that posits and pursues ideal beauty is seeking its own death. Thus the shadow of beauty, so positive in *Hymn*, becomes positively negative or demonic in *Medusa*, which represents an awful apprehension of that which ideal beauty lacks, of the nothingness that shadows it. This uncanny grace is the source of the dread in the poem.

That dread is ontological dread: the dread of something Other that must be resisted but cannot be. Although this something certainly includes the conflict of life and death, as the extra stanza in the manuscript suggests (Rogers, 1961, p. 10), it would be mistaken to conclude that *Medusa* is ultimately about the self's natural fear of and attraction for death. Such an essentially psycho-aesthetic reading would misjudge the kind, intensity, and magnitude of the dread, which the poem concentrates in the power of the evil eye.

Building the pressures of *Medusa* slowly, Shelley withholds any direct reference to evil until the third stanza, where, in the dull, flat accents of despair, he notes a 'poisonous eft' peeping 'idly' into Medusa's 'Gorgonian eyes' (25–6), which effectively multiplies by number as well as reflection the action of the evil eye, since efts, like vipers, traditionally have evil eyes. Next, he registers the power of those Gorgonian eyes: the 'hideous light', which has just cleft a cave in the rock, now ignites the midnight sky with a 'light more dread than obscurity' (29–32). Then, in an intuitive leap, he identifies the dread light as 'the tempestuous loveliness of terror', as he realises that the 'brazen glare' of the 'serpent-locks' was 'Kindled by that inextricable error, / Which makes a thrilling vapour of the air' into an 'ever-shifting mirror' reflecting the beauty and terror of Medusa: 'A woman's countenance, with serpent-locks, / Gazing in death on Heaven' (33–40).

With this expansive, sculpturesque image *Medusa* surpasses natural fear, terror, and awe. Only the language of apocalypse is appropriate to a vision in which reflection becomes judgement: or, more precisely, reflection on all levels is put under judgement. While the trembling mirror of air multiplies reflexively the terror and beauty of her face throughout the atmosphere, Medusa's mortifying and mortified eyes gaze up at Heaven, a monumental mirror-image of the relation between the gazer's petrified spirit and Medusa (see *Alastor*, 645ff.). Within the context of Shelley's concern with the self, one meaning to be distilled from this vision is that the self is discovered to be under judgement: that it belongs to the category of judgement and thus is to be judged. The passive voice is appropriate because what *Medusa* is trying to say, it cannot say directly, in the sense that the experience it works to express is only one part of an aborted process. The nature of this process must be a matter for speculation, but *Medusa* does suggest a path of approach in the description of the stages of Medusan evil: first, the self is hardened by her grace; next, the light kindled by the 'inextricable error' engraves her features onto the stony self until, in effect, her eyes gaze at her self as the gazer gazes at his self – an infinite reflection that 'thought no more can trace' (13).

This two-fold process recalls Otto's account of the two principal moments in the numinous consciousness: the *fascinans*, which is the 'stupor' of dizziness and insensibility, of benumbed amazement in the presence of the numinous; and the 'tremor' or dread, the double feeling of overwhelming awe before the numinous and of personal 'disvaluation' at its utter incommensurateness relative to the creaturely self, which thus feels reduced to 'nothingness' (Otto, 1967, pp. 26, 50). To illustrate the difference between the moments, Otto cites Mark, 10.32: 'And they were in the way going up to Jerusalem; and Jesus went before them; and they were *amazed*; and as they followed, they were *afraid*' (Otto, 1967, p. 50; my italics). Each moment, Otto says, can effect a rich diversity of kinds and degrees of feelings. Thus, the most profound response to the *fascinans* experience is the feeling of 'grace', which is the value it carries in *Medusa*, but with the difference that Medusa's grace strikes the gazer as evil. *Medusa* also displays graphically the negative power of the *mysterium tremendum*, the power to destroy the self, to engrave the Gorgon's features on the petrified spirit.

Significantly, *Medusa* stops here. It has nothing to say about the positive effect of dread, which commences in a sense of the transcendence of the Other accompanied by a corresponding feeling of creaturely unworthiness, then modulates into an awareness of sin, and culminates in the sublimity of the sanctus, the prayer of praise to the Holy, affirming the numinous to be both ontologically superior and morally good (Otto, 1967, pp. 51–2). The conspicuous absence of the positive stage is like the Sherlock Holmes dog that did not bark when it sould have, a clue to understanding both the sense and the referential meaning of *Medusa*. It returns us to the point of rupture in the process.

That point is at the medium stage in the dialectic of dread, in the sense of sinfulness: this is an intense consciousness of creaturely profaneness and unworthiness which is over and against the numinous, not particular transgressions (Otto, 1967, p. 51). Sin is associated with another mode of dread, the *ira deorum*, the formula of the Wrath of God in the Old Testament which Otto likens to the random discharge of 'stored-up electricity'; in the experience of Wrath, the supernatural and suprarational numinous 'throbs and gleams, palpable and visible' and terrible (Otto, 1967, pp. 18–19). Wrath is, in effect, the only face of God that sin can see.

This Wrath is almost viscerally palpable in *Medusa*. Its furious presence radiates from the energy of the autopsychological imagery of abysmal, baleful light, of self-convulsion, of an imprescriptible agony of spirit, which suggests that if dread is the sense of *Medusa*, then that dread refers to an unmediated experience of Wrath. What is not explicit, however, is the correlative consciousness of sin. In this regard, the sense of strain, of an excess of meaning that the poem cannot quite discharge or articulate comes, I would suggest, from a rejection or deflection of the sense of sin, a rejection that is implied in one of the possible meanings of the ambiguous, concluding image: Medusa gazing up at Heaven in stony defiance. Yet Shelley's internalisation of the Medusa moment makes the act of self-exploration and discovery into an experience of evil, a process of hardening unto death, which suggests that the self that discovers itself to be evil is the demonic self that must come under judgement. There are, nonetheless, certain clear traces of the state of sin in the poem. All the leading images collaborate to orchestrate an affrighted sense of the self as mortified, hardened to death in its brokenness, its self-concentration and autonomy, as inhumanly forlorn in its own penal solitudes, and as being brought under judgement. This much is implicit in the last two stanzas in the crepuscular 'light more dread than obscurity', which suggests the fiery abyss beneath and within; in Medusa's decapitated head gazing up at Heaven as her broken self-images spread meaninglessly throughout the frame of things; and in the conjunction of the 'brazen glare' of the serpents with the 'inextricable error', which evokes the Garden, the fall, and the consequent intermingling of good and evil.

The suggestion that the consciousness of sin is rejected or blocked in *Medusa* accords, of course, with Shelley's peculiarly vehement aversion to remorse and self-examination, as Earl

Wasserman (1971) has determined them in his construction of Shelley's metaphysic. Introspection or self-anatomy is to be shunned because it leads not to self-knowledge but to self-contempt and reproach; to 'loathe' one's own 'crime' is as wrong as loathing the 'crime' of another, both acts stemming from the 'dark idolatry of self' (*Revolt of Islam*, 3388–90). In Shelley's thought, one is not to take full moral responsibility for acts of what Wasserman calls the 'mortal self' (Wasserman, 1971, p. 182), the existential, personal self; for only the true self, immortal and impersonal, matters, and it is categorically incapable of evil. Salvation comes from true self-knowledge, which is knowing that the true self is part of the unknowable, problematical One Mind and that evil is extrinsic to it, evil's source being what Wasserman infers to be a 'continuously potential transcendent force' (Wasserman, 1971, p. 110) that works through the craven will, which mean perhaps no more than that at times Shelley uses gnostic formulations.

Self-idolatry is, then, the mistake of taking one's perishable nature seriously and, ignoring the true self, feeling guilty for one's actions, which leads in turn to the conviction that one is evil, thence to self-contempt and hatred, that amphisbaenic snake (also part of the evil-eye tradition) that kills both others and oneself (*Revolt of Islam*, 3379–87). The opposite of self-contempt is self-esteem, the possession of which, in the words of *The Cenci* Preface, necessarily makes one 'wise, just, sincere, tolerant and kind' (Shelley, 1977, p. 240); but of even greater emotional import-ance, I suspect, to Shelley's utopian idealism, it liberates one from the imprisoning past of guilt and opens up a hopeful future (*Revolt of Islam*, 3392–6). For aspiring idealism, the desire to be forever in the subjunctive mode, must have at least the horizontal sublime, the boundless future for unfettered dreaming. In a very real sense, then, everything depends on avoiding a sense of 'inextricable error' or sin, on resisting that which is irresistibly fascinating – in this case, the grace of Medusa. The true self must be protected at all costs, otherwise all hope of self-autonomy is gone.

Despite Shelley's contrary theory, however, *Medusa*, like *The Cenci*, shows the self as having, as it were, an abyss of potential evil within that exercises an urgent fascination. (Medusa's classical identity as Queen of Hell is part of the poem's originary.) This suggests strongly that evil is somehow within or contiguous with the self and that to confront that self, to look oneself in the eye, is to recognise one's own evil, to realise the self as involved in evil.

But what is that self? According to Wasserman's reading of Shelley's thought, the self in *Medusa* would be the 'mortal self' undergoing self-conviction of evil. But this, I think, misjudges the meaning of the Wrath in the poem by sticking too closely to Shelley's own self-understanding. Assuming the approximate rightness of the context we have been considering – the biographical context of Shelley's being pressed beyond the aesthetic consciousness by his life experiences and the collateral context of his concern with the problematic of self as expressed in the auto-psychological symbols in his poetry as well as in the 'Hell & Death' imagery in the paintings of the Day of Judgement and Medusa – I would hazard that the self involved in the Medusan experience is not the Shelleyan 'mortal self', but rather the true self, the ideal self of his desire for ideal beauty. The lines of force in his examination of self-reflection and the duplicity of consciousness, running from the Narcissus moment, through the permutations of the triple shadow figure, and culminating in the encounter with Wrath in the Medusa moment, argue that in *Medusa* Shelley represents the instant of recognition when the ideal self is discovered to be or turns into the false self: that is, the demonic self of desire that seduces the mortal, actual self out of life into a reflected world of beautiful, still, and dead images.

The mystery of Medusa is that she must be faced and yet not faced, resisted and yet not resisted. Her uncanniness, like her beauty and its shadow, suggests that she is the awful grace of a Nothingness that may either destroy or save but that to avoid it is to be condemned to unreality. It must have been with relief that Shelley plunged into the last act of *Prometheus Unbound*, with its intoxicated vision of the future forever free and the past safely buried, at least for the time being.

9

Metaphor and Allegory in *Prometheus Unbound*

Ross G. Woodman

I

Though *A Defence of Poetry* offers a penetrating analysis of 'the mind in creation' (Shelley, 1977, pp. 503–4), of which *Prometheus Unbound* is but one enactment among an infinite number, Shelley makes it clear that mind 'cannot create, it can only perceive' (Shelley, 1977, p. 478). Bound to an everlasting flow of sensations that has no known or knowable source (no creator), the mind endlessly arranges and rearranges these sensations in perpetual risk of arresting them into patterns or systems alien to the flow itself. But for the intervention of arbitrary signs, which is the mind's 'tribute' to the ceaseless flow (*Mont Blanc*, 5), that flow would have no existence. Existence resides in signs, the naming of what cannot be named. All names, all signs, are an arbitrary imposition of meaning, which some, like Shelley's Jupiter, would finally call 'God', and which others, like Shelley's Demogorgon, would finally call oblivion. Between the tyranny of Jupiter arresting the flow by declaring himself the Creator or God of the frozen world to which Prometheus is initially bound and the nothingness of Demogorgon who would release the flow from the potential tyranny of assigning it any name at all, Shelley's lyrical drama takes up its illusory abode.

That illusory abode is metaphor, which Shelley defines as 'before unapprehended relations of things' or 'unapprehended combinations of thought' (Shelley, 1977, pp. 482, 487). Once apprehended, metaphor is in danger of becoming familiar or 'blunted' (Shelley, 1977, p. 506), and once it becomes familiar or 'blunted' it becomes a 'curse' binding us to 'the accident of surrounding impressions' by rendering through 'reiteration' that 'accident' an immutable law, impressions becoming 'fixed and dead' (Coleridge, 1984, I, 304).

The function of metaphor, as Shelley describes it, is perpetually to restore the painted 'veil of familiarity' to 'chaos' (Shelley, 1977, pp. 505–6) or oblivion, which is itself 'the chaos of a cyclic poem' (Shelley, 1977, p. 482). Metaphor is, therefore, and must remain, 'pavilioned upon chaos' (*Hellas*, 772).

Shelley's 'mind in creation', itself an oxymoron, is as committed to chaos as it is to creation. Indeed, chaos and creation are metaphorically the same thing; the 'mind in creation' is the mind in chaos. In the exchange between Demogorgon and Asia in Demogorgon's cave, they mirror each other. Demogorgon is 'the earth without form, and void' (*Genesis*, I:2). It is 'Ungazed upon and shapeless – neither limb/Nor form – nor outline' (II.iv.5–6). Its 'mighty Darkness' (II.iv.2) is the Biblical 'darkness . . . upon the face of the deep' (*Genesis*, I.2). And though Asia may be metaphorically identified with 'the Spirit of God' that in the creation myth in Genesis 'moves upon the face of the waters' (*Genesis*, I.2), Shelley wishes in her to present that 'Spirit' in 'a before unapprehended' way, to make thereby a new metaphor out of a 'fixed and dead' one. He wishes, that is, to reduce the familiar creation myth of Genesis to the chaos from which it arose in order to release us from the tyranny it has become by its familiarity, a tyranny that Jupiter, like the Christian priesthood, is determined to preserve. Thus while Asia is initially prepared to fall down and worship the 'Power' as the Creator itself ('I could fall down and worship that and thee' [II.iii.16]), and Demogorgon, answering her catechism questions, is equally prepared to mirror back her own conventional understanding which binds Prometheus to the rock who is Peter ('God', 'God, Almighty God', 'Merciful God', 'He reigns', 'He reigns', 'He reigns' – II.iv.9–37), Asia gradually recognises what Demogorgon is determined to teach her: the blunting effect of 'reiteration'. Demogorgon by 'reiteration' has reduced her conventional wisdom to chaos, which Demogorgon calls 'the Abysm' (II.iv.114). What replaces orthodoxy, the familiar Judeo-Christian myth of creation, is an 'oracle' (II.iv.123). That 'oracle' is metaphor, the fictive voice of the 'Abysm'. When Demogorgon cries 'Behold!' (II.iv.128), the curtain goes up on a metaphorical world; a new veil replaces an old one in the manner of a palimpsest that disguises in the suspension of the metaphorical moment the 'Abysm' which it is.

The metaphorical identity of chaos and creation is nowhere more evident than in the verbal exchange in Demogorgon's cave. At the conclusion of that exchange in which dissolution becomes re-solution, Demogorgon, having announced that, for all their play of voices, 'a voice/Is wanting' (II.iv.115–16), nevertheless declares, as only metaphor can, that to name 'the revolving world' 'Fate, Time, Occasion, Time and Change' (II.iv.118–19) is merely to arrest it in metaphors that have, in Coleridge's phrase, lost 'all their life and efficiency . . . and lie bed-ridden in the dormitory of the soul, side by side, with the most despised and exploded errors' (Coleridge, 1984, I, 83). Asia's task is to substitute for these dead metaphors new and vital ones. Demogorgon can assign her a role; Asia alone can fill or perform it 'like the atmosphere/Of the sun's fire filling the living world' (II.v.26–7). The role is Love: 'To these/ All things are subject but eternal Love' (II.iv.119–20), says Demogorgon of those dead metaphors which 'stand, not o'erthrown, but unregarded now' (III.iv.179) until the end of the third act. In the added fourth act, written some six months later, they are carried off to their 'tomb in eternity' (IV.14), leaving the universe free for a time to revolve in the new metaphorical apparel Asia has provided.

It requires, Shelley suggests, a superhuman feat of the imagination to transform a 'shroud' into a 'wedding garment' (*Dejection: An Ode*, 49). Love, he writes, inhabits 'the chasm of an insufficient void'; it seeks 'to awaken in all things that are, a community with what we experience within ourselves' – within, that is, 'the chasm' itself (Shelley, 1977, p. 473). Community or relationship, which is metaphor, is pavilioned upon 'the chasm of an insufficient void' which it apparels in order to reveal. Metaphor opens to human perception 'an insufficient void' that cannot otherwise be seen. In its magical oxymoronic way, it reveals or creates nothingness, bringing it out of non-existence into an illusory existence displaying itself within and before the mind, which is in Shelley's lyrical drama an audience not of viewers but of readers, the stage being the mind itself in the theatrical or fictive display of what may be called its psychic activity.

What is that activity? It is not the creation of the mind because the mind 'cannot create, it can only perceive'. But what in Shelley's closet drama does it perceive in the act of reading? Shelley does not know. What we read are arbitrary signs arranged according to grammatical devices which Shelley calls 'a feeble shadow of the original conception of the poet' (Shelley, 1977, p. 504). It perceives as in sleep we perceive images in a dream, or as the figures in Plato's allegory of the cave in *The Republic* perceive shadows as they appear to pass by. Plato's cave becomes in *Mont Blanc* 'the still cave of the witch Poesy' where the poet seeks 'among the shadows that pass by / Ghosts of all things that are, some shade of thee [the 'Dizzy Ravine' of mind], / Some . . . faint image' (34–47). It seeks the wind in the footsteps of its departure which may be nothing at all.

Yet *Prometheus Unbound* is there even as the ravine of Arve is there. 'Thou art there' (48), Shelley exclaims in *Mont Blanc* as, arising out of 'a trance sublime and strange' quickened by the 'ceaseless motion' which is 'the path of that unresting sound', he recognises to his great surprise that his own 'separate phantasy' has its mirroring counterpart in the ravine of Arve, as 'dizzy' in its own way as himself (32–6). But what is it that is there? What is the ravine of Arve? What is *Prometheus Unbound*? If he could answer these questions, Shelley suggests in his *Hymn to Intellectual Beauty*, he would be 'immortal, and omnipotent' (39). He would, that is, be Jupiter.

The temptation to be God, to declare or believe in God, is the temptation to become the tyrant by arresting the 'ceaseless motion' following its path of 'unresting sound' by resolving it into a mythical source or dead metaphor. 'Thou art there' constitutes a sudden freeze, the death of poetry. Better that nothing be there than have the 'ceaseless flow' cease to flow or the 'unresting sound' come to rest in some final soundlessness. It is better not to know what is there, since knowing ends that 'willing suspension of disbelief for the moment, which constitutes poetic faith' (Coleridge, 1984, II, 6). Those moments of suspended disbelief, Shelley argues in his *Defence*, are 'the best and happiest moments of the happiest and best minds.' Poetry is 'the record' (Shelley, 1977, p. 504) of them, though as a 'record' they stand in need of dissolution lest they become, like the Christian myth, a creed.

II

The tyranny of truth in its imposition of meaning perverts poetry into dogma and history into nightmare. It binds Prometheus to 'a catalogue of detached facts, which have no other bond of connexion than time, place, circumstance, cause and effect'. This 'bond of connexion' or mode of relationship is the realm of dead metaphors which Shelley describes as 'a mirror which . . . distorts that which should be beautiful'; time as a 'bond of connexion' acts as 'the moths of just history', eating 'out the poetry of it' (Shelley, 1977, p. 485). The bound Prometheus of the first act struggling for 'three thousand years of sleep-unsheltered hours' (I.12) to resist by the exertion of his indominable will submission to the tyrannical rule of Jupiter thus becomes an allegory of the time span that 'nineteenth-century scientists believed separated the development of early civilisations (Egypt, etc.) from their own time' (Shelley, 1977, p. 136n). To argue, however, that Shelley's entire drama is locked within this allegorical perspective, the unbinding of Prometheus becoming thereby his release in Shelley's own time, 'from about 1789 to 1819' (Cameron, 1974, p. 486), is to ignore the movement away from an allegory of time entirely, the millennium giving way to apocalypse.

Though Milton Wilson argues persuasively that Shelley may have had this movement in mind in adding the fourth act, in practice he produced, according to Wilson, 'not the final conquest of Time and Chaos' but 'basically a celebration of the millennium' (Wilson, 1959, p. 209). Wilson's crucial word here is 'final', by which he means an end once and for all to cyclic occurrence. Such an end, however, would be the end of poetry itself. All further 'interpenetration[s] of a diviner nature through our own' (Shelley, 1977, p. 504) would cease; humankind would itself become that 'diviner nature'. Apocalypse in this sense is precisely what Jupiter has in mind in declaring that he is henceforth omnipotent. It ignores, that is, Shelley's radical understanding of the vitality of metaphor as the 'ceaseless motion' of thought present as the 'unresting sound' of poetry that continues even after the voice is still. Apocalypse for Shelley contains no sense of finality; it contains, rather, the penetration of an instant or moment in which, announced by the word 'Behold!', the mind opens to the 'Abysm', momentarily to rejoice in its own extinction as its liberation from truth other than the truth of illusion itself. Far from a 'final conquest' of 'Chaos', apocalypse for Shelley is the embracing of it. The 'chaos of a cyclic poem' is what the one 'great poem' is.

No poet was more aware than Shelley of the dangers of closure. No poet therefore clung more tenaciously to the 'Abysm' or 'void' as a perpetual opening into nothingness. Though never less than fearful of the devouring 'Abysm' that swallowed up Jonah in the labyrinthine belly of metaphor-making, Shelley's mature creative process may perhaps best be described as his conquest of fear characteristic of the knights committed to the religion of courtly love. Aware that the heroic image of that conquest descending from courtly romance through Dante and Milton and Wordsworth was in danger of becoming a creed, if indeed it had not already become one in Wordsworth, Shelley brought to the heroic the kind of irony which he admired in Cervantes' *Don Quixote*. He knew the very apparent limitations of arming himself with metaphor to fight an enemy whose metaphors had turned to stone. Writing to Peacock about his intended *Defence of Poetry* in reply to Peacock's satirical attack, Shelley described himself as 'the knight of the shield of shadow and the lance of gossamere' (Ingpen, 1909, II, 847). The full horror of that image struck him in *Adonais* when, with Plato's *Ion* in mind, a dialogue which he recommended to Peacock in that same letter, he described the poet's 'mind in creation' as 'lost in stormy visions', keeping 'with phantoms an unprofitable strife', 'in mad trance', striking 'with [the] spirit's knife [the poet's pen]/Invulnerable nothings' (345–8). What was before him on the page was the 'wrinkled sand' left by the wind waiting to be erased by the 'coming calm' (Shelley, 1977, p. 504). Better erasure, however, than closure!

Shelley, however, would be king. He would seat the imagination, that 'imperial faculty' (Shelley, 1977, p. 483), rather than Jupiter upon 'Demogorgon's vacant throne' (III.i.21). Poets, he insists, are 'the unacknowledged legislators of the World' (Shelley, 1977, p. 508). He would have them acknowledged. His *Defence* is a crowning of the poets as poet-kings. Significantly, however, his *Defence* remains a fragment; the second and third intended parts were never written. He wrote *Adonais* instead, relocating kingship in the dim pinnacle of the 'intense inane' (*Prometheus Unbound*, III.iv.204) or the now satiated 'void circumference' (*Adonais*, 420), which serve as ultimate metaphors of the abyss to which as a poet he was always committed.

III

The fragment may be described as the ideal metaphor, an arbitrary break announcing a ceaseless flow by giving a 'form' to the 'unfinished' (B. Rajan, 1985). 'Happy those for whom the fold / Of' (*The Triumph of Life*, 547–8) suggests not the turned page but the act of turning, 'ceaseless motion', 'unresting sound'. In composing *Prometheus Unbound*, however, Shelley had before him an avenue other than the fragment for avoiding closure: the Epilogue to *The Tempest* in which Prospero steps forward after the play's end to ask the audience for its applause – but not so much to affirm his achievement as to release him from it. Magic for Prospero was intimately connected to the Faustian temptation to play the tyrant and avenge himself on his enemies (a metaphor would do it), even as Prometheus's magic was for three thousand years held in the allegorical grip of contemplated revenge. Prospero therefore thought it necessary to drown his book as a kind of baptism releasing him from the sin of its grip upon him. He thought it necessary to return his book to the abyss, to Shelley's 'chaos of a cyclic poem'. For that abjuring and drowning to occur within the framework of his own frail spell, the play itself would be, however, to make the drowning not a releasing baptism but a part of the spell, a spell which may profitably be bread as Shakespeare's metaphorical enactment of his own 'mind in creation'. Working within that spell, Shakespeare could not as a dramatist release himself from it by containing Prospero's abjuration within the mythos or spell itself. What abjuration required was applause that, coming as a slap in the face, would by its very force release Shakespeare as dramatist from his metaphorical invention, which is to say from his own rough magic metaphorically mirrored in Prospero.

Assuming, then, that Prospero in delivering the Epilogue is speaking for Shakespeare himself, we may read it in the context of Shelley's later account of 'the mind in creation'. Though in the Epilogue Shakespeare's 'charms' are now 'all o'erthrown', leaving him with his own limited human strength 'which is', he says, 'most faint' – a faintness characteristic of Shelley's own account of inspiration gradually declining finally to fade away – Prospero-Shakespeare (Shakespeare as actor and dramatist) is still mysteriously confined by his audience as if the bond between them were not as yet completely broken. The reason, apparently, is that, having done all the right things within the magic sphere of the stage (pardoned the deceiver, restored Prospero's dukedom), he still dwells 'in this bare island by your spell'. He is still standing on the bare stage addressing them as if compelled now by their spell to do so. It would appear that it is now the audience who is reluctant to leave. 'But release me from my bands / With the help of your good hands', Prospero-Shakespeare pleads. He has no further 'Spirits to enforce, Art to enchant'. All that is over. And because it is over, what lies ahead, or may lie ahead, is despair, the terrible psychological aftermath of awakening from a magic spell to confront a bare stage and, indeed, by comparison with that spell, a bare life. 'And my ending is despair', continues the Prospero who speaks for Shakespeare, 'Unless I be relieved by prayer'. Applause, properly understood (even as Shakespeare now understands it), is related to prayer 'which pierces so, that it assaults / Mercy itself, and frees all faults'. And then, finally, in the most extraordinary confession of all, Prospero-Shakespeare seems to identify his 'rough magic' already abjured with the committal of a crime, as if magic were itself a mock display or imitation of the divine act of creation. 'As you from crimes would pardon'd be', Shakespeare-Prospero concludes, 'Let your indulgence set me free'.

This rather detailed reading of the Epilogue to *The Tempest* is offered for the light it casts upon Shelley's uneasy, rather sinister act of closure in *Prometheus Unbound*. There is for Shelley no release such as the Christian Shakespeare describes. The dissolution of a metaphoric spell leaves the reader, as it left Shelley, with only two alternatives: either to allow it to harden into allegory in order to live the good or moral life, or to create it anew.

With the dissolution of the spell wrought by Demogorgon, who is Shelley's Prospero, Demogorgon steps forward in Shelley's own epilogue to address the audience directly. There is, however, no audience, no theatre, no applause such as Shakespeare had enjoyed as both actor and playwright. Demogorgon is in this sense what and where it has always been: terrifyingly alone, as indeed is the Power in *Mont Blanc* which 'dwells apart in its tranquillity / Remote, serene, and inaccessible' (96–7). Explaining the action as an action in the mind of the reader, Demogorgon offers a morally instructive explanation of the 'spells' which 'the more select classes of poetical readers' with their 'highly refined imagination' (Shelley, 1977, p. 135) have just witnessed on their own inner stage. He takes it upon himself to interpret their dream, an interpretation which morally arrests the free flow of metaphor arising not from the centre of consciousness which is the will but from its periphery which is 'beyond and above' (Shelley, 1977, p. 486) it, or, if you like, below and beneath it. Metaphor, that is, is arrested by Demogorgon, fixated into a model. The beholding suddenly becomes a freeze like the declaration about the 'Dizzy Ravine' of Arve in *Mont Blanc*: 'thou art there' (34, 48).

The affirmation of the ravine as 'out there', the objective counterpart of what is in the mind, reduces metaphor to allegory by rendering its images answerable to what is external to them. It renders them answerable to 'facts' and therefore to history. Metaphor as allegory becomes simply a re-arrangement of the facts of history, the connecting modes of which are determined by consciousness and will, into a more beautiful or ideal pattern dictated by an eros without an object. The poet's eros, Prometheus's unbinding eros who is Asia and her sisters, works outside of, rather than within, history and time. It embraces chaos by arising from the 'chasm of an insufficient void' which it seeks to orchestrate into a full and dizzy intensity described by Shelley as 'the intense inane' (*Prometheus Unbound*, III.iv.204). To reduce that extraordinary activity which 'the mind in creation' cannot consciously comprehend to Demogorgon's allegorical reading is to act upon it in a manner which Shelley rejects in his *Defence of Poetry*.

'A poet therefore would do ill to embody his own conceptions of right and wrong, which are usually those of his place and time, in his poetic creations, which participate in neither', Shelley writes. He then goes on effectively to describe the 'inferior office' Demogorgon performs in the epilogue for a more popular audience of readers than the one Shelley's Preface invokes:

> By this assumption of the inferior office of interpreting the effect, in which perhaps after all he might acquit himself but imperfectly, he would resign the glory in a participation in the cause [which is the 'Abysm' itself]. There was little danger that Homer, or any of the eternal poets, should have so far misunderstood themselves as to have abdicated this throne of their widest dominion. Those in whom the poetical faculty, though great, is less intense, as Euripides, Lucan, Tasso, Spenser, have frequently affected a moral aim, and the effect of their poetry is diminished in exact proportion to the degree in which they compel us to advert to this purpose.   (Shelley, 1977, p. 488)

Demogorgon's address to the audience of readers reveals Shelley's temptation to resign 'the glory' of 'participation in the cause'. It reveals his temptation to abdicate the 'throne of widest dominion' and join those lesser poets with whom in the final stanzas of *Adonais* he includes both Keats and himself as 'the inheritors of unfulfilled renown' (397). By turning back upon himself imperfectly to contemplate the moral meaning of an action which is, like Nietzsche's transvaluation of values, beyond moral meaning, Shelley in Demogorgon holds up to the reader a distorting mirror of what in its own proper sphere is beautiful. He sends his reader back into history armed with a moral and political allegory of the reader's and Shelley's own period, even as Shakespeare-Prospero sends the audience out of the theatre into a Christian reality which the drama itself magically invokes as a 'dark conceit'.

Within the 'spells' of his own rough magic, Shelley could point to no such Christian reality. On the contrary, he could only annihilate it by releasing the oblivion it attempted to conceal as a stone conceals an empty sepulchre. If Demogorgon in the epilogue speaks for Shelley as Prospero speaks for Shakespeare, then Shelley too has betrayed metaphor in the name of moral truth. Had he remained true to metaphor instead of apparently in Demogorgon reverting to allegory, he would have sent his reader down into the 'chasm of an insufficient void', there to confront the 'Dizzy Ravine' of mind in a manner less ominous and sinister than Demogorgon's and indeed Jupiter's image of vulture and snake twisted 'in inextricable fight' (III.i.73). Such an image – the struggle to 'reassume / An empire o'er the disentangled Doom' through the moral determination of the three thousand year-old, sleep-un-sheltered, unregenerate, Promethean will 'neither to change nor falter nor repent' – is more suitable to a Marxist than a visionary nihilist. Shelley as an allegorical 'Marxist' remains in Shelley's lyrical drama Don Quixote's Sancho Panza.

IV

The struggle within Shelley between embracing 'visitations' from an unknown and unknowable source, which is profusely productive of a 'vitally metaphorical' language in the lyric mode, and the conscious dedication of those 'visitations' to moral reform, which is equally productive of allegory in the agonistic mode, is described in his *Defence* and enacted in his lyrical drama. Shelley's lyricism embraces metaphor even as his drama or agon embraces allegory. In *Paradise Lost*, Shelley witnessed as reader the struggle of Milton's 'mind in creation' between the dictation of his 'unpre-meditated song' [sic] which constitutes its 'inspired moments', and the 'artificial connexion of the spaces between their suggestions by the intertexture of conventional expressions' (Shelley, 1977, p. 504), which constitutes the moral action of the conscious will. For Shelley, the 'artificial connexion of the spaces between' its inspired moments relies, however, not merely upon 'the intertexture of conventional expressions' of the sort which derive almost directly from Satan's defiance of God in *Paradise Lost*, but, far more pervasively, upon the blunting habits of grammar, habits which force the mind into passive submission to an endlessly reiterated conception of reality. Grammar for Shelley reinforces tyranny.

'I am afraid', writes Nietzsche in *Twilight of the Idols*, 'that we are not rid of God because we still have faith in grammar' (Nehamas, 1985, p. 96). 'But what he [Nietzsche] considers necessary for belief in God [as the ultimate substance]', Alexander Nehamas explains, 'is not only grammar but *also* faith in it. And this faith is just the assumption, common to friends and foes of metaphysics alike, that language makes of its own nature ontological claims upon its users' (Nehamas, 1985, p. 96). The liberation of language from the ontological claims of grammar is for Shelley the chief function of 'unpremeditated song'. By means of spell and incantation the tyranny of grammar is at least momentarily suspended; its ontological claims are dissolved 'into a Sea profound, of ever-spreading sound'. That profound sea is the home and element of Shelley's Oceanides, Asia, Panthea and Ione. Whenever, as in the second act, they enter their own proper element, their souls, led by Asia, become

> an enchanted Boat
> Which, like a sleeping swan, doth float
> Upon the silver waves of thy sweet singing,
>   And thine doth like an Angel sit
>   Beside the helm conducting it
> Whilst all the winds with melody are ringing.
>   It seems to float ever – forever –
>   Upon that many winding River
>   Between mountains, woods, abysses,
>   A Paradise of wildernesses,
> Till like one in slumber bound
> Borne to the Ocean, I float down, around,
> Into a Sea profound, of ever-spreading sound.
>   (II.v.72–84)

That Demogorgon's epilogue should follow fast upon his thorough dissolution of a spell that awakens the oblivion that metaphor evokes ('thy words waken Oblivion' – IV.543) suggests how quickly the mind can revert to allegory; the conscious will arises to confront the threat of its own extinction, an extinction enacted by Asia's descent to Prometheus, which is at the same time her ascent from Demogorgon's cave in the descending-ascending Car of the Hour. Once again we see that 'the chaos of a cyclic poem' is what for Shelley 'the mind in creation' enacts. Allegory, on the other hand, is the mind's attempt to recover what it mistakenly considers its own lost ground, not only by binding itself to history and to objective fact, but by constructing from it an ontology of the absolute.

Shelley's metaphor-making arises from an anarchistic desire to live unhistorically in the moment by severing the bonds of connection which narrative provides ('time, place, circumstance, cause and effect'). In his attempt in the added fourth act radically to abolish the past, an abolition proclaimed with the intense fervour of prayer in the final couplet of *Hellas* ('the world is weary of the past,/O might it die or rest at last!'), Shelley anticipates the Nietzsche of Paul de Man. And both as poet and critical theorist, he anticipates Deconstruction. Not surprisingly, therefore, Deconstruction has made the 'herd-abandoned deer struck by the hunter's dart' (*Adonais*, 297) the new leader of the pack, particularly as the 'hunter's dart' that struck the 'herd-abandoned' Shelley was not the attack of the critics that killed Keats, but his own critical awareness of what language and writing are. Shelley in *Adonais* could metaphorically perceive his pen upon the page as a 'spirit's knife' striking 'invulnerable nothings' (347–8). The agon of composition under the sometimes frail disguise of 'the best and happiest moments of the happiest and best minds' (Shelley, 1977, p. 504) made him one of Deconstruction's recognisable and acknowledged founding fathers. The world that Shelley's poetry and critical prose legislated into existence is now at last amongst us, though Shelley himself as its 'trumpet' probably at the time 'felt not' what he inspired. Indeed, he might today be 'most sincerely astonished at its manifestations' (Shelley, 1977, p. 508).

Addressing himself in *Literary History and Literary Modernity* to what he calls 'the radical impulse that stands behind all genuine modernity when it is not merely a descriptive synonym for the contemporaneous or for a passing fashion' (de Man, 1983, p. 147), Paul de Man turns to Nietzsche, particularly to his polemical essay, *On the Use and Misuse of History for Life*. Life, Nietzsche argues there, is (in de Man's rendering) 'the ability to *forget* whatever precedes a present situation' (de Man, 1983, p. 146). 'Moments of genuine humanity', de Man continues, 'thus are moments at which all anteriority vanishes, annihilated by the power of an absolute forgetting' (de Man, 1983, p. 147). That 'power' attributed to Nietzsche was bequeathed to modernity by Shelley working within the larger framework of that one great self-destructing Biblical poem which concludes by obliterating its own history in a vision of the descent of the New Jerusalem in whch 'the former things are passed away' (Revelation, 21.4). 'He that sat upon the throne' (Shelley's 'unseen Power', called Demogorgon in *Prometheus Unbound*) declares, 'Behold, I make all things new' (21.5), just as Demogorgon in answer to Asia's question, 'When shall the destined hour arrive?', declares 'Behold' (II.iv.128). What she beholds are the cleaving of the rocks that held Prometheus captive and the arrival of two Cars, one to take her to Prometheus, the other to take Demogorgon to Jupiter. She beholds in that instant all things in the process of being made new, the 'mind in creation' giving birth to new metaphors 'undreamt of by the sensual and the proud' (*Dejection: An Ode*, 70).

'Modernity', de Man continues,

> exists in the form of a desire to wipe out whatever came earlier, in the hope of reaching at last a point that could be called a true present, a point of origin that marks a new departure. This combined interplay of deliberate forgetting with an action that is also a new origin reaches the full power of the idea of modernity. Thus defined, modernity and history are diametrically opposed to each other in Nietzsche's text. Nor is there any doubt as to his commitment to modernity, the only way to reach the meta-historical realm in which the rhythm of one's existence coincides with that of the eternal return. Yet the shrill grandiloquence of the tone may make one suspect that the issue is not as simple as it may at first appear.   (de Man, 1983, p. 148)

The complication, as de Man explores it, illuminates Shelley's own dilemma. It lies in the fact that the generative power obliterating the past in an originating Now characterised by the word 'Behold' is itself engaged 'in a generative scheme that extends far back into the past' (de Man, 1983, p. 150). Nietzsche resorts to the image of a chain when he speaks of history just as Shelley describes humanity bound together as generic 'Man' as 'a chain of linked thought'

(IV.394). 'It becomes impossible', de Man argues, 'to overcome history in the name of life or to forget the past in the name of modernity, because both are linked by a temporal chain that gives them a common destiny.' Nietzsche, he therefore concludes, had finally 'to bring the two incompatibles, history and modernity (now using the term in the full sense of a radical renewal), together in a paradox that cannot be resolved, an aporia that comes very close to describing the predicament of our own present modernity' (de Man, 1983, p. 150).

Shelley had also 'to bring together the two incompatibles', which, in the context of the argument of this essay, are allegory ('history') and metaphor ('modernity'). The Now of metaphor threatens the individual mind with an extinction that is, for Shelley, inherent within it because 'the existence of distinct individual minds similar to that which is employed in now questioning its own nature, is ... a delusion' (Shelley, 1977, p. 477). Can indeed, as de Man himself asks, 'Man' remain a 'chain of linked thought / Of love and might to be divided not' when he is already radically divided from his 'no more remembered' (*Prometheus Unbound*, III.iv.169) past? When the veil falls the chain breaks.

Unlike Shelley and, indeed, unlike Nietzsche, de Man considered allegory worthier than metaphor because, he argued, allegory rejected the delusory desire to coincide by establishing its language 'in the void of this temporal distance', between the story being told and its historical counterpart (de Man, 1983, p. 207). On the other hand, he argues, following Roman Jakobson, that metaphor 'is an exchange or substitution of properties on the basis of resemblance.' This 'exchange or substitution' propelled by a Romantic nostalgia for a unity of experience creates a 'proximity or an analogy so close and intimate that it allows the one to substitute for the other without revealing the difference necessarily introduced by the substitution' (de Man, 1979a, p. 62).

De Man, however, ignores the enormous emphasis both Shelley and Nietzsche place upon 'the void of this temporal distance'. Metaphor, far from creating 'a proximity or an analogy' so close that it conceals the 'difference necessarily introduced by the substitution', does, as this paper has argued, precisely the opposite. Metaphor for both Shelley and Nietzsche opens rather than conceals the 'void'. Where allegory protects the mind from the 'Abysm' of its own encounter with itself by binding it to historical and moral forces, metaphor removes all such reassuring props which, while clearly establishing and maintaining difference, do so by removing the Shelleyan and Nietzschean terrors of the deep. Allegory is the guardian of the individual mind against the void of its own non-existence.

Indeed, it may now be legitimately argued, de Man may have turned to allegory in order allegorically to distance himself from a history with which he had become metaphorically identified, an identification that 'radically suspends logic and opens up vertiginous possibilities of referential aberration' (de Man, 1979a, p. 10). His rejection of metaphor as he himself defined it may indeed have been influenced by his own early failure to maintain that distance between the story that, from 24 December 1940 to 28–29 November 1942 he wrote for *Le Soir*, a Belgium evening newspaper under German control, and the history aberrationally fused for a time with his youthful Romantic longings. Allegory, again as de Man defines it, may quite properly be described as an illuminating meditation upon the power of metaphor to delude. It is surely at least partly because Shelley in his final fragment himself explored that delusion as it called into doubt his entire career as a poet that de Man has written one of the most penetrating analyses of it, an analysis in which allegory serves as Shelley's critical tool for a profoundly disturbing examination of the dangers of a metaphoric life which drowning, as de Man suggests, most completely enfolds, leaving allegory to dispose of the body (de Man, 1979b, p. 67).

V

Unlike the poets to whom he was most indebted, Plato ('essentially a poet' – Shelley, 1977, p. 484), Dante, Milton and Wordsworth, Shelley could not unite into one the 'two irreconcilables', argument and song. Though, as he points out in his Preface to *Prometheus Unbound*, he 'had rather be damned with Plato and Lord Bacon, than go to Heaven with Paley and Malthus' (Shelley, 1977, p. 135), it would be a mistake to insist that either Bacon or Plato had much influence on his poetry. 'But it is a mistake', he continues,

> to suppose that I dedicate my poetical compositions solely to the
> direct enforcement of reform, or that I consider them in any
> degree as containing a reasoned system on the theory of human

life. Didactic poetry is my abhorrence; nothing can be equally well expressed in prose that is not tedious and supererogatory in verse. My purpose has hitherto been simply to familiarize the highly refined imagination of the more select classes of poetical readers with beautiful idealisms of moral excellence; aware that until the mind can love, and admire, and trust, and hope, and endure, reasoned principles of moral conduct are seeds cast upon the highway of life which the unconscious passenger tramples into dust, although they would bear the harvest of his happiness. Should I live to accomplish what I purpose, that is, produce a systematical history of what appear to me to be the genuine elements of human society [allegory], let not the advocates of injustice and superstition flatter themselves that I should take Aeschylus [whom he did take in the composition of *Prometheus Unbound*] rather than Plato [whom he did not take] as my model.   (Shelley, 1977, p. 135)

The relative absence of a 'reasoned system on the theory of human life' as anything more than 'the contagion of the world's slow stain' (*Adonais*, 356) left Shelley not only without a metaphysical ground for his poetry, but, far more than that, led him as a poet, as it led Nietzsche and the Deconstructionists after him, to reject such a ground. Shelley's and Nietzsche's 'vitally metaphorical' language depends for its vitality upon its liberation from truth, which is to say its liberation from logic and metaphysics. Like Nietzsche after him, Shelley recognised that poets could no more escape logic and metaphysics than they could escape grammar; it did not exclude them from using metaphysics and logic against themselves. Thus, in his *Hymn to Intellectual Beauty*, Shelley uses the language of religion ('consecrate', 'grace', 'truth', 'vowed'), as well as the ritual attitude of worship ('to one who worships thee, / And every form containing thee' – 81–2), against its traditional object in order, finally, to refute that object by declaring it to be what the poem itself is: a frail spell.

The 'thee' that is worshipped is the 'Spirit of Beauty', 'the awful shadow of some unseen Power' that 'Floats though unseen amongst us' (1–2, 13), even as Asia, the 'radiance' of whose 'beauty' Panthea can 'scarce endure' ('I dare not look on thee; / I feel but see thee not'), floats unseen like the vibration of air the instant the curtain of metaphor rises upon the word 'Behold!'. Panthea dare not look upon the radiance of Asia because, like 'light

from the meridian Sun' (II.iv.4), it would, in revealing 'in a flash'
the shared invisible world of Plato, Dante, Milton, Wordsworth
and Shelley, put out 'the light of sense' (*The Prelude*, VI.600–2)
even as it put out Milton's eyes. The 'radiance' which Panthea
cannot see is the 'celestial light' that usurps the light of the natural
sun. 'The sun will rise not until noon', says the Spirit of the Hour,
who is the Hour of Prometheus's release, itself the duration of
Asia's metaphoric spirit-performance. In the reality-illusion of
metaphor that 'Hour' is a single instant, the 'best and happiest'
moment, in which the 'coursers' that drive the Car that takes Asia
to Prometheus fly 'swifter than fire', drinking 'the hot speed of
desire' (II.v.2–10). In a stage note Shelley has the Car pause 'within
a Cloud on the Top of a snowy Mountain' (II.v). That snowy peak
is metaphorically Wordsworth's peak of Snowdon (far too accessible and familiar to suit Shelley's purposes) and Shelley's peak of
Mont Blanc, the place where for Shelley 'Power dwells apart in its
tranquillity / Remote, serene, and inaccessible' (*Mont Blanc*, 96–7).
That 'tranquillity', in turn, is the imagined pause 'on the brink of
the night and the morning', the instant in the countdown to zero
before the release of the new metaphor from the hard shell of
allegory, which Shelley compares to Asia standing 'Within a
veined shell', releasing at her 'uprise' metaphor's full vitality 'like
the atmosphere / Of the sun's fire filling the living world' (II.v.22–
7). That full vitality Shelley calls love, which is an allegory-ridden
word. Asia becomes in her 'uprise' its 'oracle'. Metaphor is the
splitting of the psyche ('cloven at thy uprise') to release its energy
too long congealed in allegory.

Clearly humanity cannot inhabit this apocalyptic instant. On
viewing the first atomic explosion in White Sands, New Mexico, in
1944, Robert Oppenheimer instantly transformed what he saw into
metaphor. He uttered words from the *Bhagavad Gita* describing the
appearance of the Godhead: 'Brighter than ten thousand suns'
(Arguelles, 1975, p. 249). He further extended the metaphor by
adding other words from the *Gita*: 'I am Death, the Destroyer of
worlds'. His imagination embraced Shelley's exact understanding
of what metaphor is. '*Life no argument.* – We have arranged for
ourselves a world in which we can live', writes Nietzsche in *The
Gay Science* (121), 'by positing bodies, lines, planes, causes and
effects, motion and rest, form and content; without these articles of
faith nobody could now endure life. But that does not prove them.
Life is no argument. The conditions of life might include error'

(Nehamas, 1985, p. 53). Nietzsche here claims what Shelley again and again as poet confronted: 'our basic beliefs, whatever their value to life, are false' (Nehamas, 1985, p. 53). We cannot both live well and in truth because, as Nietzsche argues in *The Will to Power* (487), 'A belief, however necessary it may be for the preservation of the species, has nothing to do with truth' (Nehamas, 1985, p. 53).

Allegory is for Shelley neither preferable to nor worthier than metaphor. It is simply necessary to life if one is to live with its 'contagion'. By choosing metaphor over allegory, Shelley, it may be argued, chose death over life, without, however, the comfort of a metaphysics of death, the comfort of a transcendental signified which would have contained metaphor in the shell of allegory even as Asia was contained before her 'uprise' in the 'veined shell' which 'Proteus old / Made Asia's nuptial boon, breathing within it / A voice to be accomplished' (III.iii.65–7). Shelley's *Prometheus Unbound* is that voice 'accomplished', an action 'above and beyond consciousness' that filled him as much with terror as with love, knowing as he did that 'a voice / Is wanting' (II.iv.115–16).

10

Seduced by Metonymy: Figuration and Authority in *The Cenci*

Stuart Peterfreund

As Barbara Groseclose observes, in one history of the Cenci family saga that Shelley consulted, Lodovico Muratori's *Annali d'Italia* (1749) vol. X, 'Incest was not, in fact, an aspect of the original story.' Her conjecture as to why Shelley altered Muratori's original is that, 'Dramaturgically, the decision was a necessity' (Groseclose, 1985, pp. 222, 225, 226). Shelley did indeed perceive a need to enhance the play's dramaturgical values. As he says in the 'Preface' to *The Cenci* (1819), 'The person who would treat such a subject must increase the ideal, and diminish the actual horror of the events, so that the pleasure which arises from the poetry which exists in these tempestuous sufferings and crimes may mitigate the pain of the contemplation of the moral deformity from which they spring' (Shelley, 1977, pp. 239–40).[1]

To argue, however, that Shelley's alteration is intended to mitigate the gravity of Beatrice's actions is to part ways with Shelley himself who, while endeavouring to render faithfully the moral universe of late sixteenth-century Rome, nevertheless makes it clear that nothing in that moral universe should be taken to excuse or justify the actions portrayed therein. He characterises the actions of all the play's principals, including Beatrice, as springing from 'moral deformity' and declares, moreover, that 'Revenge, retaliation, atonement, are pernicious mistakes' (Shelley, 1977, p. 240). Arguments such as Groseclose's for mitigating circum-stances ('Shelley needed to link serious provocation with the magnitude of the crime' [Groseclose, 1985, p. 226]) tend to wrench the tragedy out of its late sixteenth-century Roman moral universe and thrust it into the respective moral universes of commentators who, in their turn, argue over the presence and significance of such circumstances.[2]

More important, however, arguments in mitigation of Beatrice's violent vengeance fail to acknowledge an important *caveat* that follows from Groseclose's observation. If Count Cenci was guilty of lewd misconduct and of attempted incestuous rape, but not of incestuous rape itself, perhaps there is some other motive, whether symbolic, thematic or dramaturgical, underlying Shelley's decision to alter the original historical account. Yet most commentators have failed to acknowledge the existence of such a *caveat*, let alone to heed it. Although he specifies Shelley's goal as one 'dictated by artistic purposes rather than a desire for historical accuracy', Ronald Tetreault has no qualms about declaring, without qualification, that *The Cenci* is 'a drama . . . based on actual historical circumstances' (Tetreault, 1987, pp. 129–30). Stuart Sperry takes Beatrice's incestuous rape as a purely literal fact, arguing indeed 'that Beatrice's tragic flaw is her idealization of her own virginity' (Sperry, 1988, p. 135). Such conclusions simply ignore an important dimension of the social critique mounted in the play.

This chapter will argue that although Beatrice's seduction can be taken as a literal seduction perpetrated by her father out of the need to satisfy his appetitive will to power, it can also be read as a symbolic one consummated by Beatrice's adoption of the metonymic language of reification and self-empowerment spoken by her patriarchal society in general and by her father Count Cenci in particular. The seduction illustrates how, in Shelley's poetry, one may easily be led astray by language used habitually and unreflectively by a speaker not fully aware that language is as much the agent that constitutes the object as the referential apparatus that points to it.[3]

Although never 'named' as such in Shelley's poetry or prose, metonymy occupies an important place in his taxonomy of figuration generally and in the thematic content of *The Cenci* in particular. The absence of that 'name' is revealing. Metonymy often functions as a self-consuming trope, the primary purpose of which is to figure forth the 'real', in contrast to metaphor, the primary purpose of which is to figure forth the vividly imagined and/or ardently desired. Roman Jakobson has challenged linguistic and literary studies to move beyond the study of 'the metaphorical style of romantic poetry' and take up the study of 'the metonymic texture of realistic prose' (Jakobson, 1960, p. 375), but in posing his challenge Jakobson seems unaware of the concealed power of metonymy to fabricate an ideology of the real,[4] a power which was not then (and is not now) reckoned adequately.

The failure of reckoning results from metonymy's chief effect: self-concealment by means of repetition and naturalisation.[5] One case in point with relevance to the issue of patriarchal oppression in *The Cenci*[6] is the Christian creed: 'I believe in one God, Father Almighty, Maker of heaven and earth.' Divinity that is patrilineal in descent – from Father to Son – *and* originally preached by an all-male discipleship, *and* ratified by a Lord's Prayer now thought to have been attributed to Jesus by a disciple rather than uttered by him, is not to be shared with women – so one argument goes.[7]

Shelley execrated the lot of women oppressed by a patriarchal culture (Brown, 1979, pp. 200–1), and he may well have harboured sympathies with the gnostic analysis of the cause of and cure for religious oppression.[8] To be sure, his comments in the *Essay on Christianity* (1815–19?) assume a heretical position *vis-à-vis* the orthodox Christian conception of God the Father. Shelley argues in the *Essay* that

> the word *God* according to the acceptation of Jesus Christ unites all the attributes which these denominations contain and is the interfused and overruling Spirit of all the energy and wisdom included within the circle of existing things ... The Universal Being can only be defined by negatives which deny his subjection to the laws of all inferior existences. Where indefiniteness ends, idolatry and anthropomorphism begin.
>
> (Shelley, 1954, pp. 201–2)

God, in other words, is manifested 'within the circle of existing things' as an immanent principle responsible for the articulate and apprehensible deployment of those 'things' – the harmonious arrangements of language, for example, or that of dyads such as mother-father (or destroyer-preserver). But God is not contained within or totalised by that 'circle', and the attempt to 'name' him metonymically using a perceptible attribute found within the 'circle' is to reduce that principle by anthropomorphising it.

Shelley's mature art expresses a keen awareness of how deeply implicated figuration is in the creation and establishment of normalised, apparently 'natural' power relations. Although he points to the closely related trope of synecdoche rather than metonymy, Jerrold E. Hogle says a good deal about Shelley's understanding of the implications of figuration for such power relations – those between men and women, for example – and the systems of social control that follow from them: 'The most pervasive subordination repeated from class to class is undoubtedly the subjection of women by men, and the poet encounters this imposture as a synecdoche indicating the nature of all others in *A Vindication of the Rights of Women* by . . . Mary Wollstonecraft' (Hogle, 1988, p. 90).[9]

The insidious attractiveness of metonymy's part-for-whole logic and its potential for reduction and reification make it so dangerous and, arguably, the object of Shelley's remarks in the 'Preface' to *The Cenci* about 'the restless and anatomizing casuistry with which men seek justification of Beatrice, yet feel that she has done what needs justification' (Shelley, 1977, p. 240). A strong latinist such as Shelley most likely knew that the root of *casuistry* is *casus* (*case, occurrence*, with a strong accessory sense of *falling*). Accordingly, 'anatomizing casuistry' implies somewhat more than Reiman and Powers' useful gloss defining *casuistry* as 'that part of ethics which resolves cases of conscience, applying the general rules of religion and morality to particular instances in which circumstances alter cases, or in which there appears to be a conflict of duties' (Shelley, 1977, p. 240n). Shelley's understanding implies a falling off, a killing-by-anatomy of a 'living', human-made ethical precept, the metaphoric 'spirit' of which is lost in the application of the metonymic (and, often as not, anthropomorphic) 'letter' to a specific instance in need of justification.

In *A Treatise on Morals* (1815–21?) Shelley demonstrates the way that 'anatomizing casuistry' operates in 'the abuse of a metaphorical expression to a literal purpose':

A common sophism which, like many others, depends on the abuse of a metaphorical expression to a literal purpose, has produced much of the confusion which has involved the theory of morals. It is said that no person is bound to be just or kind, if, on his neglect, he should fail to incur some penalty. Duty is obligation. There can be no obligation without an obliger. Virtue is a law to which it is the will of the lawgiver that we should conform, which will we should in no manner be bound to obey, unless some dreadful punishment were attached to disobedience. This is the philosophy of slavery and superstition.

(Shelley, 1954, p. 188)

Shelley's most complete prose elaboration of the 'living' metaphor/ 'dead' metonymy distinction is found in *A Defence of Poetry* (1821). Shelley distinguishes between the language of poetry, which is 'vitally metaphorical; that is, it remarks the before unapprehended relations of things and perpetuates their apprehension', and the metonymic language of naturalised authority. The latter descends from that hitherto 'vitally metaphorical' language, much as the metonymic (heroic) phase of Vico's poetic logic descends from the metaphoric (originary) phase.[10] Thus the words marking 'the before unapprehended relations of things . . . become through time signs for portions or classes of thoughts, instead of pictures of integral thoughts; and then if no new poets should arise to create afresh the associations which have been thus disorganized, language will be dead to all the nobler purposes of human intercourse' (Shelley, 1977, p. 482).

Polysemous terms such as 'apprehension' and 'intercourse' suggest that the 'living' metaphor/'dead' metonymy distinction has implications for the social world of subject and object relations no less than for the history of poetry in the West. In fact metaphor, defined in part by Leslie Brisman in his study of Shelley's reinterpretation of the Christian concepts of faith, hope and love as 'a vehicle for making or crossing a certain figurative distance, like the distance between biological life and imaginative life, or earthly life and eternal life' (Brisman, 1981, p. 392, 389), issues an ethical imperative no less than it creates an aesthetic effect. Metaphor is 'an expanded form of transference' (Gumpel, 1984, p. 134). It provides a working linguistic model for what Hogle calls 'the distribution of transference', a 'continuous going-out to others beyond any present circle' (Hogle, 1988, p. 230). Metaphor is, in Shelley's terms, an enactment of 'The great secret of morals', which is 'love, or a going out of our own nature and an identification of ourselves with the beautiful which exists in thought, action, or person, not our own' (Shelley, 1977, p. 487).

Under the influence of metaphor, apprehension involves knowing through being with the other while at the same time respecting its otherness or difference to the end of fostering true and loving equality (see Hogle, 1988, p. 231), not literalised grasping or subjection of the other. Intercourse occurs between peers as a celebration of multeity-in-unity and equality-in-difference, not as the reification of the other as the proper appetitive object of the self. Dichotomies such as subject/object and mind/body simply are not operative; dyads such as mind-body and subject-object are. Loving knowledge obtained under the influence of metaphor is holistic, not dialectical.

But just as a necessarily unreflective childhood gives way to a wilfully unreflective adulthood, metaphor gives way to metonymy. Speaking of the poetic reverie characteristic of childhood (and of those who are reflective and courageous enough to persevere as true poets), in the essay *On Life* (1812–14?), Shelley observes:

> Those who are subject to the state called reverie feel as if their nature were dissolved into the surrounding universe, or as if the surrounding universe were absorbed into their being. They are conscious of no distinction. And these are states which precede or accompany or follow an unusually intense and vivid apprehension of life. As men grow up, this power commonly decays, and they become mechanical and habitual agents. Their feelings and their reasonings are the combined result of a multitude of entangled thoughts, of a series of what are called impressions, planted by reiteration. (Shelley, 1977, p. 477)

As the moist, subliminally sexual atmospherics of the metaphors 'dissolved' and 'absorbed' suggest, there is no reification in such a state of reverie because there are no discrete 'things' or objects, only continuous, evanescent and complete processes of transference. However, when it is too often repeated, a 'living' metaphor announcing these processes 'dies' into metonymy, and human beings begin to conceive of themselves not as one with the other, but as one among others – in this case as discrete, hard, corpuscular objects ('mechanical and habitual agents'), alienated and devoid of immanence in a Newtonian universe of matter, force and motion, and marked by distinctions such as those of gender, wealth and class, much as the corpuscles of Newtonian matter – or, better yet, the atoms of Lucretian matter – are marked with the distinctions to be observed in the material universe.[11] An impression 'planted by reiteration' – actually, the reified detritus ('the combined result of a multitude of entangled thoughts') of metaphor and the full range of transference that it symbolises –

makes individuals feel like 'signs for portions or classes of thoughts' instead of 'pictures of integral thoughts'. Otherness, both reified and fetishised, causes 'apprehension' and 'intercourse' to become exercises in power relations by those whose recollections of childhood might lead them to behave better and otherwise rather than exemplifications of loving knowledge. The metaphor in which the mind's knowing its equal is likened to the hand's grasping (its equal?) is literalised to grasping the passive object. And the metaphor in which the mind's unitive knowledge of its object is likened, in the root Latin sense of *intercourse*, to the running between characteristic of Shelley's moistly atmospheric, subliminally sexual ideal – an ideal presented, as Hogle suggests, 'in the third act colloquy between Ocean and Apollo' (1988, p. 197) in *Prometheus Unbound* – is literalised as the act of a hard, phallic, active male running the phallus between the legs of a soft, vaginal, passive female.

Sadly enough, the establishment of such unequal power relations between the two genders has, for Shelley at least, the tacit consent of both (see Hogle, 1988, p. 91). In *The Cenci*, dissolution into the universe or absorption of it – the options available under the influence of loving metaphor – give way under the influence of a patriarchal hegemony to metonymic occlusion and reification. The atmospherics of dissolution and absorption take on a palpability and a tainted, overtly sexual range of connotation. Although she at first denies responsibility for participating in such metonymic occlusion and reification, Beatrice, about to put it off and participate in the evanescent change of state signalled by death, ultimately admits her complicity in wrapping herself 'in a strange cloud of crime and shame' (V.iv.148).

In the first manifestation of the occlusion and reification, however, Beatrice denies any responsibility on her part for creating the 'clinging, black, contaminating mist' that appears to reify her as a unitary object ('it glues / My fingers and my limbs to one another') in the very act of apparently poisoning her 'inmost spirit of life!' (III.i.17–23). Sequentially, if not causally, the 'mist' follows from the metonymic blood that marks Beatrice as a woman subject to menarché and the rupture of the hymen that may accompany the loss of virginity if it does not occur prior to that loss, as well as one who, under the sway of metonymy, will adopt the ethos of retributive justice – blood for blood, in other words. The metonym works revealingly, interfering with the ability to see clearly and ultimately tainting any hope of transcendence, even as it prepares the way for the onset of the 'mist' of which Beatrice complains. At first, Beatrice implores Lucretia, 'My eyes are full of blood; just wipe them for me . . . /I see but indistinctly' (III.i.2–3). Revealingly, Lucretia underscores the fictive status of the metonym, stating that the blood of which Beatrice speaks is 'only a cold dew/That starts from your dear brow' (III.i.4–5). Ultimately, the metonym subverts such evanescent options as atmospheric dissolution and absorption, leading to a topsy-turvy vision of contamination and death: 'The beautiful blue heaven is flecked with blood!/The sunshine on the floor is black!' (III.i.13–14).

Metonyms do lead to one another. Beatrice does not idealise her virginity as much as Sperry argues; rather, she reifies it as a repository of universally acknowledged value – as, indeed, virginity was a component of the value that, along with a dowry, determined the exchange value of a woman of the upper classes upon entering into the marriage contract. The metonym or symbol of the exchange value of virginity, as Sperry correctly notes, is the wearing of one's hair bound up (Sperry, 1988, p. 135). Shortly after noting the presence of the metonymic blood, Beatrice asks:

> How comes this hair undone?
> Its wandering strings must be what blind me so,
> And yet I tied it fast.
>
> (III.i.6–8)

As with the mist, so with the metonym of hair: at the conclusion of the play, Beatrice realises that virginity is a state of mind – that, as Shelley writes in the play's Preface, 'no person can be truly dishonoured by the act of another' (Shelley, 1977, p. 240). Declaring that she has 'Lived ever holy and unstained' (V.iv.149), despite her circumstances and the actions to which they gave rise, Beatrice follows by symbolically reclaiming her purity, if not the literal physical fact of her virginity, by asking Lucretia to 'bind up this hair/In any simple knot' (V.iv.160–1), thus purging the metonym of bound hair of its power to reify and to create externally imposed standards of value. In fact, the metonym here reverts to a prior condition of figural polysemousness and mutuality. Moreover, to the extent that bound hair signifies innocence, Shelley's implication would seem to be that it is a state reattained by a loving mutuality that causes two or more individuals to

become one by being 'dissolved' or 'absorbed' into one another by
dint of the mutuality of their actions.

Allowed to proceed unchecked or uncorrected by 'new poets'
who 'arise to create afresh the associations which have been thus
disorganized' (Shelley, 1977, p. 432), the movement from
metaphor to metonymy has the force of making the world seem
much as it does for Blake's prophetic avatars after the (temporary)
failure of poetic vision: stony, petrific. Shelley's best synopsis of
the process is found in *Prometheus Unbound*, where Asia, following
her interview with Demogorgon, expresses her understanding of
the Promethean donation of language and its consequences:

> He gave man speech, and speech created thought,
> Which is the measure of the Universe;
> And Science struck the thrones of Earth and Heaven
> Which shook but fell not; and the harmonious mind
> Poured itself forth in all-prophetic song,
> And music lifted up the listening spirit
> Until it walked, exempt from mortal care,
> Godlike, o'er the clear billows of sweet sound;
> And human hands first mimicked and then mocked
> With moulded limbs more lovely than its own
> The human form, till marble grew divine,
> And mothers, gazing, drank the love men see
> Reflected in their race, behold, and perish.
>
> (II.iv.72–85)

The Promethean donation 'create[d]', in a pristine human environment, 'the associations' that subsequently had to be 'create[d]
afresh'. These associations are what speak the universe into
'measure[d]' coherence. Continued without let, such speech might
have resulted in the full knowledge ('Science') necessary to eradi-
cate the will to power in the gods and humanity alike. But 'the
thrones of Earth and Heaven / . . . shook but fell not'. Thus when
the 'associations' are re-created as moistly atmospheric 'billows of
sweet sound', that will to power metonymised and anthropomor-
phised 'With moulded limbs more lovely than its own' the same
divine essence that was responsible for 'The human form' and had
caused 'the listening spirit' to walk 'Godlike'. A state of petrifaction, the real emblematic of the imaginative, in which 'marble grew
divine', set in. Not able to become what they behold, the humanity

oppressed by this state (*state* in several senses) of petrifaction – significantly 'mothers', the passivised, ready recipients of the liquid 'love' that the uprightly phallic statue of Jupiter or some other male god throws off – took in ('drank') that sexualised infusion and, like 'properly' sexually responsive women of the eighteenth and early nineteenth centuries, lost themselves in rapturous yet submissive orgasm – that is, 'perish[ed]' in 'love'.

As G. Kim Blank has shown, the dynamics of struggle in *Prometheus Unbound* is informed by Oedipal issues, particularly 'that of a son attempting to contend with a tyrannical father' (Blank, 1988, p. 141). Stuart Sperry suggests quite rightly that the difference between the two dramas is more nearly that of mode – 'the esoteric' in *Prometheus Unbound* versus 'the exoteric' in *The Cenci* (Sperry, 1988, p. 127) – than that of theme. It is not surprising, then, that the description of the Pope Clement's response to pleas for clemency, as it were, recreates in historical time the heroic marble statuary of Asia's description in visionary time, while implying that his metonymically underwritten position of authority renders him somewhat less than human. As Cardinal Camillo reports,

> The Pope is stern; not to be moved or bent.
> He looked as calm and keen as is the engine
> Which tortures and which kills, exempt itself
> From aught that it inflicts; a marble form,
> A rite, a law, a custom: not a man.
> (V.iv.1–5)

Seen, for example, from the perspective of eternity assumed by the speaker of *Adonais* (1821), who views the marble cityscape of the same Rome that so oppressed Beatrice Cenci, petrifaction is contingent and mutable rather than absolute and immutable: 'And grey walls moulder round, on which dull Time/Feeds, like slow fire upon a hoary brand' (442–3). But from Beatrice's perspective, the patriarchal culture she lives in is stony, constrictive, oppressive, and utterly impervious to transcendence or evanescence. It is at once patriarchal and petriarchal. Beatrice's tragedy lies not in how she perceives this oppression, but in how she reacts to it: she does all the wrong things for all the right reasons.

It is with considerable and complex tragic irony that Beatrice does exactly what she enjoins Orsino not to do in the very first words she utters: 'Pervert not truth' (I.ii.1).[12] To 'pervert', from the Latin *vertere* (to turn) plus the intensive *per*, suggests a pun on the antecedent Greek noun *tropos* (turn) and verb *trepein* (to turn). Ultimately, it is impossible to speak the truth in anything but tropes, especially if the object of discourse is that 'Universal Being [who] can only be [described or] defined by negatives'. Thus Beatrice's injunction is, on one level, impossible to heed. On another level, however, the injunction, as the intensive *per* suggests, has to do with a distinction between tropes that are willed and those that arise spontaneously, a distinction that is isomorphic, if not precisely synonymous, with the distinction between metaphor and metonymy. Willed tropes, as Shelley makes clear in *A Defence*, are not poetry: 'Poetry is not like reasoning, a power to be exerted according to the determination of the will' (Shelley, 1977, p. 503). What is willed is 'ethical science', which 'arranges the elements which poetry has created, and propounds schemes and proposes examples of civil and domestic life: nor is it for want of admirable doctrines that men hate, and despise, and censure, and deceive, and subjugate one another' (Shelley, 1977, p. 487).

Lurking behind Beatrice's injunction is the spectre of 'the adverting mind' (100) of *Mont Blanc*, which would naturalise the text of 'Poetry [that] lifts the veil from the hidden beauty of the world and makes familiar objects be as if they were not familiar' (Shelley, 1977, p. 487) and 'read' it, much as the natural theologian (or the apostolic succession of the Catholic Church before him) claims 'to read' books – the natural and the scriptural alike – for 'God's truth'.[13] That 'truth' is presumed to be an aggregate made up by the metonymic bits, just as the natural or scriptural text is, on the literal level, made up of little bits – rocks, stones, trees and mountains in the former instance, and letters, words, verses and chapters in the latter.

In the crucial fourth act of *The Cenci*, 'God's truth' and the little bits thereof are very much in evidence. When, for example, Lucretia attempts to protect Beatrice from the Count by alleging that Beatrice has had a vision of divine retribution exacted against him for his deeds, then allows that 'It was a feint' (IV.i.70) uttered 'to awe' (IV.i.72) him, Cenci rebukes Lucretia with 'Vile palterer with the sacred truth of God' (IV.i.73). 'Palterer' means, among other things, 'equivocator', 'shuffler', or 'haggler' (*Oxford English Dictionary*, VII.ii.407). But, as the *OED* remarks of the root verb form *palter*, 'no suitable primitive *palt* is known' (VII.ii.407). It seems probable that Shelley construes this word, which appears in two crucial instances in Act IV, as derived from something like one of the probable roots for 'paltry', the Early Frisian *'palter, pulter*, a rough or broken piece (e.g. of wood or stone)' (*OED*, VII.ii.408). Paltering with 'God's truth', then – especially when it is an activity engaged in by a woman such as Lucretia – is, from Cenci's perspective, playing fast and loose with the metonyms that may be interpreted authoritatively only by the patriarchy. One might even say that the wood- or stone-splitting activity of paltering makes lesser metonyms of metonyms, further problematising the task of 'reading' the 'book' in question to a certain (and authoritative) end.

The second instance of the use of 'palterer' is in Scene iii, when Beatrice calls the assassins Marzio and Olimpio 'Base palterers!' (IV.iii.25) for their reluctance to kill the sleeping Count. Lucretia's alleged paltering is viewed by Cenci as an attempt to divert him from the goal of subjecting Beatrice's mind and body to his will and thus making his seduction of her complete. By identifying with the aggressor by speaking his metonymic language, Beatrice becomes the aggressor and seducer. Seeing Beatrice in this way means understanding that 'to seduce', dissevered from its sexual connotations, means simply 'to lead astray', something that Beatrice cannot help but do, 'wrapped' as she is 'in a strange cloud of crime and shame' that prevents her from seeing, let alone following, the proper way of proceeding. Beatrice views Marzio and Olimpio's equivocating failure to act as an indication that she has not succeeded in seducing their minds and bodies to perform the task of blood-for-blood retribution, which is in its own right a form of absolute and violent possession, albeit of a thanatic rather than an erotic nature.

As with name-calling in general, 'palterer' suggests the strategy of projection and denial. If the object of address is a palterer, then the subject is saved from any imputation that s/he might be one as well, with the corollary inference that one who is demonstrably not a palterer has access to and command of 'God's truth'. It is no coincidence, then, that shortly after Beatrice successfully exhorts Marzio and Olimpio to return to the Count's bedroom and finish the job, she explains to the two of them, and Marzio in particular, 'Thou wert a weapon in the hand of God / To a just use' (IV.iii.54–5). The two imputations of paltering, and especially the effect of that notion on Beatrice, offer another instance of how Beatrice's conviction that she is authorised to speak 'God's truth' serves to 'contort[s] her into the patterns of patriarchal language', ultimately making 'her standard/rival the supreme incarnation of mimetic violence so that she can justifiably, as God's true agent (miming the Count's similar claim), commit such violence against him herself under the cover of acting by the dictates of the highest authority' (Hogle, 1988, pp. 154, 158).

To return to the patriarchy/petriarchy dyad: Count Cenci himself sounds the note of stony obduracy when he responds to Cardinal Camillo's question, 'Art thou not/Most miserable?'

> Why, miserable? –
> No. – I am what your theologians call
> Hardened ...
> (I.i.91–4)

Cenci's prolepsis notwithstanding, the exchange, with its use of the word 'miserable', recalls in part the reaction of Milton's Satan when he first views Eden:

> Me miserable! which way shall I fly
> Infinite wrath, and infinite despair?
> Which way I fly is Hell; myself am Hell ...
> (Milton, 1957, IV, pp. 73–5)

That hell, it should be noted, is located in a petrific landscape, a 'Region dolorous', replete with 'many a Frozen, many a Fiery Alp,/ Rocks, Caves, Lakes, Fens, Bogs, Dens, and shades of death' (Milton, 1957, II, pp. 619–21). After hearing Cenci minimise his murderous exploits by claiming in a manner at once horrific and relevant to the notion of stony enclosures, 'I rarely kill the body which preserves,/Like a strong prison, the soul within my power' (I.i.114–15), Camillo tellingly responds,

> Hell's most abandoned fiend
> Did never, in the drunkenness of guilt,
> Speak to his heart as now you speak to me ...
> (I.i.117–19)

The petriarchy that vindicates a patriarchy which maintains itself in power by speaking in anthropomorphic metonyms about ultimate (and ultimately unknowable) truths is incrementally oppressive. Praising 'the great father of all' (I.iii.23), who has ostensibly answered his prayers, Cenci reveals to his dinner guests that the cause of his glee is the news that two of his four sons are dead. The former of these, 'Rocco' (rock-o? – one Italian word for 'rock' is *roccia*), is of particular interest, as he

> Was kneeling at the Mass, with sixteen others,
> When the Church fell and crushed him to a mummy,
> The rest escaped unhurt.
>
> (I.iii.58–61)

What better evidence could there be that the patriarchal God of Rome and its Church is with Cenci and against his worthless progeny? Whatever causes the stones of the church in which Rocco prays to fall apparently singles him out with an especial vengeance, not only killing him, but effacing his merest resemblance to other human beings by reducing him to 'a mummy', which Reiman and Powers define as 'a pulpy substance or mass' (Shelley, 1977, p. 250n).

Moreover, when Cenci himself is en route to Petrella – 'that lonely rock, / Petrella, in the Apulian Apennines' (III.i.239–40) – the very name of which combines the Italian word for 'stone' (*pietra*) with a dimunitive (and feminine) suffix that ironises the castle's looming, louring prospect and aspect, he passes unscathed by that

> mighty rock,
> Which has, from unimaginable years,
> Sustained itself with terror and with toil
> Over a gulph, and with the agony
> With which it clings seems slowly coming down . . .
>
> (III.i.247–51)

As Sperry explains, 'The stone never descends, for Count Cenci passes by the intended spot an hour too soon. The lines describe Beatrice herself as a kind of failing Prometheus, slowly giving way to the insupportable weight of her miseries as they drag her down into despair' (Sperry, 1988, p. 136). What Sperry does not say is that Prometheus is able to rise from and transcend his own rocky situation – the '*Ravine of Icy Rocks in the Indian Caucasus*' (Shelley,

1977, p. 136) – with the innumerable (if desexualised) agonies perpetrated by the ravishments of the Furies,[14] because he is able to unsay a curse that treats of God, fate, ultimate justice, and other matters of which human beings can have no knowledge, let alone control. Beatrice, on the other hand, continues to view the events of her life as governed by a God, fate, and ultimate justice of which she can have knowledge and, with that knowledge as a basis for her actions, a modicum of control.

The description of the rock has an historical, symbolic and prophetic dimension to it as well as the naturalistic – a dimension revealing the logic of the patriarchy/petriarchy dyad that makes it more than an opportunistic pun. As Timothy Webb observes, Shelley's examination of 'the mind of Italian Catholicism' reveals 'a close connection between power, wealth and authority, a nexus of self-interest which binds together Count Cenci, the Pope, and God' (Webb, 1977, p. 135). That each is a patriarch is beyond question: Cenci is the father of his Children; the Pope, Holy Father of the congregated faithful; God, the Heavenly Father whose will the Pope and Cenci each, in is degree, presumes to interpret to those in his charge. But each is a petriarch as well: Cenci is, by his own admission (and not without sexual innuendo), 'hardened', and Beatrice remarks both his obduracy and the futility of seeking 'by patience, love and tears / To soften him' (I.iii.115–16); the Pope, the inheritor of the Keys of Peter, is the original rock upon which Jesus would build his church (Matthew, 16.18), not to mention the 'marble form' glimpsed at the beginning of V.iv; God himself is the 'rock and . . . fortress' of Psalm 18.1, as well as the 'Rock of Ages' celebrated in Augustus Montague Toplady's 1775 hymn of the same title.

The 'mighty rock', then, is the petriarchal emblem of the patriarchal hegemony that has, 'from unimaginable years, / Sustained itself with terror and with toil' – not its own, but rather the terror and toil of those who are oppressed in the name of the patriarchal/petriarchal hegemony, yet who are nevertheless 'supporters', albeit without a choice, of that 'rock'. (Similarly, the 'agony / With which it clings' is that of the oppressed.) The rock becomes, in this description of it, a type of naturalised erection that symbolises both the terror and illegitimacy of the patriarchal/petriarchal hegemony and of the threat of phallocentric violence that underwrites it. What makes the real rock of the description memorable is not merely its size and looming aspect, but also its lack of any solid grounding: it appears to loom 'Over a gulph'. Implicit in the description is the question that Shelley sees as being begged by the patriarchy/petriarchy that he interrogates: what solid foundation or 'grounding' justifies its eminence? The answer is that none does; the illusion that any does exist is itself an effect of metonymic projection.

Yet the 'mighty rock' does not fall – not on Cenci, nor on anyone else – while the stones of a church in Salamanca do fall, crushing Cenci's son Rocco beyond recognition. More perplexing and ironic still, shortly after Marzio and Olimpio have dispatched the Count, the Papal Legate Savella arrives at Petrella, bearing, on Lucretia's report of the whispered rumour, 'a warrant for his [Count Cenci's] instant death' (IV.iv.28). Without the intervention of Beatrice, her stepmother, and the assassins, it appears as though the inheritor of the keys of Peter, the 'rock' on which the Catholic Church is founded, had sent his legate and troops to fall on Count Cenci at last. What is one to make of the 'heartbreaking, all but unthinkable possibility' that Beatrice's 'promised deliverance was immediately at hand' (Sperry, 1988, p. 134), had she only been able to persevere in her forbearance, secure in the knowledge that 'no person can be truly dishonoured by the act of another'? Is there, as D. Harrington-Lueker argues, 'an evil that is a persistent and pressing potentiality, made actual if man's will is in some measure weak or misguided', an 'evil [that] can be willed away in the sense that it is not inherent in man as Judeo-Christian theology would have it' (Harrington-Lueker, 1983, p. 179)?

The apparent answer to the dilemma is that stones fall, not subject to our will or understanding, but subject to a causal chain that originates with a 'Universal Being' who, as characterised in the passage from the *Essay on Christianity* quoted above, 'can only be described or defined by negatives which deny his subjection to the laws of all inferior existences'. That is, the workings of divine justice, if they are what is behind the question of who is to live and who is to die, operate beyond the ability of human beings, whether they be popes or lesser mortals, to comprehend. In this sense, then, Michael Worton is correct in his assertion that Savella's arrival is 'a means of undermining all notions of justice and of the sanctity of the Pope' (Worton, 1982, p. 117). Shelley would have had no difficulty with Newton's invocation of the law of parsimony in the 'Rules of Reasoning in Philosophy' that preface Book III of the *Principia*. There, Newton offers as an example of '*natural effects*' bespeaking the presence of '*the same cause[s]*' that of stones affected by the force of gravity: 'the descent of stones in *Europe* and in *America*' (Newton, 1966, p. 398). However, Shelley did have a good deal of difficulty with Newton's ascription, in the 'General Scholium' of the *Principia*, of the final cause of gravity to a 'Lord God *Pantokrator*, or *Universal Ruler*' in whom 'all things [are] contained and moved' (Newton, 1966, pp. 544–5). As Eusebes argues in *A Refutation of Deism* (1814), imperfectly quoting the words of Newton last cited,

> We are incapacitated only by our ignorance from referring every phenomenon, however unusual, minute or complex, to the laws of motion and the properties of matter; and it is an egregious offence against the first principles of reason to suppose an immaterial creator of the world, *in quo omnia moventur sed sine mutua passione*: which is equally a superfluous hypothesis in the mechanical philosophy of Newton and a useful excrescence on the inductive logic of Bacon.   (Shelley, 1954, pp. 133–4)[15]

In killing her father, Beatrice becomes what she beholds – a vengeful, stony patriarchist (if not a patriarch) with a pantocratic will-to-power that is not hers to possess. As she says to Lucretia just prior to the return of Savella's troops with Marzio in custody, in phrasing that evokes Newton's characterisation of God and her father's of himself as 'hardened':

> I am as universal as the light;
> Free as the earth-surrounding air; as firm
> As the world's centre. Consequence, to me,
> Is as the wind which strikes the solid rock
> But shakes it not.
>
> (IV.iv.48–52)

Unlike her father, however, Beatrice is, before her death, able to free herself from the delusion that by her actions she carries out the will and work of God. She goes from the *Gott mit uns* ideology of oppression to a very different view of God as her own death approaches. After their conviction but prior to sentencing, Lucretia contemplates the consequences of murdering Cenci and laments the conspirators' decision to do so. Beatrice rejoins in part:

Take cheer! The God who knew my wrong, and made
Our speedy act the angel of his wrath,
Seems, and but seems to have abandoned us.
Let us not think that we shall die for this.
                                                      (V.iii.113–16)

However, after Camillo brings the sentence and the warrant for the
conspirator's immediate execution, Beatrice's views alter radically.
At first, she doubts God's existence, while at the same time
expressing her worst fear: that the metonymic patriarchy that
presumed to speak for God also holds sway in the afterlife, devoid
of any delusions regarding its access to a divine source.

Sweet Heaven, forgive weak thoughts! If there should be
No God, no Heaven, no Earth in the void world. . .
If all things then should be . . . my father's spirit
His eye, his voice, his touch surrounding me;
The atmosphere and breath of my dead life!
If sometimes, as a shape more like himself,
Even the form which tortured me on earth,
Masked in grey hairs and wrinkles, he should come
And wind me in his hellish arms, and fix
His eyes on mine, and drag me down, down, down!
For was he not alone omnipotent
On Earth, and ever present?
                                                      (V.iv.57–69)

The horrific spectre of being condemned to unending incestuous
rape in the afterlife shakes Beatrice's ready identification of God as
a powerful patriarchal figure. Though she tells Lucretia, 'I hope I
do trust in him. In whom else / Can any trust?' (V.iv.88–9), Beatrice
no longer associates trusting in God with bearing witness to any
special manifestation of his potency or efficacy.

No difference has been made by God or man,
Or any power moulding my wretched lot,
'Twixt good or evil, as regarded me.
                                                      (V.iv.82–4)

If 'No difference has been made by God or man', it follows that
Beatrice has not been 'truly dishonoured by the act of another' –

has not suffered the 'difference' of loss of honour to her father or before God. In this last scene, Beatrice comes to realise that her repeated protestations of innocence in the aftermath of the discovery of Cenci's murder and her trial and conviction for that murder are true, although not in the sense she originally (and wilfully) intended. Ultimately, Beatrice is truly innocent – not *innocens*, or unharming, since she is responsible for instigating her father's murder, but *innocendum*, or unharmed, her honour unimpaired by the violence that has been done and is about to be done to her.

With this understanding of her innocence as essentially inviolable and intact, Beatrice accepts her impending death and that of her mother as 'the reward of innocent lives; / . . . the alleviation of worst wrongs' (V.iv.110–11), trusting that she is leaving behind both patriarchy and petriarchy for softly maternal presence and ceaseless evanescence and transference. After characterising man as 'Cruel, cold, formal . . . righteous in words/In deeds a Cain' (V.iv.108–9), and lamenting in part that 'hard, cold men, / Smiling and slow, walk through a world of tears' (V.iv.112–13), Beatrice says no more of God or man, even though she has more than two long speeches and an appropriate forum and audience for doing so. Instead, she turns to Death and woman, for reasons very much like those underlying the song of the captive Greek women in *Hellas* (1822), in which the song is 'an alternative to the repetition of sameness, a countersong that thoroughly recasts the roles of . . . women' (Hogle, 1988, p. 293). In this specific instance, Beatrice's speech revises the earlier spectre of her father's shade winding her in his 'hellish arms':

> Come, obscure Death,
> And wind me in thine all-embracing arms!
> Like a fond mother hide me in thy bosom,
> And rock me to the sleep from which none wake.
>   (V.iv.115–18)

Not surprisingly, in turning from God and man to Death and woman – and restoring the balance and alleviating the confusion between the erotic and the thanatic in the process – Beatrice also turns from figuration that is primarily metonymic and synecdochic to figuration that is primarily metaphoric ('Death['s] . . . arms') and similic ('Like a fond mother'). The speech also bears witness to the re-emergence of authentic desire, manifested in the form of what

Hogle, with a little help from Freud, characterises as 'every person's longings ... for the "original" place, the body and embrace of the Mother, to which Freud claims we seek a return in death so as to reach a state prior to our differentiation from the womb' (Hogle, 1988, p. 310).

Unlike *Prometheus Unbound*, in which unsaying one's high language suffices as the first step in setting the world right, Beatrice's renunciation of the metonymic language of oppression does not change the world in which she lives. It is a world of obduracy and gravity, under the influence of which things fall, stones and the executioner's sword alike. But then again, Beatrice is one who has been led astray by her own high language to the extent that she is unable 'To suffer woes which Hope thinks infinite; / To forgive wrongs darker than Death or Night' (IV.570-1) – at least not to the extent of eschewing the opportunity for revenge. Nevertheless, at the very end of the play 'the once hardened Beatrice ... for the very first time since the earliest portions of the play ... initiates acts of simple human kindness' (Harrington-Lueker, 1983, p. 188). That kindness suggests the transcendent value of Beatrice's insights about the language of oppression and the acts that follow from it for other ages – Shelley's, to be sure, but our own as well, and every subsequent one until the renewal of the 'great age' and return of 'The golden years' (1060-1) glimpsed in *Hellas* finally come to pass.

11
Poetic Autonomy in *Peter Bell the Third* and *The Witch of Atlas*
Jean Hall

In his prefatory poem to *The Witch of Atlas*, Shelley claims there can be no comparison between his graceful Witch, with her 'Light ... vest of flowing metre' (37) and Wordsworth's Peter Bell, 'a lean mark hardly fit to fling a rhyme at; / In shape a Scaramouch, in hue Othello' (44–5). But if Peter Bell and the Witch appear to be antithetical figures, in a deeper sense they are related – as a comparison of *The Witch of Atlas* (1820) and *Peter Bell the Third* (1819), Shelley's parody of Wordsworth's *Peter Bell*, reveals. Both Shelley's Witch and his Peter Bell practise a poetry of autonomy. They live imaginative lives that aspire to a condition of self-sufficiency, and they attempt to exist without significant engagement with the world. On the one hand, Peter Bell the Third materialises poetry by trying to possess the world rather than relate to it, and ends by becoming so absolutely self-absorbed that he obliterates mind and puts his world to sleep. At the opposite extreme, the beautiful Witch of Atlas is so immortally perfect in body and soul that she needs nothing beyond herself and must transcend the mortal world lest it make her weep. Both of Shelley's protagonists produce poetry – Peter's is small and solid, neat verbal 'pipkins' (447) that are an outgrowth of his potter's trade; whereas the Witch of Atlas, like her descendant the Lady of Shalott, sits in splendid isolation in her poetic cave 'aloof ... broidering the pictured poesy / Of some high tale upon her growing woof' (*The Witch of Atlas*, 249–53).

I begin by considering the poetry of possessiveness anatomised in *Peter Bell the Third*, and then go on in the second part of the chapter to consider the poetry of radical transcendence embodied by the Witch. The final part moves beyond Shelley's pairing of

Peter Bell the Third and *The Witch of Atlas* to consider briefly how his treatment of poetic autonomy in these poems illuminates his general attitude towards the imagination.

I

Shelley's Peter Bell is his parodic portrait of the later Wordsworth, the man who laboured on the affected *Peter Bell* for nineteen years and also produced a flood of Tory poetry. *Peter Bell the Third* charts Wordsworth's fall from a journeyman poet making his modest poetic 'pipkins' to a party man willing to write the 1815 *Ode on Waterloo*, which Shelley sees as authorising the bloody Peterloo massacre. This Peter Bell suffers his terrible decline because from the beginning he lacked an essential poetic attribute – he was 'unimaginative' (308). His lack of imagination is described through the metaphor of the closed circle:

> He had a mind which was somehow
> At once circumference and centre
> Of all he might feel or know;
> Nothing went ever out, although
> Something did ever enter.
>
> (293–7)

Here is a vision of autonomy as an inexorably centred self which establishes a 'circumference' or circular boundary: the self cannot leave its own orbit and irresistibly draws the outside world within. Whatever Peter 'saw and felt', whatever 'came within the belt / Of his own nature, seemed to melt / Like cloud to cloud, into him' (273–7). Shelley describes a distinctive poetic way of seeing, a tendency to convert anything that is perceived into a version of oneself. In *Peter Bell the Third* the Wordsworthian egotistical sublime is portrayed as a species of possessiveness, an ungiving and unsociable attitude that renders Peter 'a kind of moral eunuch' (314), 'A solemn and unsexual man' (551). Peter's lack of sexual desire is the predominant symptom of a general disinclination to relate to other people, so that his poetic thought becomes a portentous process of 'the outward world uniting / To that within him', an operation 'Considerably uninviting / To those, who medi-tation slighting, / Were moulded in a different frame' (278–82).

Peter's autonomy swiftly assumes an entrepreneurial cast, as he becomes the Devil's footman in 'Hell's Grosvenor square' (263), a position from which he will rise to dominate the world of letters. As aspiring poet he easily becomes the possession of the Devil, for he himself practices poetry as a species of possessiveness – he always is a man who has his price. As such, he is at home in 'Hell . . . a city much like London' (147), a society itself permeated by the possessive principle, which constantly provokes everyone to make profit out of everyone else. The result is an incessant struggle to rise to the top, a perennial warfare of 'the oppressor and the oppressed' (253). As autonomous poet, Peter lives in a society characterised by autonomy. Everyone operates on the principle of self-interest, attempting to best all others – and the exemplar of this attitude becomes the Devil himself, the monarch of Hell, who enjoys the world as his possession.

But in Shelley's poem the Devil has neither Miltonic sublimity nor penetration. Instead, he is an hyperbolic version of Peter's own solemn dullness, 'a leaden-witted thief – just huddled / Out of the dross and scum of nature; / A toadlike lump of limb and feature, / With mind, and heart, and fancy muddled' (339–42). This dim-witted, materialised being does not know himself – and Shelley presses the point literally; for the devil believes himself to be 'a slop-merchant from Wapping' (92), and his creature, Peter Bell, fancies himself born 'In the fens o' Lincolnshire' (113). Both are spuriously idealised beings, deluded by an 'upper stream of thought, / Which made all seem as it was not' (108–9). These possessive selves are formed as an unconscious, lumpish centre radiating illusory streams of thought: ironically, in attempting to possess the world, they have lost touch with themselves. But the Devil is dimly aware of a profound disturbance, for he longs for 'the peace he could not feel, / Or the care he could not banish' (135–6). The populace of his Hell feel similar subterranean agitations; as 'Each pursues what seems most fair', their acquisitive instincts turn against themselves, making them mine 'like moles, through mind, and there / Scoop palace-caverns vast, where Care / In throned state is ever dwelling' (260–2). Within the hollowed-out core of themselves, Care rules over these possessive beings, rendering the circle of self a vast illusory palace – an empty globe.

Because it issues from his possessive instincts, even the best of Peter's poetry is tainted by the materialised spirit and lack of self-knowledge endemic in Hell. At times he manages slightly to lighten the burden of materiality; his 'mind's work, had made alive/The things it wrought on ... Wakening a sort of thought in sense' (310–12). But when he creates poetry it is 'without a sense/ Of memory' (423–4), from a hidden past life which issues as an unconnected series of 'obscure remembrances' (418) that make him sing 'of rocks and trees', or 'Many a ditch and quickset fence', or 'pedlars tramping on their rounds,/Milk pans and pails' (421–30). The Wordsworthian poetry of memory, those great meditations which build the poetic sense of a profound and abiding self, in Shelley's comic version truly become a miscellany of poetic 'pipkins' – disconnected trees, pedlars, pans endowed with the spark of life, mildly warming 'a cold age' appreciative of 'songs for all the land/Sweet both to feel and understand' (435–46). In Peter's poetry, autonomy assumes the character of the fragmentary; for instead of creating the poet's own coherent sense of self, his meditations can only give a mysterious and faintly ludicrous life to things. Like the other inhabitants of Shelley's Hell, Peter strives to be self-sufficient and to promote his own self-interests, but the paradoxical result is the disintegration and loss of selfhood.

When the reviewers attack his poetry, Peter breaks down even further. Now the Care that always sat enthroned at his centre becomes strong agitation, and perhaps madness. Like Wordsworth's Peter Bell, he sets off on horseback, 'Lashing and spurring his tame hobby...High trotting over nine-inch bridges,/With Flibbertigibbet, imp of pride,/Mocking and mowing by his side' (549–56). The aftermath of this strange disturbance is exhaustion, and increased dullness – for at last, in order to vivify his profoundly materialised and obscure self, Peter must resort to manipulation. His earlier poetic meditations had spontaneously awakened a sort of thought in sense, but now the crazed Peter must deliberately inflict pain in order to feel any sense of life. One of his poems takes pleasure in the 'death hues of agony/ Lambently flashing from a fish' (584–5), and for this Shelley in a footnote directs us to *The Excursion*: 'That poem contains curious evidence of the gradual hardening of a strong but circumscribed sensibility, of the perversion of a penetrating but panic stricken understanding' (Shelley, 1977, p. 342).

This is the poet who writes Odes to the Devil, which glory in the Peterloo massacre. In his degenerate state Peter's possessiveness has been replaced by destructiveness, for if he cannot own the world at least he can destroy it. The antagonism that was latent in his earlier attempts at autonomy now is made painfully evident. At this point Peter Bell can retain his vitality only through 'perversion'; but his vicious Tory poetry turns out to win him the worldly success he always desired. He takes the place of the Devil and reaps the profits that buy a 'house, . . . plate, and made / A genteel drive up to his door' (688–9). But ironically, in finally winning the world Peter entirely loses himself. In his extraordinary dullness, so 'Concentred and compressed so close' (720), he becomes a materialising power that puts everything to sleep. From his self's centre streams a somnolence that narcotises everyone around him, and even deadens nature – 'The woods and lakes, so beautiful, / Of dim stupidity were full, / All grew dull as Peter's self' (740–2). At the end of *Peter Bell the Third* Peter's world sinks into slumber as Pope's world does in *The Dunciad* – but where Pope describes this in a satirically sublime vision wherein 'universal darkness buries all', the dim world of Peter Bell ends as an absurdly small affair – a globe 'Seven miles above – below – around' (768) centred on Peter himself. The autonomous poet has made a shrunken world that mirrors his own deadly and constricted circle of self.

II

The Witch of Atlas certainly is a more appealing figure than Peter Bell the Third, but, like him, she is autonomous. Once again Shelley uses the metaphor of the circle to illustrate this point. Where Peter's mind is 'At once circumference and centre', a locus where 'Nothing went ever out, although / Something did ever enter' (*Peter Bell the Third*, 294–7), the Witch too becomes a centre that draws in everything. Peter functions in this way because of his possessive instincts; but the Witch's influence is due to her intellectual beauty. It is the world that moves towards her, not the other way around, for to see the Witch of Atlas is to love her:

> her beauty made
> The bright world dim, and every thing beside
> Seemed like the fleeting image of a shade:
> No thought of living spirit could abide –
> Which to her looks had ever been betrayed,
> On any object in the world so wide,

On any hope within the circling skies,
But on her form, and in her inmost eyes.
                                            (137–44)

As poetic centre the Witch embodies the principle of attraction, the polar opposite of Peter's possessiveness. Aware of her profound effect on the beings betrayed to her gaze, she responds not by trying to possess them but by weaving 'a subtle veil . . . A shadow for the splendour of her love' (151–2). When the creatures persist in adoring her she explains that as an immortal she cannot bear to love the dying generations, for 'If I must sigh to think that this shall be – / If I must weep when the surviving Sun / Shall smile on your decay – Oh, ask not me / To love you till your little race is run' (234–7). For the Witch, engagement with the world would be an emotional encumbrance, a tie that would cause her to 'sigh' and 'weep'. Therefore she withdraws to her cave of poetry where she 'sate aloof . . . broidering the pictured poesy / Of some high tale upon her growing woof' (249–53).

The Witch's art is autonomous because she is perfect and immortal, and as such does not require the world. Where Peter Bell acts as a needy soul, an incomplete being struggling for completion through his incessant acquisitiveness, the Witch does the opposite – she banishes the world because its imperfection could sully her divine self-sufficiency. Like the Poet's visionary lover in *Alastor*, Emily in *Epipsychidion*, and the Shape all Light in *The Triumph of Life*, the Witch is one figure in a long line of transcendental beauties celebrated by Shelley. But in this visionary company the Witch enjoys one distinction: she is the protagonist of her poem. The others are the visions of the poems' heroes, men who briefly glimpse the ideal and are drawn into a passionate, poetic search for it. Their journeys are hardly comparable to the history of Peter Bell the Third, for unlike him these men are true lovers – but still there is one significant point of resemblance. Like Peter Bell, Shelley's lovers are mortal men, incomplete beings who need love and practise their poetic pursuit of perfection as an action not wholly unrelated to Peter's lust to possess the world. The difference is that where Peter materialises mortal struggle, Shelley's lovers idealise it.

If the neediness of the mortal condition is a flaw, nevertheless inhabiting this imperfect situation does offer one advantage: it makes significant action possible. Those who lack something vital will have something to do, for they always can strive for what they need. It is exactly this kind of action that is denied the Witch. Because she is complete in herself, her art also must be autonomous – it does not alter anything; it cannot grow; it is not a part of history. Only mortals can participate in history, for it is the mortal condition that involves incompleteness and hence produces change. Shelley's Witch is the true progenitor of Tennyson's Lady of Shalott and the narrator of *The Palace of Art*, figures who establish a profound rift between the worlds of human history and the enclosed perfection of artistic activity. But where Tennyson is anguished by this split, Shelley is more interested in exploring its possibilities and limitations. What would art become in a perfect world? He suggests that it would be perceptive play. His Witch becomes the pure, the absolute avatar of disinterested aesthetic contemplation – the perfect Kantian.

There are splendid advantages in this position. Freed from the mortal need for possession, the Witch can practise a poetry of absolute moral purity, for in her plenitude she is incapable of taking anything away from anyone. Her imaginative energies can be entirely liberated – and so, unlike the retired and melancholy Lady of Shalott, she soon abandons weaving her poetic 'woof' to take to her magic boat. She speeds 'down the earthquaking cataracts which shiver / Their snowlike waters into golden air' (377–8), mounts upward to the river's source, and flies into the stormy sky, reversing the natural hydrological cycle and establishing a triumphal cloud pavilion 'Which rain could never bend, or whirl-blast shake' (426). Being able to transcend nature, she can play with it, braving the sublime turbulence of cataract and storm with imaginative grace. Unlike Shelley's crabbed and self-protective Peter Bell, the Witch is a great risk-taker, a sort of imaginative sportswoman. Her imagination is endlessly joyful, ebullient – she is a generous being.

Although in the main this generosity is an autonomous quality, an inclination to regard the world as her plaything rather than engage with it, she does come near to engagement with the Egyptians when she visits them in their sleep, perceiving each person's 'naked beauty of . . . soul . . . the inner form most bright and fair' (571–3). Her imaginative penetration is matched by her creativity; for when she sees each person's soul she fashions a dream appropriate to his essential being. Once again Shelley revisits a scene common in his poetry of mortal love, but this time views the action from the stance of the ideal. Where his mortal lovers, such as the *Alastor* Poet, dream of the perfect beloved and wake to find her vanished, the Witch is herself the artist of transcendence, the maker of the images that visit human dreams. In this capacity she is potentially related to the world, but only through the prospect of human activity. Shelley suggests that our dreams are a mortal version of the Witch's disinterested aesthetic contemplation, a generous play of possibility that can instigate a variety of waking action. Although in Shelley's other poetry such action may be creative, it is not necessarily so: if Asia dreams of love in *Prometheus Unbound* and wakes to follow out her desires through the revolutionary recreation of a harmonious world, on the other hand the *Alastor* Poet wakes to renounce the world and eventually sinks into self-destruction and death.

But these serious responses to dreaming are not part of *The Witch of Atlas*. Shelley remains true to the purely transcendental perspective of the Witch, showing her impact as a short-circuiting of mortal striving, a consummation of each person's nature not dependent on his activity – for when the dreamers awake, their visions simply come true. In a transcendental key, then, human dreamings become wish-fulfilment. To the good the Witch 'gave / Strange panacea in a chrystal bowl . . . / They drank in their deep sleep of that sweet wave – / And lived thenceforward as if some control / Mightier than life, were in them' (593–7); and after death their corpses do not decay but remain suspended in a trance, living in 'dreams beyond the rage / Of death or life' (613–14). True lovers 'who had been so coy / They hardly knew whether they loved or not / Would rise out of their rest, and take sweet joy', not realising that they had acted, not dreamed, until 'the tenth moon shone' – but then 'the Witch would let them take no ill . . . and so they took their fill . . . in marriage warm and kind' (649–60). This liberation of true love through a supposed dream that turns out to be reality may well be Shelley's transposition of *The Eve of St. Agnes* (1820), and if so he would be aware that Keats's poem pointed out the need for mortal striving – for Porphyro deliberately constructs the conditions for Madeline's wish-fulfilment, and in turning her desires into actuality makes the couple's further action necessary. They must exit their dream, escape Madeline's castle, and brave the storm of life that awaits them outside.

The transcendence of activity that marks the dreams of the good also is a feature of evil dreamings. For some of the Egyptians are oppressors, and their dreams are not wish-fulfilments but strange self-subversions. In the hands of the Witch their 'harsh and crooked purposes' become 'more vain/Than in the desert is the serpent's wake/Which the sand covers' (619–21). The priests dream that they undo themselves, writing 'How the god Apis, really was a bull/And nothing more; and bid the herald stick/The same against the temple doors, and pull/The old cant down' (627–30). The king is moved to 'dress an ape up in his crown/And robes, and seat him on his glorious seat' (633–4), and soldiers 'dreamed that they were blacksmiths, and/Walked out of quarters in somnambulism' to beat 'their swords to ploughshares' (641–5). As transcendental opponent of tyranny the Witch does not instigate the kind of serious, engaged imaginative activity undertaken by Asia in the second act of *Prometheus Unbound*, which is prelude to revolutionary world change. Instead she enacts imagination as play – and when she visits the oppressors, the result is pure mischief.

In short, an important element in the Witch's imaginative ebullience is her entire lack of seriousness. This is not a flaw; it is merely a mark of her transcendence. Shelley makes the point most clearly when he shows how she fashions her hemaphrodite. Like Shelley's mortals who make an idealised image of themselves in their dreams, the Witch creates a companionable form. But where mortal poets passionately fall in love with their own dreamings, the Witch forms a 'sexless thing' possessing 'no defect/Of either sex, yet all the grace of both' – an image of 'perfect purity' (329–36) who becomes a playmate rather than a lover. Oddly enough, like Shelley's Peter Bell, that 'solemn and unsexual man' (*Peter Bell the Third*, 551), the Witch prefers to remain chaste. Peter Bell does so because of his ungenerosity, his reluctance to share anything of himself with anyone; but the Witch takes her autonomous stance for opposite reasons. In her unlimited generosity and imaginative abundance she forever must give herself away freely to the world – which means that she cannot restrict her gifts to one lover. She is 'a sexless bee/Tasting all blossoms and confined to none', which is why 'Among those mortal forms the wizard-maiden/Passed with an eye serene and heart unladen' (589–92).

Unfettered generosity perforce must be shallow because it forecloses the possibility of investing deeply in any one relationship, any one endeavour. And so Shelley leads us to the surprising realisation that eternity is lighthearted because its only action is incessant play, whereas it is mortality, for all its imperfections, which has the capacity for serious engagement. At first the generous and witty play of the Witch appears to be the opposite of Peter Bell the Third's dull versifying, and especially his painful Odes to the Devil; but on closer inspection, both figures can be seen to practise a poetry of manipulation rather than a poetry of true engagement. Instead of involving themselves with their creations, Peter and the Witch prefer to remain separate and autonomous, to be untouched by what they make. Although the Witch's ebullience seems far from Peter's sadism, the link between the two becomes evident in the Witch's trifling with the Egyptian dreamers. By giving the evil people what they deserve, the Witch devises pure mischief, a transcendental transformation of Peter's poetry of cruelty. These jokes at the expense of the oppressors reflect on them, not on the Witch herself, who simply makes their dreams come true. In doing so she is able to expose evil without becoming contaminated by it.

A detached posture, then, offers certain advantages. If the immortal Witch never can be a true and passionate lover like the mortal narrators of *Epipsychidion* and *Adonais*, nevertheless her transcendental frolics can unveil and confound evil. This potential should direct our attention to the narrators of *Peter Bell the Third* and *The Witch of Atlas*; for like Peter and the Witch, these speakers operate from a stance of detachment. Where the Witch and Peter are limited by their autonomous postures, Shelley's narrators in these poems employ detachment as a narrative position which liberates vision by harmlessly exposing evil.

In particular, the narrative detachment of *Peter Bell the Third* functions to disarm cruelty, to make the poem much closer to comedy than to satire. Shelley's *Fragment of a Satire on Satire* (1820) suggests his discomfort with the genre, which he associates with 'gibbets, axes, confiscations, chains, / And racks of subtle torture' (Shelley, 1970, p. 625). Satire becomes 'The strokes of the inexorable scourge' applied 'Until the heart be naked', a materialising poetry capable only of inflicting torture and changing the human soul for the worse – for 'Rough words beget sad thoughts . . . / Men take a sullen and a stupid pride / In being all they hate in other's shame' (Shelley, 1970, p. 626).

In conceiving of satire as a direct attack meant to inflict damage, Shelley accurately assessed the spirit of the Augustan form. As David B. Morris has shown, there was a widespread assumption in

the eighteenth century that corporal punishment was the appropriate deterrent to anti-social behaviour, and that satires could and
should act as verbal substitutions for physical punishment (Morris,
1984, pp. 214–40). To replace this cruel directness Shelley adopts a
posture of detachment which converts pain into mischief. Where
Peter Bell and the society of 'Hell . . . a city much like London' (147)
lose all sense of perspective in their ceaselessly self-interested
pursuits, the narrator of *Peter Bell the Third* stands back to contemplate this curious behaviour, hoping that folly will be moved to
expose itself. As an alternative to Peter's deadly ambition which
eventually brings on his overworked dullness, the narrator offers a
light touch; his Dedication admits that 'I have spent six or seven
days in composing this sublime piece' (324). In his prefatory poem
to *The Witch of Atlas* Shelley makes a similar case to Mary, claiming
that his Witch took 'three days/In dressing', in contrast to the
laborious 'nineteen years' of 'slow, dull care' (25–37) Wordsworth
required to produce *Peter Bell*. Shelley suggests that the proper
reply to dullness is dexterity – that the rejoinder to solemnity
ought to be play. Rather than wound through satire he chooses to
lighten the heart through comedy.

Shelleyan comedy becomes a disengagement that suspends
mortal seriousness to allow for the refreshment of play. He says to
the over-serious Mary in the prefatory poem to *The Witch of Atlas*
that she is that she is 'critic-bitten . . . That you condemn these
verses I have written/Because they tell no story, false or true . . ./
What, though no mice are caught by a young kitten,/May it not
leap and play as grown cats do,/Till its claws come?' (1–7). His
poem will arrest time, telling 'no story' because stories are a mortal
form that describes change, instead frolicking like a clawless kitten
that declines to mature and become a working mouser. There is a
deliberate refusal to grow up, to become serious – but the refusal is
a temporary one confined to the poetic play of three days. Within
these limits Shelley can play like a child but at the same time not be
reproached for childishness – because he knows what he is doing.

To validly liberate poetic play in *The Witch of Atlas* Shelley
requires a narrator who is willing to frolic but also understands as
well as temporarily denies seriousness. Mortal actuality must be
present, but only by implication. The resonant version of childhood, therefore, must be a sophisticated posture that knows
realities but manages gracefully to sidestep them for a while.
Shelley's narrators in *Peter Bell the Third* and *The Witch of Atlas*

become grown-up children, and as playful conversationalists owe much to Byron. Indeed, Peter Bell's society of Hell, with its incessant social climbing and self-seeking, seems strikingly Byronic; but even clearer links can be perceived in *The Witch of Atlas*.[1]

The poem is written in ottava rima, the stanza of *Don Juan*, and the transcendence enjoyed by the Witch recalls a famous image from Canto IV of *Childe Harold's Pilgrimage*. There Byron's narrator sings 'Roll on, thou deep and dark blue Ocean', a hymn that celebrates the sea's sublime destructiveness. Ocean dashes man to pieces, 'Spurning him from thy bosom to the skies, / [Thou] sends't him, shivering in thy playful spray / And howling, to his Gods' (Byron, 1986, p. 199; Canto IV. 179–80). But where some men sink into the depths, Byron's narrator will skim the rolling surface, skilfully ride the waves, and exuberantly survive. Shelley invokes this image in *The Witch of Atlas*, as the Witch remarks, 'the strife / Which stirs the liquid surface of man's life' (543–4) and the narrator adds,

> And little did the sight disturb her soul –
>   We, the weak mariners of that wide lake
> Where'er its shores extend or billows roll,
>   Our course unpiloted and starless make
> O'er its wild surface to an unknown goal –
>   But she in the calm depths her way could take
> Where in bright bowers immortal forms abide
> Beneath the weltering of the restless tide.
>
> (545–52)

Where Byron's narrator dexterously rides the waves, Shelley's Witch does something even more marvellous: she walks in 'the calm depths', an impossibility for human beings. This mark of her immortality – her serene transcendence of mortal turbulence – is repeated in other images of the poem. She has a pool of emerald and a pool of fire, and is accustomed to lie within them in immortal trance while 'The fierce war / Of wintry winds shook that innocuous liquor' (281–2); and her pavilion in the clouds becomes a 'windless haven' untouched by the storm that whips 'the outer lake beneath the lash / Of the wind's scourge' (429, 441–2).

The serenity that comes naturally to the immortal Witch becomes an achievement on the part of Shelley's narrator – he too manages to keep his heart light, although he is aware of life's grim realities.

The play of *The Witch of Atlas* is markedly gentler than the antics of *Don Juan*, but the poems do resemble each other in narrative posture. Byron and Shelley both aim to create a flexible, sophisticated narrator who can sport with life's turbulence and so avoid being overcome by it. But where Byron's narrator often functions by materialising the spurious ideal, pointing out that men's ideologies frequently are a function of their physical needs and greediness, Shelley's narrator enacts sophistication as an idealising activity. In this sense, the poem also refers to the lumpish protagonist of *Peter Bell the Third*, that materialised Wordsworth who in possessing the world lost all self-knowledge. Peter Bell is dark to himself, but the idealising narrator of *The Witch of Atlas* demonstrates how the exuberant creation of gossamer fantasy can be an adaptive quality, not a permanent escape from reality. For as Shelley put it in the Preface to *Prometheus Unbound*, acquainting ourselves 'with beautiful idealisms of moral excellence' liberates human capacities; because 'until the mind can love, and admire, and trust, and hope, and endure, reasoned principles of moral conduct are seeds cast upon the highway of life which the unconscious passenger tramples into dust' (Shelley, 1977, p. 135).

III

Reading *Peter Bell the Third* and *The Witch of Atlas* as a pairing which indicates the range of poetic autonomy yields a strong antithesis: Shelley sees that autonomy can be a self-centred posture that materialises the world in attempting to possess it, or a purely disinterested stance possible only to the immortals, which in its limitless generosity endlessly gives itself away in ideal play. If this were all we could derive from comparing Shelley's two poems, it would be interesting enough; but in adapting the Witch's transcendental stance to human circumstances through the creation of her poem's narrator, Shelley considerably broadens his meditation on autonomy, and provides a useful perspective for placing some of the other major works in his canon.

The gracious narrator of *The Witch of Atlas* knows mortal encumbrance and yet temporarily can liberate his imagination in immortal sport. His sophistication allows him to remain detached from, yet connected to life – and this becomes an adaptive posture, for it permits his imaginative expansion while keeping him in touch with human circumstances. A stance such as this is vital for an idealising poet like Shelley; without it, one's ideals might be overwhelmed by human history, or alternatively, emasculated through transcendental abstraction.

Like *Peter Bell the Third* and *The Witch of Atlas*, *The Cenci* and *Prometheus Unbound* can be viewed as companion poems that meditate on the imagination's stance by placing it within history or, alternatively, detaching it. Shelley describes the story of Beatrice Cenci as a 'sad reality' (Shelley, 1977, p. 237), for this beautiful woman, the mortal analogue of such figures as the Witch of Atlas or the *Alastor* Poet's visionary beloved, is an idealist who is confined by what Shelley considers the local and corrupt Catholic thought of sixteenth-century Rome. Therefore, when she is raped by her father, she retaliates by causing him to be assassinated, basing her righteousness on false religious authority and thereby corrupting her own good nature without realising what she has done. In adamantly maintaining her purity she becomes a spurious idealist, a disturbing example of autonomy who is dark to herself and ends in betraying her own best nature (see Hall, 1984).

Seen in this context, *Prometheus Unbound* becomes an alternative poem partially detached from history, and yet still significantly connected to it – a placing related to the narrative stance of *The Witch of Atlas*. Although Shelley's great lyrical drama unfolds in a fictional world, it is not purely ideal, for a multiplicity of historical references can and should be read into it. The poem becomes an example of adaptive idealism, for it provides ways of helping us to think about a variety of historical situations. In particular, the French Revolution is present in this poem only by implication, and yet it was the great contemporary historical event that Shelley constantly sought to come to terms with in his work, for he wished to acknowledge the mistakes made by the revolutionaries, and yet retain the sense of hope their movement had kindled. In Jerome McGann's terms, Shelley's strategy of detachment in *Prometheus Unbound* provides an example of the Romantic ideology, an attempt to cope with history through a posture of partial transcendence (McGann, 1983).

Similar observations can be made about *A Defence of Poetry*, which contains an abundance of transcendentalising language but also retains a strong historical orientation, for, indeed, in the main part of the essay Shelley writes a complete history of European poetry. The *Defence* has been attacked for inconsistency, for an

incoherent mingling of Platonist and empirical thought; but I
would suggest that it might better be regarded as an essay in
adaptive idealism.[2] Shelley began writing it as a reply to the
utilitarianism advocated in Peacock's *The Four Ages of Poetry*, in
which he saw a materialising taint reminiscent of Peter Bell the
Third. As he says in the *Defence*, the European society of his day has
'more scientific and œconomical knowledge than can be accommodated to the just distribution of the produce which it multiplies . . .
We want the creative faculty to imagine that which we know; we
want the generous impulse to act that which we imagine; we want
the poetry of life: our calculations have outrun conception; we have
eaten more than we can digest' (Shelley, 1977, p. 502).

Shelley's aim in the *Defence* is to remove his readers from a
restrictively local frame of reference, a misplaced faith in scientific
progress which threatened to overwhelm them in a contemporary
materialism as destructive of human life as the narrow religious
superstitions of Beatrice Cenci's Rome. His alternative to utilitarianism becomes poetry, an activity central to human life because it
is the creator of culture – which at its best can be a broad vision of
things that transcends the poet's immediate time and place in a
dialogue with the poetic generations past and to come. Thus, 'A
poem is the very image of life expressed in its eternal truth', not
because it embodies pure transcendental authority, but because it
evokes ever-renewed imaginative activity. For 'Time, which destroys the beauty and the use of the story of particular facts . . .
augments that of Poetry, and for ever developes [*sic*] new and
wonderful applications of the eternal truth which it contains'
(Shelley, 1977, p. 485). Like *Prometheus Unbound*, which is not
dependent on any one historical situation and yet could illuminate
all of them, the true poem is eternal in so far as it is evocative rather
than authoritative, for it stimulates imaginative reinterpretation,
which helps us creatively to adapt our idealism to our actuality.
Potentially, poetry can redeem history by endowing us with the
power to recreate it.

Poetry also can redeem individual human lives, as works such as
Epipsychidion and *Adonais* demonstrate. I have discussed these
poems as examples of passionate mortal poetry which show
Shelley's need to engage imaginatively with the world, but now it
must be added that such engagement is fictional, and therefore
displays a crucial element of detachment. Shelley fictionalises his
life in these poems, turning Emilia Viviani into the Emily of

Epipsychidion, Keats into Adonais, and himself into the passionate narrator of their poems. This narrator learns to arrange and rearrange his fictions, creating a series of altering world visions which finally grow comprehensive enough to permit the embrace of his beloved (see Hall, 1980, pp. 102–50). Such poetry – a poetry that demands multiple reinterpretations – is related to the constantly remade great poem celebrated in the *Defence*, and the potential multiplicity of historical references suggested by a drama such as *Prometheus Unbound*. Shelley demonstrates his sophistication in these works by showing that he is able to use his fictions rather than be used by them, for his flexible poetry becomes a means of creative adaptation, not an authoritarian vision such as Beatrice Cenci's religious world view, which ends in controlling its very maker.

Shelley often aims for a happy blend of engagement and detachment, regarding poetry as a fiction which temporarily removes one from life in order better to see and cope with it. He dramatises the dangers of imaginative autonomy, showing how an attempt at complete self-sufficiency can lead to rigidity and lack of self-knowledge, a condition which can promote the follies of his Peter Bell or the tragedy of his Beatrice. At the opposite extreme from these figures the purely ideal flexibility of the Witch of Atlas betokens a lack of engagement with the world, an inhumanly transcendental and ahistorical existence that precludes the growth and development of the soul. Like the Byron of *Don Juan*, Shelley aims at a narrative stance of partial detachment that will liberate imaginative vision without rigidifying or falsifying it. Although Shelley writes a poetry of idealism, he is a sophisticated poet capable of many moods and postures, and in *The Witch of Atlas* and *Peter Bell the Third* he courts comparison with Byron by successfully writing varieties of Romantic comedy.

12

Love, Writing and Scepticism in *Epipsychidion*

Angela Leighton

Romantic love is not a central preoccupation of the Romantic poets. By comparison with the Elizabethans or the Victorians, the English Romantics wrote very few poems about that influx of inspirational feeling which attends upon the long-drawn-out courtship of the beloved. The sustained, urbane intellectualisation of love which the courtly tradition requires is at odds with the essentially pantheistic and political concerns of the Romantics. Shelley's *Epipsychidion*, with its fervent Platonism and declamatory rhetoric, is thus something of an anomaly, even by comparison with his other works. The fact of finding a beautiful woman, captive in a convent in Italy in 1821, anachronistically inspires in him a passion from the antique, and a poetry well versed in courtly formulations. Perhaps the very medieval reality of Emilia's life encouraged in her admirer an infatuation which sounds bookish, and a passion which feels *passé*. Certainly the spirit of another poet and of another book makes itself strongly felt throughout Shelley's love poem. Dante's life-long devotion to the figure of Beatrice, as critics have shown (see Webb, 1976; Schulze, 1982), is the model against which Shelley measures the strength of his own love, and composes the story of his own *Vita Nuova*. *Epipsychidion* is thus, like many romances after Dante's, a poem in the grip of an imagination and an experience which precede its own.

* * *

Though the lover's discourse is no more than a dust of figures stirring according to an unpredictable order, like a fly buzzing in a room, I can assign to love, at least retrospectively, according to my Image-repertoire, a settled course: it is by means of this *historical* hallucination that I sometimes make love into a romance, an adventure. (Barthes, 1978, p. 197)

220

According to Roland Barthes, romantic love is a random, second-hand discourse, turned into personal history by memory and retrospection. To write about love in the courtly Platonic tradition of the West is to engage in a dusty re-arrangement of 'figures', which tell an old story, but which can be 'settled' as the uniquely experienced history of the individual. This paradox of love as inescapably intertextual – as the figures of another's speech, which can be historicised by memory, and thus given at least the 'hallucination' of an individual 'course' of events – touches rather temptingly, not only on two directions which are felt in Shelley's poem, but also on two current theoretical emphases. The text of romantic love exists on a crossroad between, on the one hand, pure self-perpetuating figurativeness, and, on the other hand, related history and biography. The self-referential nature of the first seems at odds with the documentary commitment of the second. To some extent this opposition is intrinsic to all imaginative writing, but in the text of romantic love it becomes particularly acute.

The theoretical opposition which results from this doubleness finds forceful expression in two books of the 1940s: Denis de Rougemont's *Love in the Western World* (1940) and Simone de Beauvoir's *The Second Sex* (1949). De Rougemont's wide-ranging celebration of romantic love defines it as an essentially amoral, self-sustaining and self-describing passion for the tragic. Unrequited and ultimately death-bound, romantic love 'is infinite desire which takes as its object or pretext a finite individual' (de Rougemont, 1940, p. 6). Such a pretext serves, not only for intensified feeling, but also for intensified speech, or 'self-description' (de Rougemont, 1940, p. 173). Romantic love is a passion nourished not so much on experience as on words. Its energy is self-reflexive and its inspiration self-propitiating. Thus de Rougemont summarises: 'European romanticism may be compared to a man for whom sufferings, and especially the sufferings of love, are a privileged mode of understanding' (de Rougemont, 1940, pp. 51–2). Such 'understanding' has no object, time or place. It has only a self-tormenting and self-studying subject: 'man'.

This, of course, is the butt of de Beauvoir's attack. The 'privileged mode' of romantic love is not a form of transcendent 'understanding', but of gender-specific interests. De Beauvoir's purpose is to find out the hidden history of the woman whom romantic love has turned into the supremely idealised fiction. To recover 'the dispersed, contingent, and multiple existences of actual women' (de Beauvoir, 1949, p. 283) is to resist the self-sufficient and self-satisfying figures of a discourse which shifts, arbitrarily and beautifully, in the high atmospherics of the male lover's speech.

To turn speeches into facts, dreams into interests, figures into history, is to resist the 'devouring metonymy' (Barthes, 1978, p. 75) of the lover's language, and to reject the 'psychotherapeutic plenitude' (Spivak, 1988, p. 18) offered by love's object. In the face of the dedicated narcissism and figurativeness of romantic love, the feminist critic is very often driven into literal-minded detective work, which saves the text for history and for women, but which nonetheless has its drawbacks as well. The search for 'the dispersed, contingent, and multiple' facts of women's lives leads, with fruitful or merely programmatic reductiveness, altogether outside the literary purpose of the text. This problem of 'the literary' is one which feminist theory has either grounded in the sexual politics of gender, or else tactically ignored. It has thus left it in the hands of the other main theoretical perspective of today: that of deconstruction.

Romantic literature, more than any other, has readily lent itself to the anti-historical and anti-referential devices of deconstruction. Paul de Man's long and rich investment in the 'figural' nature of Romantic literature, for instance, has consistently opposed figures and history, literariness and literalism. The figurative, or 'disfigurative', reading, according to de Man, always 'resists historicism' (de Man, 1979b, p. 69). He defends deconstruction as a means of rejecting ideological complicities, and of thereby preserving the 'autonomous potential of language', or 'literariness' (de Man, 1982, p. 10) itself. Thus the fact that poetic language, and especially Romantic language, knows itself *as* a figure, as unsettling and displacing from the start, becomes the means by which it effects its own referential disaffiliations. This is the textual 'insight' which exposes the 'blindness' of the critic, so that, he argues, when 'critics think they are demystifying literature, they are in fact being demystified by it' (de Man, 1983, p. 18).

De Man's very Nietzschean fascination with 'the intralinguistic resources of figures' rather than the 'extralinguistic referent or meaning' (de Man, 1979a, p. 106) is one which presents the text, quite familiarly now, as the free-fall of an abyss, with no ontological, authorial or socio-historical ledges. That the abyss also underlies the Romantic world view is, of course, a powerful reason why

Romantic texts lend themselves to the de-privilegings of deconstruction. The figurative insecurity of this literature is one which
can readily be turned into a Derridean transcendentalism of the
depths. In the abyss of representation (the *mise en abîme*), the
infinite play of the signifier takes over from where other kinds of
infinities, particularly God's, left off. Thus Derrida claims that the
'absence of the transcendental signified extends the domain and
the play of signification infinitely' (Derrida, 1978, p. 280). Infinity,
which has been transferred from God to signifier, is still a powerful
imaginative counter. So, too, is the idea associated with it: that of
freedom. Derrida plays on the notion of 'poetic freedom' (Derrida,
1978, p. 8), of 'a certain absolute freedom of speech' (p. 12), though
the political meaning is only a residual *double entendre*. Derrida's
freedom is not Sartre's: 'the end to which [the book] offers itself is
the reader's freedom' (Sartre, 1950, p. 33), because in Derrida both
reader and author have become, like God, defunct. Deconstruction
thus seems to take freedom one step further, in liberating the text
from all clogs of reference, so that its figurative play can be made to
play endlessly.

This infinitesimalised notion of freedom is what the recent 'resistance to theory' has challenged. By asserting the free play of the
signifier, and thus releasing the text from a reductive historicism,
deconstruction has seemed to release the text from signification
altogether – as well as, in the end, from being free. To exclude the
limiting contingencies of both history and biography in the text is
to espouse, in their place, a self-referentiality which can become
dogmatically and deterministically predictable. The signifier's infinite play can be as despotic as God's infinite rule. Absence can be
as totalitarian as presence.

By comparison, the humanist Romantic model of free perception
is one which relies on the hidden, if problematic, presences of
author and reader. As Thomas Pfau puts it, deconstruction's
'substitution of structures of consciousness by structures of language' (Pfau, 1987, p. 498) denies the process of meaning which is
so central to the Romantic text: that is, *'the relation* between
structures of consciousness and those of language' (Pfau, 1987,
p. 507). Such a relation may be precarious and uncertain, merely
desired or regretted, but without that relation, the 'open' signification of literature threatens to become closed. As Tilottama Rajan
puts it, 'Words may not be substances, but they are forces,
producing relations between things' (T. Rajan, 1985a, p. 466).

Deconstruction, according to its detractors, has tilted at origins, at gods and authors, which were always only half-hearted authorities of the text, and always only part of a relational interplay of 'forces'. It has thus, too often, turned free imaginative meaning into determined linguistic anti-meaning, and the free play of the text into the repetitive clatter of structures.

Given the theoretical war that has raged over Romantic literature, it is interesting to notice that, as far as Shelley is concerned, while *The Triumph of Life* has been the object of several 'figural' readings, most notably de Man's own (but also Bloom, 1971; Leighton, 1984; Schulze, 1988), *Epipsychidion*, with its troubling and guilty weight of autobiography, has not. Theory is always tempted to draw its universals from some carefully selected example. The subject of romantic love seems inimical both to the anti-representational play of deconstruction, and to the gender-minded politics of feminism. It is, paradoxically, too biographical for the one, and too figuratively transcendental for the other. Both a literal history of the individual life, and a stirring of old figures from the literature of the past, the poem of romantic love seems liable to pose something of a contradiction to both theoretical positions.

This contradiction, however, suggests that what is needed is a theory of the relation *between* figures and history, between literary play and literal reference. The power of *Epipsychidion* derives from the fact that its 'dust of figures', from Dante, Petrarch and Keats, is countered by the '*historical* hallucination' of a life actually lived in time, and beset by disappointments, mistakes and unfaithfulness. It is not the absence of the historical in this work, but rather its constant pull, which gives to Shelley's breathlessly figured love poem a peculiar tension. Such self-delighting figurativeness is not ultimately free of biographical reference, though it is brilliantly, tactically distant from it. That distance can be either a literary strength, or a sign of sexual self-deception and evasion.

'If you are anxious, however, to hear what I am and have been, it will tell you something thereof. It is an idealized history of my life and feelings' – thus Shelley wrote to John Gisborne more than a year after the composition of *Epipsychidion*. The poem, he suggests, with a touch of self-irony, might be of interest to a personal friend. It is a 'history' of his 'life and feelings'. He then goes on to lament that the poem's object proved a delusion in real life. She was 'a cloud instead of a Juno', and the work she inspired was, consequently, like Ixion's monstrous offspring, a 'centaur' (Shelley,

1964, II, p. 434). However, the poem's history is also, Shelley claims, a little self-defensively, an 'idealized' one, and the word, as has been noted, shows the continuing presence in his thoughts of the poem which so pervasively haunts his own. Dante's *Vita Nuova* is described in the *Defence of Poetry* as 'the idealized history of that period, and those intervals of his life which were dedicated to love' (Shelley, 1977, p. 497). Thus the autobiographical nature of Shelley's poem, its sense of 'what I am and have been', is quickly confused with the notion of a distanced and improved story, an 'idealized history', not of facts but of 'feelings'. The defensive duplicity of Shelley's attitude to *Epipsychidion* is not only a result of disillusionment after the event; it is also a doubleness which the poem everywhere betrays. Between idealism and history, love and life, feeling and fact, there is an awkward split, which seems to spoil the poem's very courtly ideals. The work is, indeed, though not quite as Shelley intends it, a 'centaur'.

This sense of divided purpose is suggested by the elaborate disguise of the advertisement. Partly self-mocking and partly self-pitying, it gives an account of a poet's death which directly bears on the idealistic last section of the poem. 'The Writer of the following Lines died at Florence, as he was preparing for a voyage to one of the wildest of the Sporades' (Shelley, 1977, p. 373). The whole work is thus presented as the orphaned offspring of a man whose actual life disproves the romantic goals of his poem. By means of this intricate disclaimer, Shelley seems to invite a formalistic and self-referential reading of the poem. Its connection with human life, both his own and the Writer's, has been cut. The text remains a monument to perished ideals. This seems to be, indeed, the initiating motif of an authorial self-deconstruction. As Barthes generalises, with tempting applicability, 'the voice loses its origin, the author enters into his own death, writing begins' (Barthes, 1977, p. 142). Yet this passionately contrived 'death of the author' carries a conviction in *Epipsychidion* which exceeds its function as an autobiographical decoy.

For all its convention of anonymity, the advertisement nevertheless hints at certain personal explanations. The Writer, we are told, suffered from 'romantic vicissitudes', which rendered him the fool, or else the victim, of 'circumstances'. His pantisocratic schemes were tragically doomed. Shelley tells so much, and then abruptly castigates those readers who would reduce the story of the Writer's idealism to 'a matter-of-fact history of the circumstances'. Idealism and history are at odds in this work. Nonetheless, Shelley himself plays a cat-and-mouse game with them. Though he aristocratically snubs 'a certain other class' of reader who would literalise the story's high-minded figures, he himself then baits the reader's appetite for facts. In a last, surprising shift of tactics, he suddenly quotes Dante, who asserts that the poet should feel 'shame' if he could not reveal, under 'the garb of metaphor or rhetorical figure', an underlying 'true meaning' (Shelley, 1977, p. 373n). Shelley's clear association here of idealism with 'rhetorical figure' and of 'history' with the bare truth, in a passage which is itself an elaborate figure to 'cover up' the truth of his own autobiography, is suggestive of something which much of the subsequent poem betrays. Between rhetoric and history, figure and truth, there is a wide but connected distance, and the poem, like the advertise-ment, shifts tantalisingly within it.

These two schizophrenic directions of the advertisement, to-wards idealistic figurativeness on the one hand, and towards a 'matter-of-fact' life story on the other, are subtly reflected in the two main strands of criticism by which the poem has been interpreted. It is, above all, Shelley's depiction of women and his statements about free love that have divided critics into opposing camps. The Rev. Stopford A. Brooke's edition of *Epipsychidion*, for instance, sets a pattern for innumerable future interpretations. Brooke asserts in his preface that 'the woman and the poem belong to the ideal and not to the actual' (Brooke, 1887, p. xxi), and that therefore the work's theories cannot be 'used to promote licen-tiousness' (p. xxxi). Shelley's invitation to Emilia, to join him in a *ménage à quatre* with Mary and Claire Clairmont in some unspecific isle in the east, is a subject for complicated evasion by many critics. For Carlos Baker, 'Emilia is only, or mainly, one more metaphor of the Shelleyan epipsyche', so that those 'literalists' who have supposed the poem to be 'an invitation to adulterous elopement' are 'deceived' (Baker, 1948, p. 218). Emilia, he assures us, is 'sexless as an angel' (p. 219).

The two categories of the ideal and the literal provide the critics, as they do Shelley himself, with a useful moral distinction. Thus, for Milton Wilson, Emily is 'a figure' for some mystical and transcendent 'goal out of Time' (Wilson, 1959, p. 230). For Desmond King-Hele, she is a Jungian archetype: 'an idealized *anima*' (King-Hele, 1960, p. 271), while Ellsworth Barnard reclaims her as a symbol of 'the Christian doctrine of Grace' (Barnard, 1964, p. 264).

For Earl Wasserman she represents 'the power of the divine operating on the world of mutability' (Wasserman, 1971, p. 425), and Harold Bloom, though he acknowledges that the ending of the poem 'is undoubtedly to be taken as a pragmatic program for polygamy' (Bloom, 1971, p. 340), generally interprets the work as one in which 'the biographical situation is almost totally absorbed into the poem's mythopoeic speculations' (Bloom, 1971, p. 335). On the other side of this divide, Kenneth Neill Cameron closely correlates the poem's cosmic symbolism with the actual women in Shelley's life, including the mysterious woman by the well, who was probably a prostitute encountered in Oxford – 'for a "well" is a common symbol for learning' (Cameron, 1974, p. 280). Nora Crook and Derek Guiton make the woman at the well the cornerstone of a whole physiological interpretation of Shelley's works, though, for them, she was met 'at Eton rather than Oxford', where there was, literally, a 'well' (Crook and Guiton, 1986, p. 153).

Thus *Epipsychidion* continues to be, to a large extent, a split poem. On the one hand, it may be read as a mythological expression of the forces of Love, Imagination or Grace. On the other hand, it may be read as a biographical allegory, in which the poet's sexual history is recounted in a decipherable meteorological imagery of women. For the first group, Emily is a superhuman power: a prime mover of poems, whether angel, *anima*, grace or myth. For the second group, she is one woman among many whom Shelley turned into spiritual companions or seductive muses, in a short-lived idealism which could change to ruthless neglect.

Certainly, the true stories of these 'dream women' (Crompton, 1967) bear witness to a need of the imagination which, in the smaller details of real life, could be exploitatively disregarding. The poet's avidity for objects of romantic love met little internal challenge from his avowed feminism which, though vociferous on the evils of prostitution, and routinely scornful of the legalism of marriage, nonetheless could assert, with enthusiasm and perhaps self-congratulation, that the 'freedom of women produced the poetry of sexual love' (Shelley, 1977, p. 496). Yet Shelley's own great poem of 'sexual love' was inspired by a woman who, far from free, was confined to a convent by a patriarchal father, who was arranging her marriage. The sad story of Emilia, whom the Shelleys befriended and then forgot, and whom Medwin found, many years later, dying alone in Florence, after an unhappy marriage and the deaths of four children, is one which lies outside the scope of this poem. The literal-minded reader who searches for 'the noble and unfortunate lady' of the title will not find any literal description of her, or any account of her feelings, among Shelley's rapturous acclamations. Here she is transcendently a spirit or a bird, a seraph or a vision, a lamp or a sun. Life's 'matter-of-fact history' seems not to interrupt the brilliant profusion of figures that she inspires.

But *Epipsychidion* is neither an entirely figurative poem about inspiration, nor an entirely biographical poem about the women Shelley loved. The narcissistic element of 'self-description' (de Rougemont, 1940, p. 173) which marks out romantic love is crossed, in *Epipsychidion*, by a dragging current of personal history, which sets up its own peculiar contradictions in the work. Although Shelley embraces a fervent rhetoric of love's permanence, it is a rhetoric set in opposition to the perpetual stress of time. Thus the long, exuberant address to Emilia is retrospectively conscious of the loves of other women. The aesthetic ideal of the eternal moment is set against a self-justifying rehearsal of the past. *Epipsychidion*'s statements of emotional dedication are subtly temporised. The poem's effusive Platonism, with all its metaphysical and religious reassurances, is advanced against the grain of a constant displacement of the present into the past, the idealised into the remembered, the desired into the forgotten, the written into the erased.

Only a month or so after its composition Shelley wrote to his publisher, Ollier, disavowing the poem's emotional commitment. He wrote in terms which resonantly confirm the work's own intimations: 'it is a production of a portion of me already dead; and in this sense the advertisement is no fiction' (Shelley, 1964, II, pp. 262–3). The feeling of death runs through this love poem, not in the mystical-sexual sense of a consummating dénouement, by which 'death is revealed as having been the real end, what passion has yearned after from the beginning' (de Rougemont, 1940, p. 54), but rather in the sense of emotional exhaustion. At times, Shelley's love poem sounds like a practice ground for *Adonais*. The death of Keats, a month or so later, found Shelley imaginatively prepared for elegy. In register, *Epipsychidion* is like an elegy without an object – unless its object is something dead at the heart: 'a portion of me'.

The first lines of the work thus continue a sense of mourning which the advertisement subtly justifies:

> Sweet Spirit! Sister of that orphan one,
> Whose empire is the name thou weepest on,
> In my heart's temple I suspend to thee
> These votive wreaths of withered memory.
>
> (1–4)

This sombre address does not promise much. The poet's spirit is orphaned, the woman is weeping, the 'votive wreaths' seem funerary and, what is more, they already belong to a long-forgotten past – unless 'withered memory' means, even more disturbingly, that they have already forgotten the object of their devotion. Shelley's characteristic aesthetic of fading inspiration is here confusingly conflated with a declaration of love. Thus, the 'heart's temple' begins to sound like a tomb for one dead. The 'wreaths' of poetry sound like a *memento mori*. Shelley's circumspect imagery, which is heavy with echoes from Keats's *Ode to Psyche*, seems designed to disappoint, rather than seduce, its object. A strong 'tug of death' (Wasserman, 1971, p. 458), whether from intimations of Keats's death, from Shelley's own ill-health, or from some more latent disillusionment of the imagination, infiltrates the language of this love poem, so that its figures seem self-consciously 'withered' from the start.

Epipsychidion thus sets against its desired transcendence the pattern of a history which draws everything into the past. For all its epiphanic declarations, it seems defeated by memory. For all its feverish idealism, it feels emotionally late and cold. Emilia Viviani, in her wretched but appealingly literary imprisonment, inspires a poem which is only great because its 'autonomous potential of language', its rich 'resources of figures', cannot withstand reduction to life's matter of facts. Emilia, in her high captivity, receives one of the most ornately flagging love poems ever written.

> Poor captive bird! who, from thy narrow cage,
> Pourest such music, that it might assuage
> The rugged hearts of those who prisoned thee,
> Were they not deaf to all sweet melody;
> This song shall be thy rose: its petals pale

> Are dead, indeed, my adored Nightingale!
> But soft and fragrant is the faded blossom,
> And it has no thorn left to wound thy bosom.
>   (5–12)

It is typical of Shelley's language to give the effect of skating on a succession of similes. This 'devouring metonymy' of the imagination is one which restlessly transforms the woman into a bird, birdsong into a poem, the poem into a rose, and the rose back into a poem, which is returned, in a somewhat empty-handed gesture, to its source. 'This song shall be thy rose'. Emilia receives, by this closed circuit of figures, the rose which is only her own song again, but 'faded'. In this audibly Keatsian theft of inspiration, Emily's plight as a prisoner is turned into a figure for the poet who sings, unregarded and unappreciated by the critic-imprisoners who are 'deaf' to his song's sweetness. Shelley is readily moved by a victimisation which is both Emilia's and Keats's, but which reminds him of his own.

However, beneath this ornamental, figurative resourcefulness, there is an odd confusion of tenses: 'This song shall be thy rose: its petals pale / Are dead, indeed, my adored Nightingale!' In this tactless modesty trope, which again connects love with waning inspiration, the promise is spoiled even as it is made. Time has already taken its toll of the rose, so that the poet's love sounds late, and his song reluctant. This lover gives his mistress 'wreaths' which are 'withered', and roses which are 'faded'. Such gifts are decidedly fainthearted. The more Shelley stirs 'a dust of figures' from courtly romance, as if to weave a wreath of self-perpetuating literariness, the more strongly does his language betray the lag of time. 'Italian platonics', as Mary Shelley wryly implied (Mary Shelley, 1980, I, p. 223), have had their day, and Dante's religious constancy has given way to the Romantic's scepticism and disappointment. A real and impermanent history of love presses against the figures of Shelley's florid courtliness.

This consciousness of time everywhere underlies the poet's labouring idealism. His very addresses to the object of his love can be bewilderingly pessimistic:

> Sweet Lamp! my moth-like Muse has burnt its wings;
> Or, like a dying swan who soars and sings,

Young Love should teach Time, in his own grey style,
All that thou art.

(53–6)

Grammatically, these lines make no sense. 'Or' does not initiate
another comparison for the Muse, while, technically, the 'dying
swan' is 'Young Love' itself. Such syntactical clumsiness suggests
imaginative evasion. Figures, in this poem, come thick and fast, as
if to avoid their literal reference. But Shelley's style does contain
another reality principle. The 'Muse' is already burning, the swan
already 'dying', while the emblems of 'Love' and 'Time' have
become inextricably twinned in the idea of a passion which has
its 'own grey style'. Shelley's figurative flights are very often
expressive, not of Emily herself, but of time running out. Thus
Emily, at the end of a long series of attributions, is suddenly
addressed as 'A violet-shrouded grave of Woe' (69). Whether she is
like the violets, the shroud or the grave is a detail lost in the
baroque fantasy of the construction. The tenor, for Shelley, is very
often not a specific fact, but a pervading mood. This mood is
reinforced, for instance, by the curious direction of the lines: 'She
met me, Stranger, upon life's rough way, / And lured me towards
sweet Death' (72–3). Such negative promise is full of dread. The
real tenor of many of these flights of figurativeness is not eternal
love but passing time.

While *Epipsychidion* seems, then, to urge a flight from time,
towards the timeless island of romantic love, it is a flight weighed
down by the transience of life. Shelley's high-flown figures,
whether impelled by self-pity, sexual hypocrisy or literary imitation, are nonetheless loaded with tell-tale frictions and salutary
scepticisms. It is significant, for instance, that at each of the high
points of his continuous metaphors, the poem must fall. Such
falling passages betray the strain of a figurativeness which cannot,
in the end, carry the poet's conviction:

> I measure
> The world of fancies, seeking one like thee,
> And find – alas! mine own infirmity.
>
> (69–71)

The traditional message of such fallings-off is that the desired
object remains sublimely out of reach. The Shelleyan message,

however, is the more sceptical one of knowing that such figures cannot long outsoar the ground of real life:

> Ah, woe is me!
> What have I dared? where am I lifted? how
> Shall I descend, and perish not?
>
> (123–5)

Such stock expressions of the sublime express, in Shelley, a linguistic scepticism which measures the distance between the figure and the thing. The thing, by itself, would be death to the poet. But so, too, would the figure. The area of 'play', of the poem's open-endedness, lies *between* the two, until a principle of reality, the 'chains of lead', brings the sublime down to the bathetic at the end:

> The winged words on which my soul would pierce
> Into the height of love's rare Universe,
> Are chains of lead around its flight of fire. –
> I pant, I sink, I tremble, I expire!
>
> (588–91)

Such a weight of gravity, which is like the weight of the literal *within* those 'winged words', ends the prolific resources and the airy self-sufficiency of the poem's similes. Words themselves are chained. The landscape of the Shelleyan sublime is a linguistic one, spanning vehicle and tenor, figure and fact. But without the disenchantment which brings one down to the other, there would be no meaning to the play, and no relation to make it work. The nature of that disenchantment Shelley in his later years calls simply 'Life'.

Thus *Epipsychidion* deflates its own afflatus and grounds its own flights. However magnified into a universal cosmography of the emotions, the poem also contains a sequential survey of the past, which sets the ideal represented by Emily against a procession of delusive earlier loves. The first of these seems to be the lost original of them all, the figure of courtly love herself:

> In the words
> Of antique verse and high romance, – in form,
> Sound, colour – in whatever checks that Storm

Which with the shattered present chokes the past;
And in that best philosophy, whose taste
Makes this cold common hell, our life, a doom
As glorious as a fiery martyrdom;
Her Spirit was the harmony of truth.

(209–16)

This first woman, who is the spirit of poetry and 'romance', does not belong to life's experiences, but to dreams and books. She is a creature merely of the literary sensibility, and her role is to suspend the constant 'Storm' of the present into the past. She gives a temporary haven, in vision and dream, from the rage of time. But she only 'checks' the storm; she cannot halt it, or be, as Beatrice was for Dante, the sign of an eternal life beyond the present.

In two lines which beautifully express the precariousness of Shelley's idealism, the poet affirms that this visionary 'Being' (190) cannot redeem the miseries of the world, but can only make 'this cold common hell, our life, a doom / As glorious as a fiery martyrdom' (214–15). The sense of time can be eased by her, and life's 'cold common hell' can be made to burn with purpose. But no more. The explicit knowledge which underpins the very evanescent idealism of this figure of love is that time destroys everything, and that life has gone 'cold'. It is characteristic of Shelley in his last years to regard time as the odds against which he must write, and life as the glare against which he must dream. The whole of the subsequent story of *Epipsychidion* is a search for the copy of this first love. Yet the fear of not feeling, of having been frozen by real life, is the abrasive undercurrent of all its buoyant metaphors of desire.

The structure of *Epipsychidion*, like that of *The Triumph of Life*, is one in which each new figure of love simply erases the last. Searching for the lost creature of dreams and idealisms, Shelley finds, instead, the woman by the well:

One, whose voice was venomed melody
Sate by a well, under blue night-shade bowers;
The breath of her false mouth was like faint flowers,
Her touch was as electric poison, – flame
Out of her looks into my vitals came,
And from her living cheeks and bosom flew
A killing air, which pierced like honey-dew

> Into the core of my green heart, and lay
> Upon its leaves; until, as hair grown grey
> O'er a young brow, they hid its unblown prime
> With ruins of unseasonable time.
>
> (256–66)

That this woman is a source of 'melody', however venomous, suggests she too has some bearing on the poet's song. Her 'killing air' eerily echoes the effect of Emilia's more beneficent singing:

> And from her lips, as from a hyacinth full
> Of honey-dew, a liquid murmur drops,
> Killing the sense with passion . . .
>
> (83–5)

Just as the 'shape all light' (352) in *The Triumph of Life* first dances like a benign vision and then violently tramples the mind's thoughts 'into the dust of death' (388), and just as in Shelley's Italian tale, *Una Favola*, the veiled female shapes who negotiate between Life and Love are ambiguously 'spectres of [the poet's] own dead thoughts, or the shadows of the living thoughts of Love' (Shelley, 1954, p. 359), so, in *Epipsychidion*, one woman shades into another woman, good shades into evil, and Love shades into Life. The relativism of Shelley's Romantic vision finds ample support in the indiscriminate recurrence of his figures. Thus the woman by the well may be not so much Emilia's moral opposite, but her spectral double, seen from another angle: the dead thought behind the living one. She may therefore represent that ruinous disenchantment which attends on all love: life's brutal history, which, everywhere in this poem, blasts the poet's 'heart' with 'unseasonable time'. The underlying anxiety of *Epipsychidion* is that life's matter of fact, its 'cold common hell', may be not only the destroyer of love, but also its prevailing context and reality.

'What is Love?', Shelley asks at the begining of his essay *On Love*, and answers that it is 'that powerful attraction towards all that we conceive or fear or hope beyond ourselves when we find within our own thoughts the chasm of an insufficient void' (Shelley, 1977, p. 473). Where Dante's allegory of Love rests firmly on the fixed point of a pre-Copernican universe – 'The love that moves the sun and the other stars' (Dante, 1949–62, III, p. 145) – Shelley's allegory moves restlessly across the 'chasm' and the 'void' which open up below. The whole unstable geography of *Epipsychidion*, its careless fervour and hectic symbolism, its effect of too high altitudes and doubling repetitiveness, all serve to undermine with irony, as Earl Schulze points out (1982, p. 197), its Dantesque philosophy of eternal love. The Romantic world view is one which, for all its visionary idealism, readily splits open. In the *Defence of Poetry*, for instance, the very delighting action of poetry arises from a famine of the abyss within: the poet's 'thoughts of ever new delight . . . form new intervals and interstices whose void for ever craves fresh food' (Shelley, 1977, p. 488). At the end of *Epipsychidion* the proof of having found the ideal at last is that the 'smile' of the 'Eternal' (479) fills the 'bare and void interstices' (482) of nature. To gloss and smooth those 'interstices' is the aim of Shelley's sexual idealism. However, the last two hundred lines of the poem suggest that such idealism, when freed from the fretful scepticism of life, becomes somnambulantly dull. Unlike Keats, whose work still haunts lines like 'Till you might faint with that delicious pain' (452) and 'Blushes and trembles at its own excess' (476), Shelley's poem stagnates with sensuousness. Such time-free love lacks conviction. Without those 'interstices', those geological and imaginative 'faults' of vision which break the trance of the ideal in Shelley, his poetry begins to sleep-walk on the sound of its own metre. The evidence of the verse is that the utopian isle, like the one in *Prometheus*, is a less good place for poetry than the insecure terrain of disappointment and loss:

> What storms then shook the ocean of my sleep,
> Blotting that Moon, whose pale and waning lips
> Then shrank as in the sickness of eclipse; –
> And how my soul was as a lampless sea,
> And who was then its Tempest; and when She,
> The Planet of that hour, was quenched, what frost
> Crept o'er those waters, 'till from coast to coast
> The moving billows of my being fell
> Into a death of ice, immoveable; –
> And then – what earthquakes made it gape and split,
> The white Moon smiling all the while on it,
> These words conceal . . .
>
> (308–19)

The Comet, identified as Claire, here eclipses Mary's Moon, in a 'disfigurement' which erases one thing by another, in a movement which suggests an endless substitution. The new love erases the old, and is itself soon 'quenched'. Yet Shelley's imagery radically confuses the sequential order, so that one woman seems like another again. For instance, it is Emily who was earlier described as a 'Moon beyond the clouds!' (27) and as 'the Moon' which 'Burns, inextinguishably beautiful' (82). In this chaotic universe, the moon can be either constant or changeable, burning or icy. The history of love, which Shelley seems to trace with methodical, biographical purpose, is, at the level of the poem's imagery, a history of merely repetitive changeableness.

Yet it is in these passages of disillusioned idealism that Shelley's poetry is at its best. The effect of the Comet is to open up those 'intervals and interstices' which make the emotional texture of desire seem to crack: 'And then – what earthquakes made it gape and split' (317). Here, the constancy of the 'white Moon smiling all the while' (318) offers a fearful parody of Emily's constancy. Under that Moon's detached forgetfulness, the 'earthquakes' of feeling reveal the void beneath. This 'chasm of an insufficient void' in love makes Shelley's poem, not Dantesque in the end, but truly Romantic. Its idealism, its worship of Emily, is founded on hollow ground. Beneath the work's paratactic profusion of similes, there is an emotional void. Life's actual history opens up the 'faults', which no courtly creed or Platonic inspiration can truly hide. Shelley's 'dust of figures' would be nothing *but* dust, without this unique, underlying failure of imaginative nerve. Such an intimation of failure characterises his poetry of love, which the various 'magnetic ladies' of the imagination move and control.

Shelley's repeated use of a particular word in his later poetry expresses in miniature the deep ambivalence of his aesthetic of romantic love. It is not only the placing of Emily in a sequential, sexual history of other women which makes *Epipsychidion* so anomalous a love poem; it is also her association with the self-conscious and self-referring act of writing. At the start of the poem, Emily is envisaged as weeping over the 'name' of the poet, whose text, whether poetic or epistolary, she already holds in her hand. From this situation, the poet goes on to figure her as the inspiration of the poem which is being written:

> Thou Mirror
> In whom, as in the splendour of the Sun,

All shapes look glorious which thou gazest on!
Aye, even the dim words which obscure thee now
Flash, lightning-like, with unaccustomed glow;
I pray thee that thou blot from this sad song
All of its much mortality and wrong,
With those clear drops, which start like sacred dew
From the twin lights thy sweet soul darkens through...

(30–38)

This is indeed the 'devouring metonymy' of the courtly poet, who seeks to bind the cosmic with the domestic, in a 'conceited' sort of literariness which has a long and well-worn history. Shelley adopts the traditional weather imagery of Renaissance love-poetry, but applies it not so much to an emotional situation as to an aesthetic one. The real subject under scrutiny here is not Emily, but a poem. Her tears, for which there was good reason in real life, become caught up in the self-descriptive figures of writing. She weeps, not in the past or in the future, but in the elaborate present of the moment of composition. Thus the poet looks not to the 'wrong' in her life, but to the 'wrong' in his own poem, which her beautifully rarefied tears will 'blot'.

In this word, the literary displacement of the woman into a helpful muse, into a weather of the imagination, becomes grotesquely literal. Poetry is a form of words on paper, a delicate but material object, which tears, or rain, or dew, will 'blot'. The word is one which, increasingly in Shelley's later poetry, bears the weight of a drama which is both narcissistically self-serving, but also profoundly anxious. If the means substitutes the end, the love poem the love object, the 'sad song' the sad woman, then how evanescent and inconsequent are its light patterns. That they may be blotted out altogether is a fear which *Epipsychidion* seeks to hide, but which some of Shelley's other late poems clearly reveal.

Throughout Shelley's writing, it is possible to trace a developing metaphor of the mind in creation as a page, a shore, or a desert to be written on. In *The Revolt of Islam* (1817) the poet, like Christ, writes strange signs on the sand: 'Clear, elemental shapes, whose smallest change / A subtler language within language wrought' (3111–12; Shelley, 1970). These inscriptions on the sand are, for the young Shelley, indeed a kind of dust, which sifts into ever 'subtler' variations of meaning. But in the later poetry there is an after-movement, like an after-thought, which destroys the mind's writing.

In *The Zucca* (1822), for instance, Shelley writes of

> beauty, which, like sea retiring,
> Had left the earth bare, as the wave-worn sand
> Of my lorn heart . . .
>
> (5–7; Shelley, 1970)

At about the same time, he writes in *Fragments of an Unfinished Drama*, of the 'dream' (151)

> Like a child's legend on the tideless sand,
> Which the first foam erases half, and half
> Leaves legible.
>
> (152–4; Shelley, 1970)

The famous description of inspiration as a god walking on the sea in the *Defence* is similarly one in which 'the coming calm erases' the god's 'footsteps' to leave only 'traces' (Shelley, 1977, p. 504). However, the great culmination of this double movement of writing and erasing is to be found in *The Triumph of Life*, where the mind's devices of forgetting and repressing are described in terms of a natural imprint which is then substituted by another:

> And suddenly my brain became as sand
>
> Where the first wave had more than half erased
> The track of deer on desert Labrador,
> Whilst the fierce wolf from which they fled amazed,
>
> Leaves his stamp visibly upon the shore . . .
>
> (405–9)

Here, Shelley's idiosyncratic use of the Actaeon myth, to describe the flight of thought on thought as a process of predatory forgetfulness, is one which brilliantly subjects poetic vision to the action of time. In *The Triumph of Life*, his most insistently historicised phantasmagoria, the time-bound imagination hunts itself, erasing the precarious calligraphy of vision, in an action which is sceptically repeated, not only throughout life (hence its harsh triumph) but also throughout history (hence Shelley's re-enactment of Rousseau's loss).

The feminisation of this aesthetic of writing and erasing belongs to Shelley's last years, particularly the years after the composition of *The Witch of Atlas* (1820). The Witch herself, who is the playful, insouciant creature of a knowledge which precedes 'Error and Truth' (51), is a muse who writes 'strange dreams upon the brain' (617). She is the figure of a capricious, morally purposeless inspiration, which is written like an incarnate language on the brain. However, it is Dante who gives Shelley the notion of a double movement, expressive and then repressive, in the act of creation. Shelley's own translation of the first Canzone of the *Convito* renders Dante's lines as 'That thought is fled, and one doth now appear/Which tyrannizes me with such fierce stress' (19–20; Shelley, 1970). Dante's 'combination of two ladies and a soul', which gives Shelley some 'problems' as a translator (Webb, 1976, p. 296), also gives him the main dramatis personae of *Epipsychidion*. But even more pertinent to the duplicitous muses of his later years is Dante's description of Matilda in the *Purgatorio* (see Webb, 1976, p. 318). Matilda makes the poet drink from two rivers, because, in Sayers' very Shelleyan translation, 'This side blots all man's sins from memory;/That side to memory all good deeds restores' (Dante, 1949–62, II, pp. 128–9). (In neither Dante's original, nor in Cary's translation, is this figure of memory as a written script present.) Unlike Dante's experience, however, the erasure of one vision by another in *The Triumph of Life* brings about no moral improvement. Quite the opposite. Here, the fragile figure of the 'track of deer' is erased and substituted by the 'stamp' of the 'wolf'. All that remains of Dante's moral scheme is the arbitrarily destructive passage of time.

This double movement recurs in Shelley's late poems. In *To Jane: The Recollection* (1822), for instance, a thought of love is blanked out by a subsequent thought:

> Until an envious wind crept by,
> Like an unwelcome thought,
> Which from the mind's too faithful eye
> Blots one dear image out.
>
> (81–4)

Paradoxically, although *another* thought blots the 'image', the mind's being 'too faithful' is also curiously to blame. The erasure comes not only from the temporal passage of one thought on another, but also from the eye's very intensity of faithfulness. Thus, the inevitability of disillusionment is found right at the heart of the lover's steadfast gaze. The mind is blotted also by being '*too* faithful'.

In his later works, Shelley frequently returns to this figure of a writing which does not shift endlessly into a 'subtler language', but which is simply erased. The extent to which this calligraphic metaphor of inspiration is closely connected with memory and time is suggested by a fragment in the poet's Notebooks, possibly from *Charles I* (1822):

> Time who outruns & oversoars whatever
> Is swiftest, & whose tramp is
>   like a warsteeds armed heel
> Whose wings are like the shadows of a cloud
> Which blots the sunshine from [. . .]
> Time – in whose path thy name is stamped in light
> Blots not thy story with his languid plumes
> Soils not   with his erasing feet.
>   (Buxton Forman, 1911, I, p. 185)

The recurrence of the word 'blot' in association with the action of the woman muse, and especially with the relentless passage of her passing feet, suggests how far the act of writing, as well as the act of loving, for Shelley, is doomed to a scepticism which leaves nothing indelible, and no ideal protected from the tread of history.

> And still her feet, no less than the sweet tune
> To which they moved, seemed as they moved, to blot
> The thoughts of him who gazed on them, and soon
>
> All that was seemed as if it had been not,
>   As if the gazer's mind was strewn beneath
> Her feet like embers, and she, thought by thought,
>
> Trampled its fires into the dust of death,
> As Day upon the threshold of the east
> Treads out the lamps of night . . .
>   (382–90)

The female figure of the 'shape all light' focuses, in *The Triumph of Life*, the ambiguous and complicit connection between vision and time, dream and glare, stars and sun, which is the connection already forming between the various female figures of *Epipsychidion*. It is she who first traces the beautiful pattern of a 'sweet tune' upon the mind with her dancing feet; but it is also she who can subsequently 'blot' the 'thoughts' of the poet she inspires. The writing on the mind's sand, which Shelley punningly describes as the movement of the muse's 'feet', is as quickly erased as it is written; so quickly, in fact, that in a kind of hologram effect, the erasure and the writing are part of the same process. It is the same 'sweet tune' which inspires and destroys. The muse of visionary poetry is also, for the late Shelley, the muse of time. It is time that she measures with her moving 'feet'. This is both the metrical time of poetry, but also, quite simply, the time which passes, and turns thoughts to 'embers', 'fires' to 'dust', 'night' to 'Day'. This same figure 'all light' is both the light of the stars and the light of the sun. She is both the kindly muse of dream and the violent muse of waking. She is Emily, Mary, Claire, and the woman at the well all in one. Just as in *Epipsychidion* the feminised cosmos of stars and moon and sun merge and succeed each other, in a passage of time which is Shelley's admission of a 'matter-of-fact history' which cannot be idealised, so, in *The Triumph of Life*, the single woman muse is a configuration of dreaming and forgetting, loving and not loving, idealising and literalising, which is the underlying good faith of his own sceptical imagination.

Thus, in the end, Shelley refuses to separate vision and history, figure and fact. Instead, he brings them into close and frictional relation. The delicately figured dreams of the night are blotted out by the day's cold common light. Yet it is precisely by this movement that dreams are also, in a strange way, saved: 'like day she came, / Making the night a dream' (392–3). While *Epipsychidion* still tries to distance the ideal from the real, the permanent from the temporal, it is in *The Triumph of Life* that the two warring perspectives of Shelley's sceptical Romanticism finally come together. The muse who governs this great last work is one who violently, yet truthfully, combines, without choice or differentiation, both vision and disenchantment, both love and life, both the timeless moment and the routine losses of time.

Appendix
A Shelley Survey: Which Shelley Now?

G. Kim Blank

In the Preface to *Prometheus Unbound* Shelley notes that creative individuals are inescapably the creators and creations of their own age. As a
poet, then, Shelley saw himself as a producer and product of the particular
historical moment. But Shelley saw poets as creators and creations of
circumstances beyond their lifetime. When Shelley says at the end of the
Defence that poets use 'words which express what they understand not'
(Shelley, 1977, p. 508), he is opening poetry up to a scene of eternal
interpretations. Thus the Shelley of 1822 is created anew as, for example,
the Shelley of 1889, 1936 or 1990. Shelley knew that he would become at
least as much a product of circumstantial biases and changing views of
literary and critical worth as a creation of his own time. By virtue of being
taught, written about and anthologised, Shelley has thus become institutionalised, ideologised, constituted and reconstituted – all, of course, to
justify various pedagogical, critical, theoretical and often political ends
and needs. Behind all of this lurks a question: why teach Shelley at all? We
don't necessarily have to fall back to ask the larger, overwhelming
question (i.e. why teach literature?), but while admitting that Shelley has
become canonised, we can formulate a question which, in the context of
The New Shelley, is appropriate to address: which Shelley is being taught?

A survey was carried out in an attempt to discover which Shelley is
being perpetuated in upper-level undergraduate courses in the USA,
Canada and Great Britain. Much university teaching is carried out in a
kind of vacuum, and often we tend to teach what we were taught or what
text books direct us to teach. The results of this survey will aid teachers of
Romanticism in contextualising their classroom practices.

I THE SURVEY

Questionnaires were sent out to just over 100 randomly chosen universities
in the USA, Canada and Great Britain. Eighty-four completed responses
were returned, although a few more were returned only partially completed
but with some usable information. The objective was to determine which
of Shelley's works are represented in upper-level undergraduate courses
taught under the auspices of 'Romanticism' or 'English Romantic Poetry'.

The survey also intended to solicit candid responses not just about Shelley as a poet, but about Shelley's status as a poet relative to that thing called 'Romanticism' and to the other major Romantic poets. The very idea of comparing these poets by 'rank' under the guise of 'importance to Romanticism' was considered offensive enough to provoke charged comments. Many respondents did indeed jump, and in this respect alone the survey contains results that openly express the critical attitude towards Shelley in the late 1980s.

II WHICH TEXTBOOKS?

The textbook selected by an instructor obviously influences course content. Instructors teaching courses like 'Romantic Poetry' normally have two choices: they can use either a period anthology or an individual volume for each poet. In the case of the former, there are of course restrictions on the number of works included, as well as problems with the potentially unrepresentative quality. On the other hand, if individual volumes for each poet are used, there is usually a choice between 'selected' or 'complete' editions. The 'selected' editions often present the same problem as anthologies, while the justification for having students purchase a 'complete' text when they may only use a fraction of the material may be wanting.

The table below, which breaks down particular course texts into the percentage of time used, shows that Shelley is more or less divided in being taught out of anthologies and collections of his poetry. A number of respondents indicated that they vary their texts, and this accounts for the total number of responses exceeding 84. The table is to be interpreted in such a way that, taking the first line as an example, we read it: the Perkins

% of the time used

	Total 100	USA (48 responses)	Canada (27 responses)	UK (25 responses)
Perkins[1]	27	31	44	—
Reiman[2]	17	25	11	8
Webb[3]	9	—	4	32
Norton[4]	12	17	11	4
OSA[5]	3	4	—	4
Bloom/Trilling[6]	8	8	8	8
Cameron[7]	5	6	8	—
Heath[8]	2	—	8	—
Noyes[9]	3	4	4	—
Butter[10]	2	—	—	8
Other	8	5	2	20
No text	4	—	—	16
	100%	100%	100%	100%

Notes 1–10: see chapter notes for full details.

text is used 27% of the time in courses on Romanticism, which breaks down into 31% of the time in the USA, 44% of the time in Canada, and 0% of the time in the United Kingdom (UK).

It must first of all be remembered that undergraduate studies in English Literature at UK universities do not often employ the numbered course system; rather, there are a series of required papers in chosen areas. This very much changes the requirement of 'set' textbooks.

In North America it appears that David Perkins' *English Romantic Writers* (1967) has stood up well over two decades, taking 31% of the market share in the USA and 44% in Canada. Besides the fact that some of the texts of individual poems are faulty in light of advances in more recent Shelley textual scholarship, it could be argued that the selection of the works is reasonably representative. However, it may be regrettable that *The Revolt of Islam* (or *Laon and Cythna*) and *The Cenci* do not appear even in an appended or selected passages version; and it is certainly regrettable that only the first 211 lines of *Julian and Maddalo* are given – in other words, we are without the problematical centre of the poem: the Maniac's words. The Norton Critical Edition (*Shelley's Poetry and Prose*) edited by Donald H. Reiman and Sharon B. Powers has done almost as well on Romantic courses as Perkins' anthology; it is especially popular in the US market, although in Britain it is not nearly as popular as Timothy Webb's *Selected Poems*. Perhaps the other item worth noting is that the Oxford Standard Authors (OSA) edition (edited by Thomas Hutchinson and corrected by G. M. Matthews) has probably lost much ground in the last ten years or so, and will continue to lose the Shelley market until (or unless) a new edition is prepared in the relatively new Oxford Authors series.

III   WHICH WORKS?

Respondents were asked to list which works by Shelley they teach. The survey reveals that the *Ode to the West Wind* is the most popular, appearing in courses on Romanticism 83% of the time. A grouping of four other works are taught betwen 70 and 80% of the time: *Adonais*, *A Defence of Poetry*, *Mont Blanc*, and the *Hymn to Intellectual Beauty*. Two other poems are taught more than 60% of the time: *Prometheus Unbound* and *To a Sky-Lark*.

Below is the complete listing and the percentage of times the work is taught. Works taught less than 5% of the time are not included.

1.	*Ode to the West Wind*	83%	11.	*Ozymandias*	32%
2.	*Adonais*	80%	12.	*Epipsychidion*	29%
3.	*A Defence of Poetry*	77%	13.	*England in 1819*	27%
4.	*Mont Blanc*	71%	14.	*Julian and Maddalo*	27%
5.	*Hymn to Intellectual Beauty*	70%	15.	*The Cloud*	24%
6.	*Prometheus Unbound*	67%	16.	*Lines . . . Euganean Hills*	19%
7.	*To a Sky-Lark*	62%	17.	*Lift Not the Painted Veil*	18%
8.	*Alastor*	44%	18.	*Stanzas – April 1814*	13%
9.	*The Triumph of Life*	33%	19.	*The Cenci*	12%
10.	*The Mask of Anarchy*	33%	20.	*Song to the Men of England*	12%

21. On Life	11%	27. The Witch of Atlas	5%
22. The Sensitive-Plant	10%	28. Lines: 'When the lamp is shattered'	5%
23. Mutability (1814)	9%	29. With a Guitar. To Jane	5%
24. On Love	8%	30. Queen Mab	5%
25. Ode to Liberty	7%	31. Hellas	5%
26. To Jane ('The keen stars...')	6%	32. To—('Music, when soft...')	5%

Note that *Alastor* stands more or less on its own at 44%, and is followed by another close grouping of seven other works ranging between 24 and 33%. Everything else gets taught less than 20% of the time, with only *Lift Not the Painted Veil* and *Lines written among the Euganean Hills* showing any noteworthy popularity. The average number of works by Shelley taught in courses on English Romanticism is ten, with the range being 0 (!) to 37.

This list shows some good things and some bad things. It is a good sign that *A Defence of Poetry* ranks so highly: Shelley's poetics should be put into the context of his own work and nineteenth-century literature theories of poetic production. At the same time it is disappointing that poems like *Julian and Maddalo* (27%) and *Epipsychidion* (29%) are not taught more frequently. Both poems can be seen as central in terms of negotiating the autobiographical-allegorical problems in Shelley's poetry as well as displaying the parameters and style of narrative tone and distancing in his poetry. Based on the infrequency that *Hellas* (5%), *The Cenci* (12%), and *Lines written among the Euganean Hills* (19%) are taught, the space in the otherwise excellent Reiman and Powers Norton Critical Edition granted to essays on these poems hardly seems warranted. (An essay on *The Triumph of Life* might have been more appropriate.) It is also surprising that *Alastor* is not taught more frequently, since scholarship generally recognises it as Shelley's first important poem; moreover, most of Shelley's subsequent poetry can be directly traced back to *Alastor*. Perhaps the biggest disappointment is that Shelley's *Peter Bell the Third* is not mentioned as being taught by any of the respondents, despite the poem's demonstration of Shelley's satirical skills and his expressed attitude towards the contemporary literary and socio-political scene. *Peter Bell the Third* is not in the Perkins anthology. In sum, the top ten selections can be seen as not adequately representing the remarkable range of tone, style and topics of which Shelley was capable.

IV RANKING

As mentioned, one of the issues that the survey hoped to tap was Shelley's 'importance as a Romantic' relative to the other major Romantic poets. Predictably, Wordsworth is overwhelmingly considered the most important Romantic, receiving a ranking of first 80% of the time. Coleridge is behind Wordsworth, being ranked second 40% of the time. Determining the third-ranked Romantic is not quite so clear-cut. Although Blake is ranked second 22% of the time, and Keats and Shelley receive 12% and 10% respectively at this ranking, the added rankings at third and higher show that Blake gets 44% of his share at third or higher (10% + 22%

+ 12%), Keats gets 44% (0% + 12% + 32%), and Shelley gets 40% (2% + 10% + 28%). To put it another way, no significant numbers put Keats or Shelley in the top two places, but both are considered third in importance about one-third of the time. On the other hand, Byron takes a beating, getting a total fifth and sixth ranking 74% of the time. The complete results are given below.

	Wordsworth	Coleridge	Blake	Keats	Shelley	Byron
1st	80%	8%	10%	0%	2%	0%
2nd	16%	40%	22%	12%	10%	0%
3rd	4%	18%	12%	32%	28%	6%
4th	0%	12%	22%	20%	32%	14%
5th	0%	12%	16%	18%	20%	34%
6th	0%	10%	18%	18%	8%	46%
	100%	100%	100%	100%	100%	100%

V   COMMENTS

The survey asked that respondents make some comments regarding their ranking of the individual poets. One respondent wondered why the survey was conducted at all, since, as he said, the issue of Shelley 'has long been settled'. But not at all so. As another respondent stated, 'Shelley's position [as a first-rate Romantic] remains greatly diminished by Leavis' criticism'. A number of respondents suggested that Shelley is 'the most difficult' Romantic, that 'students generally dislike Shelley', and that 'he gets least attention from panicky students'. Likewise it was said that the 'qualities embodied in Shelley strike few chords in a present-day audience . . . Shelley has very few takers among my students'.

Two further rather glum bottom-lines were that 'Shelley is the one Romantic poet we could spare and do the least violence to the period', and that 'Shelley is not influential . . . and not globally expressive of the central tenets/concerns of Romanticism'. But others suggested that Shelley is the 'great gloss for Romantic concepts', and that he is 'central to Romanticism'. In fact, one respondent said that Shelley is 'the least understandable outside the context of Romanticism'. Those who found Shelley peripheral to Romanticism tended to be vague in stating reasons; those who found Shelley central tended to point to his importance relative to his great contemporaries: he is seen as 'epitomizing the irony that distinguishes the second generation from Wordsworth and Coleridge' or having a 'skeptical response to Wordsworthian and Coleridgean concerns'. Shelley was also contextualised from the perspective of illustrating 'the ethereal characteristics of early 19th-century poetry'. Many comments painted Shelley in glowing colours: 'a great technician, brilliant philosopher and social critic'; 'quickest mind in poetry'; 'most interesting as a craftsman and personality'; 'broadest range'; 'wrote the most important theoretical statements'.

VI CONCLUSION

There remain, then, some doubts about Shelley's worth and relevance, but it also appears that Shelley plays an important role in the Romantic canon. He has found his way, having suffered and survived the post-Arnoldian and New Critical slings and arrows. His reputation will nevertheless be forever dented: so much said by so many powerful voices will always remain with Shelley. Perhaps at this particular moment, and with *The New Shelley*, we have even reached one summit in Shelley's reputation, with post-modernist criticism and theory heralding Shelley as one of its champions. It might be remembered that *Deconstruction and Criticism* (by Harold Bloom, Paul de Man, Jacques Derrida, Geoffrey Hartman and J. Hillis Miller), hailed as a 'manifesto' of contemporary hermeneutics, was originally conceived as a book about Shelley (Bloom, 1979, p. ix). Thus qualities in Shelley's writing and thinking that were at one time condemned – for example, the privileging of language at the expense of meaning, the density and regressive nature of his figurative formulations, the radical scepticism – are today often considered exemplary, both in terms of promoting the theory and illustrating it in a particular style of poetry.

Notes

Notes to the Introduction

1. Wasserman's indebtedness to Pulos is relegated to a footnote that appears more than one-quarter of the way into his study: 'How firmly Shelley's thought was based on skepticism has been amply demonstrated by C. E. Pulos in his *The Deep Truth: a Study of Shelley's Scepticism* . . . It is from Pulos' analysis, and not from any supposedly fundamental Platonism, that any study of Shelley's thought must begin' (Wasserman, 1971, p. 136n). Lloyd Abbey's *Destroyer and Preserver: Shelley's Poetic Skepticism* (1979), Donald Reiman's chapter on Shelley in *Intervals of Inspiration: The Skeptical Tradition and the Psychology of Romanticism* (1988), and Terence Allan Hoagwood's *Skepticism and Ideology: Shelley's Political Prose and its Philosophical Context from Bacon to Marx* (1988) each in its own way further connects Shelley to the sceptical tradition. Today it is no longer such a safe overview of Shelley to refer to him as a 'natural Platonist' (as is promoted, for example, in Grabo, 1936; Notopoulos, 1949; and Rogers, 1956). What seems more 'natural' for Shelley is his sceptical disposition.
2. Leavis in his personal feelings towards Shelley never went quite so far as Eliot, who said of Shelley: 'I find his ideas repellant'; 'some of Shelley's views I positively dislike' (Eliot, 1933, pp. 80, 83).
3. Except when noted otherwise, all quotations from Shelley's poetry are from Shelley (1977).

Notes to Chapter 1: Shelley: Style and Substance

1. Proving he can abandon himself to beauty, Jacques Derrida eloquently expresses the way presence is haunted by absence when he writes that 'the order of the signified is never contemporary, is at best . . . discrepant by the time of a breath from the order of the signifier' (Derrida, 1976, p. 18). With some sympathy for human fallibility, he warns that 'contrary to what our desire cannot fail to be tempted into believing, the thing itself always escapes' (Derrida, 1973, p. 104).
2. Shelley's 'most productive poetic impulse', writes Keach, 'is neither to deny by transcending nor to despair at moments of fading, dissolving and erasing, but to articulate them as indispensable images in the drama of human perception and signification . . . Shelley presents us with a sequence of fadings and erasings: an original paradisal imagery is replaced by an interdependent succession of substitutions' (Keach, 1984, pp. 152–3).

248

3.   In *Of Grammatology*, Derrida says: 'We think only in signs ... One could call play the absence of the transcendental signified as limitlessness of play, that is to say as the destruction of onto-theology and the metaphysics of presence' (1976, p. 50).

4.   Brian Nellist explains the importance of play in the poem in 'Shelley's Narratives and *The Witch of Atlas*' (Nellist, 1982, pp. 170–6). I concur with Nellist in thinking that 'it is when Shelley allows his narratives to hover on the edge of different possibilities and interpretations that he is most successful' (Nellist, 1982, p. 173).

5.   Though unsympathetic to deconstruction, Eugene Goodheart draws an important distinction between de Man and Derrida: 'One feels an ambivalence in Derrida's deconstructions, which, on the one hand, demystify philosophy's truth claims and, on the other, enter sympathetically in to the metaphoric movement of thought itself, thereby revealing its "poetic" character ... Rigorously ascetic in his readings, de Man almost scornfully resists the seductive claims of metaphor' (Goodheart, 1984, p. 115). More in tune with Derridean modes of thought, Howard Felperin calls deconstruction 'nothing other than language skepticism in the mode of play' (Felperin, 1985, p. 131).

6.   Keats, who may have shared something of the guilty Rousseauistic attitude to language, distrusted the power of Shelley's style and considered it too extravagant. It will be remembered that he wrote to Shelley with advice to 'curb your magnanimity and be more of an artist, and "load every rift" of your subject with ore' (Keats, 1958, II, p. 323).

Notes to Chapter 3: The Nursery Cave: Shelley and the Maternal

I am grateful for the suggestions and encouragement given me by a number of friends while I was engaged in the writing of this essay: Michelle Cliff, Clark Emery, George Dekker, Mary Favret, Albert Gelpi, Herbert Lindenberger, Anne Mellor, Marjorie Perloff, Robert Polhemus, Adrienne Rich, and David Riggs.

1.   For bibliography and commentary on the advice books directed to women, see St Clair (1989, pp. 504–11).

2.   Hogle takes it that Nathaniel Brown (1979) has established Shelley 'as the most protofeminist among the major male Romantic poets', though admitting that there are 'some telling limitations in the poet's personal attitudes and actions' (Hogle, 1988, p. 347). I would say rather that the problem lies behind those attitudes and actions in the conceptualisation of women's subjectivity that characterises the 'liberal' social theory to which Shelley ardently adhered.

      Carole Pateman's argument in *The Sexual Contract* is important here. She points out that the social contract theorists desirous of implementing a change from a hierarchically ordered society built on patriarchal control of a kin group to a contractual society in which the 'individual' is the fundamental unit, did not want thereby to surrender male dominance. They found a rationale for its maintenance in the theory that women's vulnerability to male sexual aggression makes it necessary that they have male protection, while men's sexual right to women underlies their status as 'individuals' privileged to be members of the fraternal social contract of the civil sphere (Pateman, 1988, p. 113). A discussion of Shelley's protofeminism would need to consider the degree to which he subscribed to this doctrine, as evidenced by his fear, expressed in *A Philosophical View of Reform*, that 'the admission of females to the right of suffrage ... seems somewhat immature' (Reiman, 1973, p. 1046).

3. Paul Friedrich's *The Meaning of Aphrodite* summarises theories regarding the origin of the goddess and describes her attributes and associated signs or images. Of particular relevance to Shelley's work are Aphrodite's association with the Dawn, with liminality, and with a sexualised maternity (Friedrich, 1978, pp. 43–9, 134–48, 181–4).

4. Space does not permit the recounting of particular plots, but even such titles as 'The Libertine Reclaimed' (Anon., 1795), 'The Triumph of Patience and Virtue' (Anon., 1799b), 'The Unfeeling Father' (Anon., 1803) and 'Three Years after Marriage' (Anon., 1808a) suggest their theme. There was also 'trading' from country to country of works that contrast feminine virtue with masculine brutality and/ or irresponsibility. Johann Friedrich Pestalozzi's *Leonard and Gertrude*, a classic rendition of the theme, was translated into English in 1800, and volume XXXIII (1802) of *The Lady's Magazine* carried a serialised translation of Augustus La Fontaine's 'The Rigid Father; or, Paternal Authority Too Strictly Enforced'.

    'Life' brought its own corroborations to the fantasies of 'art'. Joachim Campe's description of Caroline, Princess of Wales and mother of Princess Charlotte, who lived separately from the licentious Prince Regent, was reprinted in the March 1806 issue of *La Belle Assemblée* (Campe, 1806). In it Campe makes no overt allusion to the Prince, but his sketch of Princess Caroline draws all its lineaments from images of the virtuous mother/educator. In 1808 *La Belle Assemblée* carried a memoir of Carolina Matilda, 'married in 1766, at the age of fifteen to Christian VII of Denmark' (Anon., 1808b) – a much more harrowing version of the familiar story, and here discretion did not make it necessary to veil the husband's viciousness.

5. Work such as Fenn's is clearly setting the pattern for the 'elaborated' speech of a family controlled through the 'personal' as opposed to the 'positional' mode of interaction, as described by Basil Bernstein and further analysed by Mary Douglas (Douglas, 1982, pp. 21–32). Of further interest and importance in regard to the mother's role in the acquisition of language is Friedrich Kittler's 'The Mother's Mouth' in his *Discourse Networks* (Kittler, forthcoming).

6. The contrast I am delineating here between Lacanian and Bakhtinian theories about the formation of subjectivity in relation to the acquisition of language owes much to Andrea Nye's lucid exposition of the issues involved (Nye, 1987, pp. 664–86).

7. As my language suggests, I am reading Shelley's lines through the lens of Herbert Marcuse's Chapter 10, 'The Transformation of

Sexuality into Eros' in *Eros and Civilization* (Marcuse, 1974, pp. 197–221).

8. I am indebted to Margaret Homans both for the term 'literal language' and for the example from Woolf. I disagree with Homans, however, when she makes this 'literal language' available to girl children as it is not to boys, since mothers or mother surrogates are in our society the caretakers from whom infants of both genders acquire speech. For the same sociological reason, I think also that there is nothing intrinsically 'feminine' about 'literal language'.

Notes to Chapter 4: 'These Common Woes': Shelley and Wordsworth

1. See Blank (1988, pp. 30–2) on how Shelley's poem is unique in its attempt to appropriate a Wordsworthian style and subject.
2. See, for example, Mueschke and Griggs's early (1934) article, as well as Wasserman (1971, p. 16). See also Cameron's suggestion about Coleridge's 'pervasive' influence on Shelley (Cameron, 1974, p. 208).
3. Blank, pp. 40–2, discusses in detail Shelley's developing interest in Wordsworth between 1812 and 1816.
4. See Lucy Newlyn's (1986) volume on Coleridge and Wordsworth for a more detailed account of the two poets' allusions to one another's work. I am also grateful to Dr Vernon Shetley for insights on the relationship between Coleridge and Wordsworth in the poems discussed here.
5. For a convincing argument that Shelley would have read Wordsworth's poem, see Gohn's (1979) article, 'Did Shelley Know Wordsworth's *Peter Bell?*'

Notes to Chapter 5: The Web of Human Things: Narrative and Identity in *Alastor*

The edition used for *The Revolt of Islam* is Thomas Hutchinson (ed.) (1905) *Poetical Works* (Oxford: Clarendon Press).

1. For a thorough discussion of the Wordsworth–Shelley relationship as it pertains to this poem, see Blank (1988, pp. 50–4, 98ff.) Blank links *Alastor* to *The Excursion*; I have followed a somewhat different path in linking the poem to Wordsworth's figurations of the visionary child.
2. Georg Lukács uses the terms extensive and intensive totality to describe epic and drama respectively, with the latter term indicating a completeness that is more inward and solitary than the social plenitude of the epic. The novel, by contrast, is extensive but lacks totality (1971, p. 46).
3. Schopenhauer (1966, I, pp. 248–5); Nietzsche (1967a, pp. 49–56). For a discussion of Nietzsche's concept of 'Mood', see Stanley Corngold, 'Nietzsche's Moods', *Studies in Romanticism* (forthcoming, Spring 1990).
4. I refer to the first version of the poem from MS JJ, which lacks the

lines about the boy's death. This early draft can be found in
Wordsworth (1979, p. 492).

5.   The 'symbolic' in contrast to the 'imaginary' is, according to Lacan,
the order of language and the law in which the subject finds himself
inscribed, displaced. To this dyad Kristeva adds a third category, the
'semiotic', associated with physiological drives and pulsions whose
residual presence disrupts language, being felt in terms of absence,
contradiction, silence. Where the symbolic is patriarchal, the semiotic
is associated with the mother's body, so that the feminine resistance
to male *logos* is not pleasure (as in Cixous' valorisation of the
imaginary) but rather a de-idealised difference (Kristeva, 1980,
pp. 133–4).

6.   For Nietzsche's discussion of the body see Nietzsche (1967b, pp. 271,
281). On the relation between the semiotic and the body in Kristeva
see Kristeva (1980, p. 6; 1984, pp. 25–30).

7.   Thomas Weiskel suggests that the Poet's journey falls into 'two
phases, an upward, regressive journey to origins (11.222–468), and a
downward course, following a river that is meant to image the
progress of his life' (Weiskel, 1976, p. 146).

8.   The two exceptions are 280–90 and 366–9.

Notes to Chapter 6: Shelley as Revisionist: Power and Belief in *Mont Blanc*

A few segments in this essay rework, with significant changes, the reading
of *Mont Blanc* in Hogle (1988, pp. 73–86). My thanks to the Oxford
University Press and to William Sisler, its Executive Editor, for permission
to draw upon this material. A short, initial version of this piece was also
delivered in Los Angeles during the English Romanticism Division meeting at the Modern Language Association Convention of December 1982. I
am grateful to Stuart Curran, chair of that meeting, for his sage advice
about revisions and to Kim Blank for his more recent editorial suggestions.

1.   Percy and Mary Shelley both declare Wordsworth a 'slave' to high
Anglican and Tory interests upon reading *The Excursion* in September 1814 (Mary Shelley, 1987, I, p. 25). Percy's *Peter Bell the Third* in
1819, moreover, is a pointed satire on Wordsworth's falling-off into
religious, solipsistic and conservative postures, a process in which
'Peter' seems encouraged by a Coleridge figure (*Peter Bell the Third*,
373ff). In addition, Percy quite explicitly shows his objections to
systematising in the manner of the German '*criticism of pure reason*'
during one of his letters of 1821 (Shelley, 1964, II, p. 266). Though
Coleridge's *Biographia Literaria* was not available to him before he
wrote *Mont Blanc*, Shelley knew his precursor's Kantian philosophy
by that time from reading such 1809 versions of it as Nos. 9 and 21 of
The Friend (Coleridge, 1969, pp. 122–33, 294–6). All my quotations
from Wordsworth and Coleridge come, unless noted otherwise,
from the Oxford *Poetical Works* editions of their writings. Citations
from the Bible are from the King James version.

2. See the seminal discussions of Shelley's devotion to empirical scepticism in Pulos (1954, *passim*); Reiman (1965, pp. 3–18); Wasserman (1971, pp. 131–53); Cameron (1974, pp. 150–7); and Curran (1975, pp. 95–118, 199–205). The best discussion of this scepticism in relation to *Mont Blanc* is Spencer Hall (1973, pp. 199–203). Note, too, my sense of the limits in these readings (Hogle, 1988, pp. 7–12). The notion of 'first generation' Romantics, of course, is more our construction than Shelley's, though he does see Wordsworth and Coleridge as father-figure celebrities (for example in Shelley, 1964, I, p. 201).

3. Discussions of *Mont Blanc*'s recollections of *Tintern Abbey* include Bloom (1959, p. 35); Reiman (1969, pp. 45–6); Chernaik (1972, pp. 48–9); Jean Hall (1980, pp. 43–9); and Blank (1988, pp. 171–82).

4. The progeny include Susan Hawk Brisman (1977); Leslie Brisman (1978, pp. 137–82); and Blank (1988, *passim*).

5. As discussed in Bloom (1976b, p. 105) and Blank (1988, pp. 40–4, 86–98), partly on the basis of Peacock (1970, p. 43).

6. Before Freud proposes his most famous notion of transference, wherein the patient displaces his own tendencies and repressions on to the analyst, he has to (and does) assume 'memory traces' – left from infancy and always longing for the satisfaction of very early impulses – that carry their appetites over into other and later 'mnemic images' in the face of the inevitable loss of the primal sources of satisfaction (such as the breast). I am referring here to the argument offered in *The Interpretation of Dreams* (1900). For a discussion of how much and how little Shelley's sense of transference resembles this and other Freudian kinds, see Hogle (1988, pp. 16–18).

7. Though Shelley does at times offer versions of John Locke's view that language is primarily a creation and extension of thought-patterns (as in the *Defence of Poetry* – Shelley, 1977, p. 483), we find him just as committed to the view descended from the Abbé de Condillac through Horne Tooke and even Coleridge – and expressed in this statement by Asia – that thought cannot really exist coherently without there first being the linguistic placement of different figures in a syntax. For discussions of how these two views of the thought-language interplay relate to each other in Shelley, see Cronin (1981, pp. 1–25); Fry (1983, pp. 137–43); and Hogle (1988, pp. 12–13).

8. In that letter, Shelley claims to be quoting Spinoza, perhaps from the letters in the *Opera Posthuma*, but the vision in the quotation is of an '*infinite* number of atoms ... falling ... *from* all eternity in space, till at least one of them fortuitously diverged from its track' (Shelley, 1964, I, p. 44). These words are more a clear redaction of the Lucretian fall and *clinamen* than a direct transcription of any known passage by Spinoza, though the latter does refer to such notions on the way to suggesting a *natura naturans* behind the descent and the swerve. See Hogle (1988, pp. 32–5, 349).

9. See the extensive account of the many echoes from *De rerum* in

Shelley's poem offered in Phillips (1982), despite the fact that Phillips mistakenly tries to make the presuppositions of *Mont Blanc* more Platonic and *non*-Lucretian than Shelley does himself.

10. For the beginnings of and the reasons behind Shelley's early and keen interest in Lucretius, see Cameron (1950, pp. 88–9) and Hogle (1988, pp. 32–3).

11. In discussing this and related aspects of Lucretius, I am indebted to Serres (1975).

12. This realisation refutes the long-standing tradition in readings of *Mont Blanc* which sees the Power as either the agency or the presence of an Absolute truly at one with itself. That tradition gained its strongest impetus from Vivian (1955) and reached its peak in Wasserman (1971, pp. 222–38), despite the latter's disavowal of Platonic or Plotinian readings of Shelley. To some degree, the tradition continues even in readings that view Shelley's language as ironically trying to give form to an inchoate Other which is so extra-linguistic that it has no relation to movements between differences. See particularly McNiece (1975), Leighton (1982, pp. 58–72), and Ferguson (1984). In fact, as we now see, the Power, though certainly a linguistic construct, *is* a movement between differences, a self-ironising process 'in itself', throughout Shelley's poem.

13. The reading of this phrase that edges most towards my position on it, without finally taking it, is Rieder (1981, p. 786).

14. Shelley's letter, in fact, is like the poem in that it places the scientific and the mythic in a similar juxtaposition while reacting to the sight of Mont Blanc, with the Comte de Buffon's theories about changes in the earth being alluded to in virtually the same breath as the legend of Ahriman (the dark counterpart of beneficent Oromaze in Zoroastrian accounts of the cycles through which all of life seems to pass). For where Shelley drew both ideas, see Buffon (1775–6) and the unfinished *Ahrimanes* (1812–15) in Peacock (1967, VII, pp. 422–32). See also Butler (1982).

15. I draw the term 'heteroglossia' and the picture of the reading mind connected with it – a portrait that sees consciousness as an interplay of different ideological registers – from Mikhail Bakhtin and particularly from one of the books of the 1920s that he published under a 'cover' name (Voloshinov, 1973).

16. *Mont Blanc*, in fact, promotes a version of what Keats (using the phrase I quote here) would call 'negative capability' in its truest sense, the one where 'man is capable of being in uncertainties, Mysteries, doubts' without insisting on a centred and absolutist resolution of the related differences (Keats, 1958, I, p. 193).

17. See the intriguing, if sometimes excessively Freudian, argument offered in Rapaport (1983).

18. Shelley later develops his sense of poetry's genesis as a self-transformative crossing between differences – and hence a process culturally gendered as feminine (traditionally the gender of continual otherness-from-itself) – in *The Witch of Atlas*, his very playful poem of August 1820. There and in *Mont Blanc* he thus

anticipates Alice Jardine's sense of a 'gynesis' appearing in modern
writing, an awareness of a pre-logical (feminine) otherness as the
sublimated (poetic) underwriter of rationalistic, hierarchical (male)
logic. See Hogle (1988, pp. 211–19, 381n., 117 and Jardine (1985)
pp. 31–49, 65–87, 118–44).

19. See the sense of 'forelanguage' in Cixous (1976), to whom I am
indebted for the term.

20. Prominent examples include Bloom (1959, pp. 34–5), Reiman (1969,
p. 44), Wasserman (1971, pp. 237–8), Chernaik (1972, p. 49), Hall
(1973, pp. 201–3, 219–20), Webb (1977, pp. 138–9), Leighton (1982,
pp. 70–2), and Ferguson (1984, pp. 210–14).

Notes to Chapter 7: *Julian and Maddalo* as Revisionary Conversation Poem

1. The poem was finished, according to Matthews (1963, pp. 65–6), no
earlier than December 1818, and probably no later than March 1819.

2. All quotations from Coleridge's poetry are from Coleridge (1912).

3. For this reason I read Julian's statement, 'we / Wept without shame in
[the Maniac's] society' (515–16) as a piece of naive irony: since
'society' is non-existent between observer and observed, specimen
and scientist, or spectacle and spectator, shame is impossible.

4. In words that Marjorie Levinson applies to the romantic fragment
poem, the conversation poem displays 'the concern with textual
reception as a means of controlling the social reception of the poet'
(1986a, p. 209).

5. Levinson (1986a, p. 161) and Blank (1988, p. 121) also note the resemblance.

6. Some of these resemblances between music and the language of the
Maniac are also observed by Tetreault (1987, pp. 150–4).

7. Robinson (1976, pp. 91–4) argues strongly against the prevailing view
and in favour of Byron/Maddalo as the Maniac's prototype.

8. Brisman (1977, pp. 51–62) and Bruns (1974, pp. 59–61) suggest that
the concept of *Logos* is fundamental to Shelley's theories of language.
Keach (1984, pp. 34–7) argues, and I think rightly, that the *logoisitic*
concept is fundamental only to an apocalyptic transformation of
ordinary, fallen language. On *Logos* as a Romantic ideal of discourse,
see Rajan (1980, pp. 206–7).

Notes to Chapter 8: Self, Beauty and Horror: Shelley's Medusa Moment

1. Quotations from *Medusa* and *To—* are from the Hutchinson edition
(Shelley, 1970, pp. 582–3, 525–6).

2. This essay is part of a much longer work-in-progress that will
examine, among other things, Shelley's modalities of the self and the
problematic of consciousness from various perspectives.

Notes to Chapter 10: Seduced by Metonymy: Figuration and Authority in
The Cenci

1. Michael Worton emphasises Shelley's 'consistent and deliberate
    refusal ... to *name* the catalysing action within the tragedy' as a way
    of focusing that contemplation: 'All the major events are ...
    reported rather than presented', thus directing attention to 'lan-
    guage as a purveyor of truth' (Worton, 1982, p. 107).
2. Thus Stuart Curran, although urging the reader of *The Cenci* to
    refrain from imposing upon Beatrice's 'world an ethic foreign to its
    exigencies, denying the repeated symbolism of the imagery and the
    carefully balanced structure of characterisations', ends up seeing
    Beatrice as the sort of character more usually found in existential
    fiction than in tragedy: 'Only by killing her father in line with the
    principles of divine justice can Beatrice hope for an absolution from
    the evil into which her father has plunged her' (Curran, 1970,
    p. 140). Carlos Baker sees Beatrice's actions in a much harsher light:
    'Instead, under indignities of the most horrible kind, a gentle and
    innocent girl was turned into an efficient machine of vengeance,
    coolly planning, imperiously executing, denying her part in, and at
    last calmly dying for the murder of her father' (Baker, 1948, p. 142).
       More recently, Ronald Tetreault, with a nod towards Fredric
    Jameson's thesis that a culture's common language subverts heter-
    oglossic alternatives and enforces the horizons of the dominant
    ideology, pleads for mitigation on the grounds that Beatrice,
    'Having no access to an alternative discourse ... locks herself
    into tragedy by embracing the ideology of vengeance embedded
    in the prison-house of her father's language' (Tetreault, 1987,
    p. 141). Stuart Sperry takes a harder line, turning to Shelley's
    'Preface' to note 'the inflexible moral imperative that Beatrice
    violates in carrying out the murder of her father', and characterising
    Shelley's strategy in the play as being 'to invite, indeed require,
    us to condemn Beatrice's actions unblinkingly and simultaneously
    to love her, and act incorporating but transcending mere forgive-
    ness.' If Sperry's Shelley seems to be saying, *pace* Jameson and
    Tetreault, 'hate the sin but love the sinner', so be it: Sperry holds
    that Shelley 'regarded the moral recognition of his play truer to the
    underlying spirit of Christianity than the sacrilegious politics of false
    piety and self-interest he exposes in all his work' (Sperry, 1988,
    p. 130, 140).
3. G. Kim Blank, drawing on the previous work of Ronald L. Lemon-
    celli (Lemoncelli, 1978, pp. 104–6), also sees the struggle between
    Cenci and Beatrice as having symbolic overtones, albeit overtones
    arising from Shelley's struggle with Wordsworth as a precursor
    exhibiting a failure of imaginative and political nerve rather than the
    'seduction to metonymy'. Nevertheless, Blank's argument that
    'Count Cenci can be seen as a corrupt poet, and Beatrice as his
    poem' (Blank, 1988, p. 154) shows some affinities with my argu-
    ment, given that Shelley's quarrel was principally with the metony-

mising and anthropomorphising Wordsworth of *The Excursion* (1814) and after.

4. Terence Allan Hoagwood's study of Shelley's political prose makes it clear that from the perspective of Shelley's sceptical commitment, the concept of the real or, to use Hoagwood's term, 'truth', is at best problematic and at worst extremely vexed. In the place of 'truth', the sceptic prefers to talk of the 'relative property' or 'probability' (Hoagwood, 1988, p. 8). For earlier treatments of Shelley's scepticism, see Pulos (1954) and Abbey (1979).

5. Eugenio Donato reveals how metonymy produces naturalisation – indeed, produces the very ideological construct of 'Nature' itself – through repetition. Speaking of the undertaking of Bouvard and Péchuet in mounting the exhibits in France's Museum of Natural History, Donato observes: 'By displaying plants metonymically selected and metonymically ordered, it meant to produce a *tableau* of Nature' (Donato, 1979, p. 230).

6. Eugene R. Hammond (1981, pp. 25–32) reads the play in terms of Beatrice's successive betrayal by three hierarchically ordered fathers: Count Cenci, her biological father; Pope Clement VIII, her Holy Father; and God, her Heavenly Father.

7. See Pagels (1979, pp. 28, 60) for a fuller discussion of the way in which the creed suppresses gnostic alternatives and, with them, alternative constructions of gender and belief.

8. In *The Assassins* (1814), Shelley sympathetically describes a small band of early Christians who hold 'opinions [that] considerably resembled those of the sect afterwards known by the name of Gnostics. They esteemed the human understanding to be the paramount rule of human conduct; they maintained that the obscurest religious truth required for its complete elucidation no more than the strenuous application of the energies of the mind' (Shelley, 1966, p. 145). See also Rieger (1967, p. 133).

9. It is often the case that one person's metonymy is another's synecdoche. M. H. Abrams' *A Glossary of Literary Terms* defines metonymy as a figure in which 'the literal term for one thing is applied to another with which it has become closely associated. Thus "the crown" or "the scepter" can stand for a king'. The *Glossary* defines synecdoche as a figure in which 'a part of something is used to signify the whole, or (more rarely) the whole is used to signify a part... Milton refers to the corrupt clergy in *Lycidas* as "blind *mouths*"' (Abrams, 1988, pp. 66–7). Both figures operate on the principle of substitution – part for whole or one thing closely associated with another for another – as contradistinguished from metaphor, which operates on the principle of non-substitutive interaction (Black, 1981, pp. 77–9). Following the lead of Quintilian, who says that metonymy and synecdoche are 'not very different' (Quintilian, 1876, p. 129), and that of Liselotte Gumpel, who speaks of the ' "metonymic" relation of carefully spaced parts to the whole' (Gumpel, 1984, p. 139) in a manner calculated to amalgamate metonymy and synecdoche, I should argue that Hogle's insight

about Shelley's understanding of the uses of synecdoche holds
equally – indeed, interchangeably – well for his understanding of
the uses of metonymy, if indeed Shelley himself draws any distinction between the operative logic of the two figures.

10.   As Vico wrote,

> Metonymy of agent for act resulted from the fact that names for
> agents were commoner than names for acts. Metonymy of subject
> for form and accident was due to the inability to abstract forms
> and qualities from subjects. Certainly, metonymy of cause for
> effect produced in each case a little fable, in which the cause was
> imagined as a woman clothed with her effects: ugly Poverty, sad
> Old Age, pale Death.   (Vico, 1968, p. 130)

Shelley might also have taken his notion of tropaic decline from
William Warburton's *The Divine Legation of Moses Demonstrated*
(Warburton, 1738–41, pp. 150–1). Shelley's reading of Warburton is
documented in Shelley (1964, I, pp. 69, 77; II, p. 487).

11.   In the thirty-first query of his *Opticks* (4th edn, 1730), Newton
argues that 'it seems probable . . . that God in the Beginning form'd
Matter in solid, massy, hard, impenetrable, moveable Particles, of
such Sizes and Figures, and with such other Properties, and in such
Proportion to Space, as most conduced to the end for which he
form'd them' (Newton, 1952, p. 401). Carl Grabo is persuaded that
'Shelley was either familiar with Newton's *Opticks* or later works
derived therefrom' (Grabo, 1930, p. 15). In Book II of *De rerum natura*
(*ca.* 55 BC), Lucretius states that *'the characteristics of atoms of all
substances . . . differ in shape and the rich multiplicity of their forms'*
(Lucretius, 1951, p. 70). Hogle discusses the influence of Lucretius
among others in the development of Shelley's materialism, noting
his especial fascination with 'the way Lucretius counters the
Christian (and Gothic) idea that a "divine power" is able to "produce" everything out of "nothing" ' (Hogle, 1988, p. 32).

12.   Tetreault argues that this speech 'erects a standard to which she [i.e.
Beatrice] can never measure up, for it indicates a determinate
signified set at defiance by the moral ambiguities of her experience'
(Tetreault, 1987, p. 134).

13.   The trope of reading for 'God's truth' comes from Stephen Toulmin's characterisation of the natural theologians of the seventeenth
century: 'In their view, God's hand had written the Book of Nature
as surely as it had the Book of Scripture; and you could "read God's
mind" in the one as surely as in the other' (Toulmin, 1982, p. 232).

14.   Sperry compares Fuseli's pictorial rendering of the torments of
Prometheus with Shelley's rendering of those torments: 'In
Shelley's *Prometheus* this [i.e. the genital, and particularly the
phallically tormenting] aspect of the hero's ordeal is never treated.
In *The Cenci* the genital threat is not merely explicit but overpower-
ing' (Sperry, 1988, p. 135).

15.   Clark, who anglicises the Latin as 'In whom all things move,

without affecting each other', mistakenly attributes Holbach's *Système de la nature* (1775) as the source (Shelley, 1954, p. 134n.).

Notes to Chapter 11: Poetic Autonomy in *Peter Bell the Third* and *The Witch of Atlas*

Thanks to Jerrold E. Hogle for offering helpful observations on a preliminary version of this chapter.

1. Richard Cronin has noted the Byronic tone of *The Witch of Atlas*, and suggests that Shelley 'admired *Don Juan* as a comedy, not as a satire' and 'learned from *Don Juan* ... the possibility of employing an uneven or mixed style, so that the reader is prevented from finding a point of reference in any one of the poem's styles and forced to consider the relation between styles as the poem's meaning' (Cronin, 1981, pp. 57, 58). Three other recent interpretations of the poem are worth mentioning. The first two are by Jerrold Hogle. He suggests that 'the poem is "about" (in the process of) the sheer release of further transfigurations from the potentials in existing metaphors, so much so that every image comes less from a "seed" or "cause" and more from ways that metaphor shifts beyond or beside itself into new analogies repeating old ones with some differences' (Hogle, 1980, p. 330). His second essay amplifies on this theme, arguing that the Witch's 'destiny is to veil her already self-veiling emergence from innumerable relations in new reopenings of whatever denies her gaiety' (Hogle, 1988, p. 219). The third is Andelys Wood, who points to the poem's 'Ambiguities in diction, image, and symbol', which 'call attention to unresolved tensions between the ideal of immortality and reconciling love and the reality of death and dividing change', dislocations which render the work an example of Romantic irony (Wood, 1980, p. 74). Obviously none of these critics see *The Witch of Atlas* as an example of poetic autonomy; for the classic statement of that case see Harold Bloom's chapter on the poem in *Shelley's Mythmaking* (Bloom, 1959).
2. The classic statement is M. H. Abrams' 'Romantic Platonism', in *The Mirror and the Lamp: Romantic Theory and the Critical Tradition* (1953).

Notes to Appendix: A Shelley Survey: What Shelley Now?

1. *English Romantic Writers*, ed. David Perkins (New York: Harcourt Brace Jovanovich, 1967).
2. *Shelley's Poetry and Prose*, eds Donald H. Reiman and Sharon B. Powers (New York: Norton, 1977).
3. *Percy Bysshe Shelley: Selected Poems*, ed. Timothy Webb (London: Dent, 1977).
4. *The Norton Anthology of English Literature* (vol. 2), eds M. H. Abrams *et al.* (New York: Norton, 1962).

5. *Shelley: Poetical Works*, ed. Thomas Hutchinson, rev. G. M. Matthews (London: Oxford University Press, 1970).
6. *The Oxford Anthology of English Literature: Romantic Poetry and Prose*, eds Harold Bloom and Lionel Trilling (London: Oxford University Press, 1973).
7. *Percy Bysshe Shelley: Selected Poetry and Prose*, ed. Kenneth Neill Cameron (New York: Holt, Rinehart and Winston, 1951).
8. *Major British Poets of the Romantic Period*, ed. William Heath (London: Macmillan, 1973).
9. *English Romantic Poetry and Prose*, ed. Russell Noyes (London: Oxford University Press, 1956).
10. *Alastor and Other Poems; Prometheus Unbound with Other Poems; Adonais*, ed. P. H. Butter (London: Collins, 1970).

Bibliography

ABBEY, Lloyd (1979) *Destroyer and Preserver: Shelley's Poetic Skepticism* (Lincoln: University of Nebraska Press).

ABRAMS, M. H. (1953) *The Mirror and the Lamp: Romantic Theory and the Critical Tradition* (London: Oxford University Press).

ABRAMS, M. H. (1971) *Natural Supernaturalism: Tradition and Revolution in Romantic Literature* (New York: W. W. Norton).

ABRAMS, M. H. (1988) *A Glossary of Literary Terms*, 5th edn (New York: Holt, Rinehart and Winston).

ADORNO, Theodor (1974) 'Lyric Poetry and Society', *Telos*, XX, pp. 56–71.

ANON (1729) *The Nurse's Guide* (London: J. Brotherton).

ANON (1795) 'The Libertine Reclaimed', *The Lady's Magazine*, XXVI, pp. 159–60.

ANON (1799a) 'Review of *A Voyage to India* and *The Works of Sir William Jones*', *The Lady's Monthly Museum*, III, pp. 477–80.

ANON (1799b) 'The Triumph of Patience and Virtue', *The Lady's Magazine*, XXX, pp. 389–90.

ANON (1803) 'The Unfeeling Father: A Fragment', *The Lady's Magazine*, XXXIII, pp. 383–4.

ANON (1808a) 'Three Years after Marriage: A Tale from the French of M. Imbert', *The Lady's Monthly Museum*, IV, n.s., pp. 28–32.

ANON (1808b) 'Memoir of Carolina Matilda, Queen of Denmark', *La Belle Assemblée*, IV, no. 29, pp. 105–7.

ANON (1808c) 'Account of the City of *Palmyra*. Collected from Various Authors'. *La Belle Assemblée*, IV, no. 37, 154–9.

ANON (1808d) 'On the Origin of the Black Art; or Magic', *La Belle Assemblee*, IV, no. 37, pp. 203–10.

ANON (1814) *Synopsis of the Contents of the British Museum* (London: R. and J. Dodsley).

ARGUELLES, Jose A. (1975) *The Transformative Vision: Reflections on the Nature and History of Human Expression* (Berkeley: Shambhala Publications).

ARNOLD, Matthew (1905) *Essays in Criticism: Second Series* (London: Macmillan).

ARNOLD, Matthew (1962) *Lectures and Essays in Criticism*, ed. R. H. Super (Ann Arbor: University of Michigan Press).

BAKER, Carlos (1948) *Shelley's Major Poetry: The Fabric of a Vision* (Princeton: Princeton University Press).

BARBAULD, Anna Letitia (1811) *The Female Speaker* (London: J. Johnson).

BARNARD, Ellsworth (1964) *Shelley's Religion* (New York: Russell and Russell).

BARTHES, Roland (1974) *S/Z*, trans. Richard Miller (New York: Hill and Wang).

261

BARTHES, Roland (1977) 'The Death of the Author', in *Image Music Text*, trans. Stephen Heath (Glasgow: Fontana/Collins), pp. 142–8.

BARTHES, Roland (1978) *A Lover's Discourse: Fragments*, trans. Richard Howard (New York: Hill and Wang).

BLACK, Max (1981) 'Metaphor' (first pubd 1955), in Mark Johnson (ed.) *Philosophical Perspectives on Metaphor* (Minneapolis: University of Minnesota Press), pp. 63–82.

BLANK, G. Kim (1988) *Wordsworth's Influence on Shelley: A Study of Poetic Authority* (London: Macmillan).

BLOOM, Harold (1959) *Shelley's Mythmaking* (New Haven: Yale University Press: reprinted by Cornell University Press, 1969).

BLOOM, Harold (1970) *Romanticism and Consciousness: Essays in Criticism* (New York: W. W. Norton).

BLOOM, Harold (1971) *The Visionary Company: A Reading of English Romantic Poetry* (revised and enlarged edn) (Ithaca and London: Cornell University Press).

BLOOM, Harold (1976a) 'Poetic Crossing: Rhetoric and Psychology', *Georgia Review*, XXX, pp. 495–524.

BLOOM, Harold (1976b) *Poetry and Repression: Revisionism from Blake to Stevens* (New Haven: Yale University Press).

BLOOM, Harold et al., (1979) *Deconstruction and Criticism*. New York: Seabury.

BRISMAN, Leslie (1978) *Romantic Origins* (Ithaca, NY: Cornell University Press).

BRISMAN, Leslie (1981) ' "Mysterious Tongue": Shelley and the Language of Christianity', *Texas Studies in Literature and Language*, XXIII, 3, pp. 389–417.

BRISMAN, Susan Hawk (1977) '"Unsaying His High Language": The Problem of Voice in *Prometheus Unbound*', *Studies in Romanticism*, XVI, pp. 51–86.

BROOKE, Rev. Stopford A. (1887) Introduction to *Epipsychidion* (London: The Shelley Society).

BROWN, Nathaniel (1979) *Sexuality and Feminism in Shelley* (Cambridge, Mass.: Harvard University Press).

BROWN, Sarah (1777) *Letter to a Lady on the Best Means of Obtaining the Milk* [London].

BRUNS, Gerald (1974) *Modern Poetry and the Idea of Language* (New Haven: Yale University Press).

BRYANT, Jacob (1775) *A New System, or an Analysis of Ancient Mythology* (London: T. Payne).

BUCHAN, William (1809) *The New Domestic Medecine . . . to which is now first added . . . his Advice to Mothers* (London: Thomas Kelly).

BUFFON, Georges Louis Leclerc Comte de (1775–6) *Natural History of Animals, Vegetables, and Minerals, with the History of the Earth in General*, trans. William Kenrick and J. Murdock (London: Bell).

BURKE, Edmund (1759) *A Philosophical Enquiry into the Origin of our Ideas of the Sublime and Beautiful* (2nd edn) (London: R. and J. Dodsley).

BUSH, Douglas (1963) *Mythology and the Romantic Tradition in English Poetry* (New York: W. W. Norton).

BUTLER, Marilyn (1979) *Peacock Displayed: A Satirist in his Context* (London: Routledge and Kegan Paul).

BUTLER, Marilyn (1982) 'Myth and Mythmaking in the Shelley Circle', *ELH*, XLIX, pp. 50–72.

BUXTON FORMAN, H. (ed.) (1911) *Note Books of Percy Bysshe Shelley* (3 vols) (St. Louis: William K. Bixby/The Bibliophile Society).

BYRON, Lord George Gordon (1986) *Byron*, ed. Jerome J. McGann (London: Oxford University Press).

CAMERON, Kenneth Neill (1950) *The Young Shelley: Genesis of a Radical* (reprinted 1962) (New York: Collier).

CAMERON, Kenneth Neill (ed) (1964) *The Esdaile Notebook: A Volume of Early Poems by Percy Bysshe Shelley*, III (New York: Alfred A. Knopf).

CAMERON, Kenneth Neill (ed.) (1970) *Shelley and his Circle: 1773–1822*, Vol. III (Cambridge, Mass.: Harvard University Press).

CAMERON, Kenneth Neill (1974) *Shelley: The Golden Years* (Cambridge, Mass.: Harvard University Press).

CAMERON, Sharon (1976) *Lyric Time: Dickinson and the Limits of Genre* (Baltimore: Johns Hopkins University Press).

CAMPBELL, Olwen Ward (1924) *Shelley and the Unromantics* (London: Methuen).

CAMPE, Joachim Henry (1806) Selection from *Travels in England*, *La Belle Assemblée*, vol. I, no. 2, pp. 66–8.

CHERNAIK, Judith (1972) *The Lyrics of Shelley* (Cleveland: Case Western Reserve University Press).

CHODOROW, Nancy and CONTRATTO, Susan (1982) 'The Fantasy of the Perfect Mother', in Barrie Thorne and Marilyn Yalom (eds) *Rethinking the Family: Some Feminist Questions* (New York: Longman), pp. 54–75.

CIXOUS, Helene (1976) 'The Laugh of the Medusa', trans. Keith and Paula Cohen, *Signs*, III, pp. 875–93.

COLERIDGE, Samuel Taylor (1912) *Poetical Works*, ed. E. H. Coleridge (London: Oxford University Press).

COLERIDGE, Samuel Taylor (1956) *Biographia Literaria*, ed. George Watson (London: J. M. Dent).

COLERIDGE, Samuel Taylor (1969) *The Friend*, in *The Collected Works*, vol. IV, part 2, ed. Barbara Rooke (Princeton: Princeton University Press).

COLERIDGE, Samuel Taylor (1976) *On the Constitution of the Church and State* [1830] (London: Routledge and Kegan Paul).

COLERIDGE, Samuel Taylor (1984) *Biographia Literaria* (2 vols), eds James Engell and W. J. Bate (Princeton: Princeton University Press).

CROMPTON, Margaret (1967) *Shelley's Dream Women* (London: Cassell).

CRONIN, Richard (1981) *Shelley's Poetic Thoughts* (London: Macmillan).

CROOK, Nora and GUITON, Derek (1986) *Shelley's Venomed Melody* (Cambridge: Cambridge University Press).

CULLER, Jonathan (1977) 'Apostrophe', *Diacritics*, VII, 4, pp. 59–69.

CURRAN, Stuart (1970) *Shelley's Cenci: Scorpions Ringed with Fire* (Princeton: Princeton University Press).

CURRAN, Stuart (1975) *Shelley's Annus Mirabilis: The Maturing of An Epic Vision* (San Marino, CA: Huntington Library).

CURRAN, Stuart (1986) *Poetic Form and British Romanticism* (New York: Oxford University Press).

DANTE Alighieri (1910) *The Vision or Hell, Purgatory, and Paradise of Dante Alighieri* (3 vols), trans. Henry F. Cary (London: Oxford University Press).

DANTE Alighieri (1949–62) *The Comedy of Dante Alighieri* (3 vols), trans. Dorothy L. Sayers (Harmondsworth: Penguin).

DARWIN, Erasmus (1794) *The Botanic Garden: A Poem in Two Parts* (2 vols, 3rd edn) [Lichfield and London].

DARWIN, Erasmus (1803) *Zoonomia; or The Laws of Organic Life* (2 vols) (Boston: D. Carlisle).

DAVIDOFF, Leonore and HALL, Catherine (1987) *Family Fortunes: Men and Women of the English Middle Class* (London: Hutchinson).

DAWSON, P. M. S. (1980) *The Unacknowledged Legislator: Shelley and Politics* (Oxford: Clarendon Press).

DE BEAUVOIR, Simone (1949) *The Second Sex*, trans. H. M. Parshley (Harmondsworth: Penguin).

DE MAN, Paul (1979a) *Allegories of Reading: Figural Language in Rousseau, Nietzsche, Rilke, and Proust* (New Haven: Yale University Press).

DE MAN, Paul (1979b) 'Shelley Disfigured', in H. Bloom *et al.* (eds) *Deconstruction and Criticism* (New York: Seabury).

DE MAN, Paul (1982) 'The Resistance to Theory', *Yale French Studies*, LXIII, pp. 3–20.

DE MAN, Paul (1983) *Blindness and Insight: Essays in the Rhetoric of Contemporary Criticism*, 2nd edn (London: Methuen).

DE ROUGEMONT, Denis (1940) *Love in the Western World* (Princeton: Princeton University Press).

DERRIDA, Jacques (1973) *Speech and Phenomena and Other Essays on Husserl's Theory of Signs*, trans. David B. Allison (Evanston: Northwestern University Press).

DERRIDA, Jacques (1976) *Of Grammatology*, trans. Gayatri Chakravorty Spivak (Baltimore: Johns Hopkins University Press).

DERRIDA, Jacques (1978) *Writing and Difference*, trans. Alan Bass (Chicago: University of Chicago Press).

DERRIDA, Jacques (1979) *Spurs: Nietzsche's Styles*, trans. Barbara Harlow (Chicago: University of Chicago Press).

DERRIDA, Jacques (1981) *Positions*, trans. Alan Bass (Chicago: University of Chicago Press).

DERRIDA, Jacques (1982) *Margins of Philosophy*, trans. Alan Bass (Chicago: University of Chicago Press).

DONATO, Eugenio (1979) 'The Museum's Furnace: Notes toward a Contextual Reading of *Bouvard and Pechuet*', in Josue V. Harari (ed.) *Textual Strategies: Perspectives in Post-Structuralist Criticism* (Ithaca: Cornell University Press), pp. 213–38.

DOUGLAS, Mary (1982) *Natural Symbols: Explorations in Cosmology* (New York: Pantheon).

DRUMMOND, William (1805) *Academical Questions* (London: Bulmer).

ELIOT, T. S. (1933) *The Use of Poetry and the Use of Criticism: Studies in the*

Relation of Criticism to Poetry in England (Cambridge, Mass.: Harvard University Press).

EMERSON, Carlyl (1986) 'The Outer Word and Inner Speech: Bakhtin, Vygotsky, and the Internalization of Language', in Gary Saul Morson (ed.) *Bakhtin: Essays and Dialogues on his Work* (Chicago: University of Chicago Press).

ENGELS, Friedrich (1958) *The Condition of the Working Class in England*, trans. W. O. Henderson and W. H. Challoner (Oxford: Basil Blackwell).

EVEREST, Kelvin (1983) 'Shelley's Doubles: An Approach to "Julian and Maddalo"', in Kelvin Everest (ed.) *Shelley Revalued: Essays from the Gregynog Conference* (Totowa, NJ: Barnes and Noble), pp. 63–88.

FELPERIN, Howard (1985) *Beyond Deconstruction: The Uses and Abuses of Literary Theory* (Oxford: Clarendon Press).

FENN, Lady Eleanor [Mrs Lovechild, pseud.] (n.d.) *Rational Sports*. In *Dialogues Passing Among the Children of the Family* (London: John Marshall).

FENN, Lady Eleanor (1797) *The Infant's Friend: A Spelling Book* (London: E. Newberry).

FENN, Lady Eleanor (1798) *Parsing Lessons for Young Children* (London: E. Newberry).

FERGUSON, Frances (1984) 'Shelley's *Mont Blanc*: What the Mountain Said', in Arden Reed (ed.) *Romanticism and Language* (Ithaca, NY: Cornell University Press).

FERNALD, Anne (1984) 'The Perceptual and Affective Salience of Mothers' Speech to Infants', in L. Feagans *et al.* (eds) *The Origins and Growth of Communication* (Norwood, NJ: Ablex), pp. 5–29.

FINE, Reuben (1986) *Narcissism, The Self, and Society* (New York: Columbia University Press).

FRAZER, James G. (1911) *The Golden Bough: A Study in Magic and Religion*, 13 vols (London: Macmillan).

FOOT, Paul (1980) *Red Shelley* (London: Sidgwick and Jackson).

FREUD, Sigmund (1961) *Civilization and its Discontents*, trans. James Strachey (New York: W. W. Norton).

FREUD, Sigmund (1965) *The Interpretation of Dreams*, trans. James Strachey (New York: Basic Books).

FRIEDRICH, Paul (1978) *The Meaning of Aphrodite* (Chicago: University of Chicago Press).

FRY, Paul (1983) *The Reach of Criticism: Method and Perception in Literary Theory* (New Haven: Yale University Press).

FRYE, Northrop (1957) *Anatomy of Criticism: Four Essays* (Princeton: Princeton University Press).

GERARD, Albert (1968) *English Romantic Poetry: Ethos, Structure, and Symbol in Coleridge, Wordsworth, Shelley, and Keats* (Berkeley: University of California Press).

GISBORNE, Thomas (1799) *An Enquiry into the Duties of the Female Sex* (4th edn, corrected) (London: W. Davies).

GOHN, Jack Benoit (1979) 'Did Shelley Know Wordsworth's *Peter Bell*?' Keats-Shelley Journal, XXVIII, pp. 20–4.

GOODHEART, Eugene (1984) *The Skeptic Disposition in Contemporary Criticism* (Princeton: Princeton University Press).

GRABO, Carl (1930) *A Newton Among Poets: Shelley's Use of Science in Prometheus Unbound* (Chapel Hill: University of North Carolina Press).

GRABO, Carl (1936) *The Magic Plant: The Growth of Shelley's Thought* (Chapel Hill: University of North Carolina Press).

GROSECLOSE, Barbara (1985) 'The Incest Motif in Shelley's *The Cenci*', *Comparative Drama*, XIX, pp. 222–39.

GUMPEL, Liselotte (1984) *Metaphor Reexamined: A Non-Aristotelian Perspective* (Bloomington: Indiana University Press).

HALL, Jean (1980) *The Transforming Image: A Study of Shelley's Major Poetry* (Urbana: University of Illinois Press).

HALL, Jean (1984) 'The Socialized Imagination: Shelley's *The Cenci* and *Prometheus Unbound*', *Studies in Romanticism*, XXIII, pp. 339–50.

HALL, Spencer (1973) 'Shelley's "Mont Blanc"', *Studies in Philology*, LXX, pp. 199–221.

HAMMOND, Eugene R. (1981) 'Beatrice's Three Fathers: Successive Betrayal in Shelley's *The Cenci*', *Essays in Literature*, VIII, pp. 25–32.

HARPER, George McLean (1925) 'Coleridge's Conversation Poems', *Quarterly Review*, CCXLIV, pp. 284–98.

HARPHAM, Geoffrey Galt (1987) *The Ascetic Imperative in Culture and Criticism* (Chicago: University of Chicago Press).

HARRINGTON-LUEKER, D. (1983) 'Imagination versus Introspection: *The Cenci* and *Macbeth*', *Keats-Shelley Journal*, XXXII, pp. 172–89.

HAYDEN, John O. (ed.) (1976) *Romantic Bards and British Reviewers* (Lincoln: University of Nebraska Press).

HEATH, Stephen (1989) 'Modern Literary Theory', *Critical Quarterly*, XXXI, no. 2, pp. 35–49.

HERODOTUS (1987) *The History*, trans. David Grene (Chicago: University of Chicago Press).

HESIOD (1936) *Hesiod, the Homeric Hymns, and Homerica*, trans. Hugh G. Evelyn-White, Loeb Classical Library; rev. edn (Cambridge, Mass.: Harvard University Press).

HILDEBRAND, William H. (1971) 'A Look at the Third and Fourth Spirit Songs: *Prometheus Unbound*, I', *Keats-Shelley Journal*, XX, pp. 87–99.

HILLMAN, James (1972) *The Myth of Analysis* (Evanston: Northwestern University Press).

HIRSCH, Bernard A. (1978) '"A Want of That True Theory": *Julian and Maddalo* as Dramatic Monologue', *Studies in Romanticism*, XVII, pp. 13–34.

HOAGWOOD, Terence Allan (1988) *Skepticism and Ideology: Shelley's Political Prose and Its Philosophical Context from Bacon to Marx* (Iowa City: University of Iowa Press).

HOGLE, Jerrold E. (1980) 'Metaphor and Metamorphosis in Shelley's "The Witch of Atlas"', *Studies in Romanticism*, XIX, pp. 327–53.

HOGLE, Jerrold E. (1988) *Shelley's Process: Radical Transference and the Development of his Major Works* (New York: Oxford University Press).

HOLMES, Richard (1975) *Shelley: The Pursuit* (New York: E. P. Dutton).

HOMANS, Margaret (1986) *Bearing the Word* (Chicago: Chicago University Press).

HOUSE, Humphry (1953) *Coleridge: The Clark Lectures, 1951–52* (London: Rupert Hart-Davis).

HUME, David (1964) *The Philosophical Works*, ed. T. H. Green and T. H. Grose (Darmstadt: Scientia Verlag Aalen).

HUNT, Leigh (1828) *Lord Byron and Some of His Contemporaries* (London: Henry Colburn).

INGPEN, Roger (1909) *The Letters of P. B. Shelley*, vol. II (New York: Charles Scribner's Sons).

INGPEN, Roger and Walter E. Peck (eds) (1965) *The Complete Works of Percy Bysshe Shelley* (10 vols) (New York: Gordian Press). (See Shelley 1926–30.)

JACOBUS, Mary (1976) *Tradition and Experiment in Wordsworth's Lyrical Ballads (1798)* (Oxford: Clarendon Press).

JAKOBSON, Roman (1960) 'Concluding Statement', in Thomas A. Sebeok (ed.) *Style in Language* (Cambridge, Mass.: MIT Press), pp. 350–77.

JARDINE, Alice (1985) *Gynesis: Configurations of Woman and Modernity* (Ithaca, NY: Cornell University Press).

JOUKOVSKY, Nicholas A. (1985) 'Peacock before *Headlong Hall*: A New Look at his Early Years', *Keats-Shelley Memorial Bulletin*, XXXVI, pp. 1–40.

KEACH, William (1984) *Shelley's Style* (New York: Methuen).

KEATS, John (1958) *The Letters of John Keats 1814–1821* (2 vols), ed. Hyder Edward Rollins (Cambridge, Mass.: Harvard University Press).

KING-HELE, Desmond (1960) *Shelley: His Thought and Work* (London: Macmillan).

KITTLER, Friedrich A. (forthcoming) *Discourse Networks, 1800/1900*, trans. Michael Metteer, with Chris Cullen (Stanford: Stanford University Press).

KRAMNICK, Isaac (1977) *The Rage of Edmund Burke – Portrait of an Ambivalent Conservative* (New York: Basic Books).

KRISTEVA, Julia (1980) *Desire in Language: A Semiotic Approach to Literature and Art*, trans. Thomas Gora, Alice Jardine and Leon S. Roudiez (New York: Columbia University Press).

KRISTEVA, Julia (1984) *Revolution in Poetic Language*, trans. Margaret Waller (New York: Columbia University Press).

LA FONTAINE, Augustus (1802) 'The Rigid Father: or, Paternal Authority Too Strictly Enforced', *The Lady's Magazine*, XXXIII.

LACAN, Jacques (1977) *Écrits: A Selection*, trans. Alan Sheridan (London: Tavistock).

LEAVIS, F. R. (1936) *Revaluation: Tradition and Development in English Poetry* (London: Chatto and Windus).

LEIGHTON, Angela (1984) *Shelley and the Sublime: An Interpretation of the Major Poems* (Cambridge: Cambridge University Press).

LEMONCELLI, Ronald L. (1978) 'Cenci as Corrupt Dramatic Poet', *English Language Notes*, XVI, pp. 103–17.

LEVINSON, Marjorie (1986a) *The Romantic Fragment Poem: A Critique of a Form* (Chapel Hill: University of North Carolina Press).

LEVINSON, Marjorie (1986b) *Wordsworth's Great Period Poems: Four Essays* (Cambridge: Cambridge University Press).

LEWIS, C. S. (1964) *The Discarded Image* (Cambridge: Cambridge University Press).

LUCRETIUS (1937) *De rerum natura*, trans. W. H. D. Rouse, Loeb Classical Library; Rev. edn (Cambridge, Mass.: Harvard University Press).

LUCRETIUS (1951) *On the Nature of the Universe*, trans. R. E. Latham (Harmondsworth: Penguin).

LUKÁCS, Georg (1971) *The Theory of the Novel*, trans. Anna Bostock (Cambridge, Mass.: MIT Press).

McGANN, Jerome J. (1983) *The Romantic Ideology: A Critical Investigation* (Chicago: University of Chicago Press).

McNIECE, Gerald (1975) 'The Poet as Ironist in "Mont Blanc" and "Hymn to Intellectual Beauty" ', *Studies in Romanticism*, XIV, pp. 311–36.

MAGNUSON, Paul (1974) *Coleridge's Nightmare Poetry* (Charlottesville: University Press of Virginia).

MAGNUSON, Paul (1988) *Coleridge and Wordsworth: A Lyrical Dialogue*. (Princeton: Princeton University Press).

MARCUSE, Herbert (1974) *Eros and Civilization: A Philosophical Inquiry into Freud* (Boston: Beacon Press).

MARRS, Edwin W., Jr (ed.) (1975) *The Letters of Charles and Mary Anne Lamb* (3 vols) (Ithaca: Cornell University Press).

MARSHALL, Mrs Julian (ed.) (1889) *The Life and Letters of Mary Wollstonecraft Shelley*, Vol. I (London: R. Bentley).

MARX, Karl, and ENGELS, Friedrich (1976) *The German Ideology* [1845–46] (Moscow: Progress Publishers).

MASSEY, Marilyn Chapin (1985) *Feminine Soul: The Fate of an Ideal* (Boston: Beacon Press).

MATTHEWS, G. M. (1963) ' "Julian and Maddalo": The Draft and the Meaning', *Studia Neophilologica*, XXXV, pp. 57–84.

MEDWIN, Thomas (1913) *The Life of Percy Bysshe Shelley* [1847], ed. H. B. Forman (London: Humphrey Milford).

MELLOR, Anne K. (1988a) Introduction to *Romanticism and Feminism* (Bloomington and Indianapolis: Indiana University Press).

MELLOR, Anne K. (1988b) *Mary Shelley: Her Life, Her Fiction, Her Monsters* (New York: Methuen).

MERLE, Joseph Gibbons (1841) 'A Newspaper Editor's Reminiscences. Chap. IV', *Fraser's Magazine*, XXIII, pp. 699–710.

MILLER, J. Hillis (1979) 'The Critic as Host', in Harold Bloom *et al.* (eds) *Deconstruction and Criticism* (New York: Seabury Press), pp. 217–53.

MILLER, J. Hillis (1982) *Fiction and Repetition: Seven English Novels* (Cambridge, Mass.: Harvard University Press).

MILTON, John (1957) *Complete Poems and Major Prose*, ed. Merritt Y. Hughes (New York: Odyssey).

MORRIS, David B. (1984) *Alexander Pope: The Genius of Sense* (Cambridge, Mass.: Harvard University Press).

MOSS, William (1794) *An Essay on the Management, Nursing, and Diseases of Children* (London: W. N. Longman).

MUESCHKE, Paul and GRIGGS, Earl L. (1934) 'Wordsworth as the Prototype of the Poet in Shelley's *Alastor*', *PMLA*, XLIX, pp. 229–45.

NEHAMAS, Alexander (1985) *Nietzsche: Life as Literature* (Cambridge, Mass.: Harvard University Press).

NELLIST, Brian (1982) 'Shelley's Narratives and *The Witch of Atlas*', in Miriam Allott (ed.) *Essays on Shelley* (Liverpool: Liverpool University Press).

NELSON, James (1756) *An Essay on the Government of Children* (London: R. and J. Dodsley).

NEWEY, Vincent (1982) 'The Shelleyan Psycho-Drama: "Julian and Maddalo"', in Miriam Allott (ed.) *Essays on Shelley* (Totowa, NJ: Barnes and Noble), pp. 71–104.

NEWLYN, Lucy (1986) *Coleridge, Wordsworth, and the Language of Allusion* (Oxford: Clarendon Press).

NEWTON, Isaac (1952) *Opticks, or a Treatise of the Reflections, Refractions, Inflections, and Colours of Light*, based on the fourth edition, 1730, ed. Duane H. D. Roller (New York: Dover).

NEWTON, Isaac (1966) *Sir Isaac Newton's Mathematical Principles of Natural Philosophy and His System of the World*, trans. Andrew Motte; rev. Florian Cajori, 1934 (Berkeley and Los Angeles: University of California Press).

NIETZSCHE, Friedrich (1967a) *The Birth of Tragedy and the Case of Wagner*, trans. Walter Kaufmann (New York: Vintage).

NIETZSCHE, Friedrich (1967b) *The Will to Power*, trans. Walter Kaufmann and R. J. Hollingdale (New York: Vintage).

NIETZSCHE, Friedrich (1974) *The Gay Science*, trans. Walter Kaufman (New York: Random House).

NIETZSCHE, Friedrich (1984) *The Portable Nietzsche*, ed. and trans. Walter Kaufmann (New York: Penguin Books).

NORRIS, Christopher (1988) *Paul de Man: Deconstruction and the Critique of Aesthetic Ideology* (New York: Routledge and Kegan Paul).

NOTOPOULOS, James A. (1949) *The Platonism of Shelley: A Study of Platonism and the Poetic Mind* (Durham: Duke University Press).

NYE, Andrea (1987) 'Woman Clothed with the Sun: Julia Kristeva and the Escape from/to Language.' *Signs: Journal of Women in Culture and Society* XII, pp. 664–686.

OTTO, Rudolf (1967) *The Idea of the Holy*, trans. John W. Harvey (Oxford: Oxford University Press).

OTTO, Walter F. (1965) *Dionysus: Myth and Cult*, trans. Robert B. Palmer (Bloomington: Indiana University Press).

OVID, (1977) *Metamorphoses*, trans. Frank Justus Miller, Loeb Classical Library, 3rd edn (Cambridge, Mass.: Harvard University Press).

PAGELS, Elaine (1979) *The Gnostic Gospels* (New York: Random House).

PATEMAN, Carole (1988) *The Sexual Contract*, Cambridge: Polity Press.

PEACOCK, Thomas Love (1967) *The Works*, 10 vols, eds Halliford Edition, H. F. B. Brett-Smith and C. E. Jones (New York: AMS).

PEACOCK, Thomas Love (1970) *Memoirs of Shelley and Other Essays and Reviews*, ed. Howard Mills (London: Hart-Davis).

PESTALOZZI, Johann Friedrich (1800) *Leonard and Gertrude* (London: S. Hazard).

PFAU, Thomas (1987) 'Rhetoric and the Existential: Romantic Studies and the Question of the Subject', *Studies in Romanticism*, XXVI, pp. 487–512.

PHILLIPS, Jane E. (1982) 'Lucretian Echoes in Shelley's "Mont Blanc"', *Classical and Modern Literature*, II, pp. 71–93.

PRAZ, Mario (1956) *The Romantic Agony*, trans. Angus Davidson (New York: Meridian).

PULOS, C. E. (1954) *The Deep Truth: A Study of Shelley's Scepticism* (Lincoln: University of Nebraska Press).

QUINTILIAN (1876) *Quintilian's Institutes of Oratory or, Education of an Orator*, Vol. 2, trans. John Selby Watson (London: George Bell).

RAJAN, Balachandra (1985) *The Form of the Unfinished: English Poetics from Spenser to Pound* (Princeton: Princeton University Press).

RAJAN, Tilottama (1980) *Dark Interpreter: The Discourse of Romanticism* (Ithaca: Cornell University Press).

RAJAN, Tilottama (1984) 'Deconstruction or Reconstruction: Reading Shelley's *Prometheus Unbound*', *Studies in Romanticism*, XXIII, pp. 317–38.

RAJAN, Tilottama (1985a) 'Displacing Post-Structuralism: Romantic Studies After Paul de Man', *Studies in Romanticism*, XXIV, pp. 451–74.

RAJAN, Tilottama (1985b) 'Romanticism and the Death of Lyric Consciousness', in Chaviva Hosek and Patricia Parker (eds) *Lyric Poetry: Beyond New Criticism* (Ithaca: Cornell University Press), pp. 194–207.

RAPAPORT, Herman (1983) 'Staging *Mont Blanc*', in Marc Krupnik (ed.) *Displacement: Derrida and After* (Bloomington: Indiana University Press), pp. 59–73.

REIMAN, Donald H. (ed.) (1965) *Shelley's "The Triumph of Life": A Critical Study*, Illinois Studies in Language and Literature No. 55 (Urbana: University of Illinois Press).

REIMAN, Donald H. (1969) *Percy Bysshe Shelley* (New York: Twayne).

REIMAN, Donald H. (ed.) (1973) *Shelley and his Circle, 1773–1822* VI. (Cambridge MA.: Harvard University Press).

REIMAN, Donald H. (1979) 'Shelley as Agrarian Reactionary', *The Keats-Shelley Memorial Bulletin*, XXX, pp. 5–15.

REIMAN, Donald H. (ed.) (1986) *Peter Bell the Third: A Facsimile of the Press-copy Transcript by Mary W. Shelley ... and The Triumph of Life: A Facsimile of Shelley's Holograph Draft* (New York and London: Garland).

REIMAN, Donald H. (1988) *Intervals of Inspiration: The Skeptical Tradition and the Psychology of Romanticism* (Greenwood, Fl: Penkevill).

RICOEUR, Paul (1985) *Time and Narrative*, trans. Kathleen McLaughlin and David Pellaver, vol. 2 (Chicago: University of Chicago Press).

RIEDER, John (1981) 'Shelley's "Mont Blanc": Landscape and the Ideology of the Sacred Text', *ELH*, XLVIII, pp. 778–98.

RIEGER, James (1967) *The Mutiny Within: The Heresies of Percy Bysshe Shelley* (New York: G. Braziller).

ROBINSON, Charles E. (1976) *Shelley and Byron: The Snake and Eagle Wreathed in Fight* (Baltimore: Johns Hopkins University Press).

ROGERS, Neville (1956) *Shelley at Work: A Critical Inquiry* (Oxford: Clarendon Press).

ROGERS, Neville (1961) 'Shelley and the Visual Arts', *Keats-Shelley Memorial Bulletin*, XII, pp. 9–17.

ROLLINS, Hyder Edward (ed.) (1958) *The Letters of John Keats, 1814–1821* (2 vols) (Cambridge, Mass.: Harvard University Press).

RYAN, Michael (1982) *Marxism and Deconstruction: A Critical Articulation* (Baltimore: Johns Hopkins University Press).

RZEPKA, Charles J. (1986) *The Self as Mind: Vision and Identity in Wordsworth, Coleridge, and Keats* (Cambridge, Mass.: Harvard University Press).

SAID, Edward (1979) *Orientalism* (New York: Vintage).

ST CLAIR, William (1989) *The Godwins and the Shelleys: The Biography of a Family* (London: Faber and Faber).

SARTRE, Jean-Paul (1950) *What Is Literature?* trans. Bernard Frechtman (London: Methuen).

SCHNEIDAU, Herbert (1976) *Sacred Discontent: The Bible and Western Tradition* (reprinted 1977) (Berkeley: University of California Press).

SCHOPENHAUER, Arthur (1966) *The World as Will and Representation* (2 vols), trans. E. F. J. Payne (New York: Dover).

SCHULZE, Earl (1982) 'The Dantean Quest of *Epipsychidion*', *Studies in Romanticism*, XXI, pp. 191–216.

SCHULZE, Earl (1988) 'Allegory Against Allegory: "The Triumph of Life"', *Studies in Romanticism*, XXVII, pp. 31–62.

SCOTT, Walter Sidney (1943) *The Young Athenians* (London: Golden Cockerel Press).

SCRIVENER, Michael Henry (1982) *Radical Shelley: The Philosophical Anarchism and Utopian Thought of Percy Bysshe Shelley* (Princeton: Princeton University Press).

SERRES, Michel (1975) *La naissance de la physique dans le texte de Lucrece: Fleuves et turbulences* (Paris: Grasset).

SHAKESPEARE, William (1964) *The Tempest*, ed. Frank Kermode (London: Methuen).

SHELLEY, Mary (1980) *The Letters of Mary Wollstonecraft Shelley*, vol. I, ed. Betty T. Bennett (Baltimore and London: Johns Hopkins University Press).

SHELLEY, Mary (1987) *The Journals, 1814–1844*, eds Paula R. Feldman and Diana Scott-Kilvert (Oxford: Clarendon Press).

SHELLEY, Percy Bysshe (1911) *Note Books of Percy Bysshe Shelley* (3 vols), ed. H. B. Forman (Boston: Bibliophile Society).

SHELLEY, Percy Bysshe (1926–30) *The Complete Works of Percy Bysshe Shelley* (10 vols.), eds Roger Ingpen and Walter E. Peck (London: Ernest Benn).

SHELLEY, Percy Bysshe (1954) *Shelley's Prose or The Trumpet of a Prophecy*, ed. David Lee Clark (Albuquerque: University of New Mexico Press).

SHELLEY, Percy Bysshe (1959) *Percy Bysshe Shelley's Prometheus Unbound: A Variorum Edition*, ed. Lawrence John Zillman (Seattle: University of Washington Press).

SHELLEY, Percy Bysshe (1964) *The Letters of Percy Bysshe Shelley* (2 vols), ed. Frederick L. Jones (Oxford: Clarendon Press).

SHELLEY, Percy Bysshe (1968) *Shelley's Prometheus Unbound: The Text and the Drafts*, ed. Lawrence John Zillman (New Haven: Yale University Press).

SHELLEY, Percy Bysshe (1970) *Shelley: Poetical Works*, eds Thomas Hutchinson and G. M. Matthews (London: Oxford University Press).

SHELLEY, Percy Bysshe (1972) *The Complete Poetical Works*, vol. I, ed. Neville Rogers (Oxford: Clarendon Press).

SHELLEY, Percy Bysshe (1975) *The Complete Poetical Works*, vol II, ed. Neville Rogers (Oxford: Clarendon Press).

SHELLEY, Percy Bysshe (1977) *Shelley's Poetry and Prose*, eds Donald H. Reiman and Sharon B. Powers (New York: W. W. Norton).

SIEBERS, Tobin (1983) *The Mirror of Medusa* (Berkeley: University of California Press).

SOUTHEY, Robert (1894) *Joan of Arc, Ballads, Lyrics, and Minor Poems* (London: George Routledge and Sons).

SPERRY, Stuart (1988) *Shelley's Major Verse: The Narrative and Dramatic Poetry* (Cambridge, Mass.: Harvard University Press).

SPIVAK, Gayatri Chakravorty (1988) 'Finding Feminist Readings: Dante-Yeats', in *In Other Worlds: Essays in Cultural Politics* (New York and London: Routledge and Kegan Paul), pp. 15–29.

STEINMAN, Lisa M. (1978) 'Shelley's Skepticism: Allegory in *Alastor*' *ELH*, XLV, pp. 255–69.

STEINMAN, Lisa M. (1983) 'From *Alastor* to *The Triumph of Life*: Shelley on the Nature and Source of Linguistic Pleasure'. *Romanticism Past and Present*, VII, pp. 23–36.

TETREAULT, Ronald H. (1987) *The Poetry of Life: Shelley and Literary Form* (Toronto: University of Toronto Press).

THOMPSON, E. P. (1969) 'Disenchantment or Default? A Lay Sermon', in *Power and Consciousness*, ed. Conor Cruise O'Brien and William Dean Vanech (New York: New York University Press, pp. 149–181).

TODOROV, Tzvetan (1984) *Mikhail Bakhtin: The Dialogical Principle* (Minneapolis: University of Minnesota Press).

TOULMIN, Stephen (1982) *The Return to Cosmology* (Berkeley: University of California Press).

VICO, Giambattista (1968) *The New Science of Giambattista Vico*, trans. Thomas Goddard Bergin and Max Harold Fisch (Ithaca: Cornell University Press).

VINGE, Louise (1967) *The Narcissus Theme in Western European Literature up to the Early 19th Century*, trans. Robert Dewsnap (Lund: Gleerups).

VIVIAN, Charles H. (1955) 'The One "Mont Blanc"', *Keats-Shelley Journal*, IV, pp. 55–65; reprinted in Shelley (1977, pp. 569–79).

VOLNEY, Constantin (1890) *The Ruins, or, Meditations on the Revolutions of Empires; and the Law of Nature* (New York: Peter Eckler).

VOLOSHINOV, V. N. (1973) *Marxism and the Philosophy of Language*, trans. Ladislav Matejka and I. R. Titunik (New York: Seminar).

WARBURTON, William (1738–41) *The Divine Legation of Moses Demonstrated* (2nd edn) (London: Fletcher Gyles).

WASSERMAN, Earl R. (1971) *Shelley: A Critical Reading* (Baltimore: Johns Hopkins University Press).

WEBB, Timothy (1976) *The Violet in the Crucible: Shelley and Translation* (Oxford: Clarendon Press).

WEBB, Timothy (1977) *Shelley: A Voice Not Understood* (Manchester: Manchester University Press).

WEISKEL, Thomas (1976) *The Romantic Sublime: Studies in the Structure and Psychology of Transcendence* (Baltimore: Johns Hopkins University Press).

WERKMEISTER, Lucyle (1967) *A Newspaper History of England 1792–1793* (Lincoln: University of Nebraska Press).

WHITE, Newman Ivey (1940) *Shelley* (2 vols) (New York: Alfred A. Knopf).

WILSON, Milton (1959) *Shelley's Later Poetry: A Study of his Prophetic Imagination* (New York: Columbia University Press).

WOLFE, Humbert (ed.) (1933) *The Life of Percy Bysshe Shelley as Comprised in The Life of Shelley by Thomas Jefferson Hogg; The Recollections of Shelley & Byron by Edward John Trelawny; Memoirs of Shelley by Thomas Love Peacock* (2 vols) (London: Dent).

WOLLSTONECRAFT, Mary [Mr. Cresswick, pseud.] (1789) *The Female Reader* (London: J. Johnson).

WOOD, Andelys (1980) 'Shelley's Ironic Vision: The Witch of Atlas', *Keats-Shelley Journal*, XXIX, pp. 67–82.

WOOD, Robert (1757) *The Ruins of Balbec. Otherwise Heliopolis in Coelosyria* [London].

WOODINGS, R. B. (ed.) (1968) *Shelley: Modern Judgements* (London: Macmillan).

WOODMAN, Ross Greig (1964) *The Apocalyptic Vision in the Poetry of Shelley* (Toronto: University of Toronto Press).

WOODRING, Carl (1970) *Politics in English Romantic Poetry* (Cambridge, Mass.: Harvard University Press).

WOOLF, Virginia (1927) *To the Lighthouse* (New York: Harcourt, Brace, Jovanovich).

WORDSWORTH, William (1876) *The Prose Works of William Wordsworth* (3 vols), ed. A. B. Grossart (London: Moxon).

WORDSWORTH, William (1959) *The Prelude*, ed. E. De Selincourt, rev. Helen Barbishire (London: Oxford University Press).

WORDSWORTH, William (1969) *Poetical Works*, ed. Thomas Hutchinson, rev. Ernest de Selincourt (London: Oxford University Press).

WORDSWORTH, William (1977a) *The Poems*, v. I, ed. John O. Hayden (New Haven: Yale University Press).

WORDSWORTH, William (1977b) *The Poems*, v. II, ed. John O. Hayden (New Haven: Yale University Press).

WORDSWORTH, William (1979) *The Prelude 1799, 1805, 1850*, eds Jonathan Wordsworth, M. H. Abrams and Stephen Gill (New York: W. W. Norton).

WORDSWORTH, William (1984) *Descriptive Sketches*, ed. Eric Birdsall, *The Cornell Wordsworth* (Ithaca, NY: Cornell University Press).

WORTON, Michael (1982) 'Speech and Silence in *The Cenci*', in Miriam Allott (ed.) *Essays on Shelley* (Totowa: Barnes and Noble), pp. 105–24.

Index